Leader Guide

Minneapolis

ISBN 978-1-4514-0118-9

Illustrator: Paul Soupiset, Toolbox Studios, Inc.

sparkhouse Team: Bethany Stolle, David Schoenknecht, Arlene Flancher, Emily Gable, Carolyn Banks, Laurel Seeling, Logan Wang, Kristofer Skrade, Timothy Paulson

Toolbox Studios Team: Paul Soupiset, Joanne Stawicki, Stacy Thomas, Steven Gonzalez, Maria Harrington

Leader Guide Team: Erin Davis, Sarah Walker Cleaveland, Kristan S. Potter, Darin Wiebe, Erik Ullestad, Tony Jones, Holly Inglis, Vicky Goplin

Video Team: Paul Soupiset, Wes Halula, Aaron Christopher, Jared Neher, Dizilu, Matthew Keller, Damian Johnson, Jill Bernard, John Goodman, Jay Ness, Shane Nelson, Mike Turner

Anti-Workbook Team: Patricia A. Stroup, Darin Wiebe, with Julia Wiebe (12), Elida Wiebe (16), Steven Boggess (17), Jacob Friehauf (13), Aidan Baack (12), Daniel Meador (10), Hannah Meador (12), Evan Bergo (12), Kenz Scobba (13), Michel Meador

Review Team: Jessicah L.K. Duckworth, Adam Walker Cleaveland, Edwin DuBose, Holly Rankin Zaher, Andrea Hall, Drew Ludwig, Erik Ullestad, Todd J. Query

Special Thanks to Tony Jones and Andrew Root for re:form's theological and biblical framework.

Special Thanks to these test congregations: Spirit of Hope United Methodist Church, St. George's Episcopal Church, Windsor Heights Lutheran Church, Williamsburg United Methodist Church, Lafayette Presbyterian Church, The Presbyterian Church of Plum Creek.

The paper used in this publication meets the minimum requirements of American National Standard for Information Sciences—Permanence of Paper for Printed Library Materials, ANSI Z329.48-1984.

Manufactured in the U.S.A.

14 13 12 1 1 10 1 2 3 4 5 6 7 8 9 10

Contents

Bible

Creed

Discipleship

Jesus

Other Beliefs

Tough Questions

What is re:form?

Encounter

First, youth encounter a concept from the historic Christian faith with the re:form DVD.

Engage

Next, the re:form Anti-Workbook activities get youth interacting with each other and exploring their faith in creative ways.

Respond

Finally, youth present their point of view by uploading their work to the re:form Gallery, at www.reformgallery.org.

What's this Leader Guide thing?

re:form confirmation

Bible Unit
Who wrote the Bible, God or humans?

Prepare

What's behind all this?

The nature of the biblical canon has been a very contentious issue throughout the history of Christian theology. The spectrum of opinions spans from those who believe that the writers were in a trance and God moved their hands to form the words to those who believe that the authors had no idea that what they were writing was even special, let alone holy.

While Paul wrote that "all scripture is inspired," it's hard to imagine he was referring to his own writings. However, in hindsight, the church determined in the early centuries that some writings testified to the gospel in a way that they considered in line with the Apostles' teaching, and was therefore authoritative. Human beings clearly put pen to parchment to create the documents that have become the Hebrew and Christian Scriptures, but as with other moments of God's grace, Christians believe that God inspired these writers in a unique way and that God guarded the process that formed the canon.

Therefore, while Christians may believe many books to be inspirational, we believe that the Bible is uniquely inspired by God and therefore the best revelation of God and the gospel that we have.

Where are kids at?

- Kids love competition. It's a great way to engage them in learning and discovery. Make sure it takes place in an environment of trust with clear ground rules.
- Tech-savvy teens are more aware than ever of other cultures and religions and may wonder what's different about the Bible and Christian writings. Encourage curiosity, and provide resources where kids can discover more—like Bible concordances, maps, dictionaries, reputable websites, etc.

2 Timothy 3:16

Where's this going?
By confronting their assumptions and biases about where the Bible came from, the group can start wrestling through them to a new understanding of the Bible.

Consider this ...
"What we have, from Genesis to Revelation, is a massive narrative structure in which, though Paul, the evangelists, and John of Patmos are, of course, extremely well aware of the earlier parts, no single author saw the whole or knew about all its other parts. It is as though engineers from different workshops were invited to produce bits and pieces of cantilevers which ended up, when put together without the different work-shops knowing of it, producing the Forth Bridge."
N.T. Wright, *Scripture's Doctrine and Theology's Bible*, p. 61.

© 2010 sparkhouse. All Rights Reserved. May be reproduced for local use only provided each copy carries this notice.

Bible Unit: Who wrote the Bible, God or humans? 1

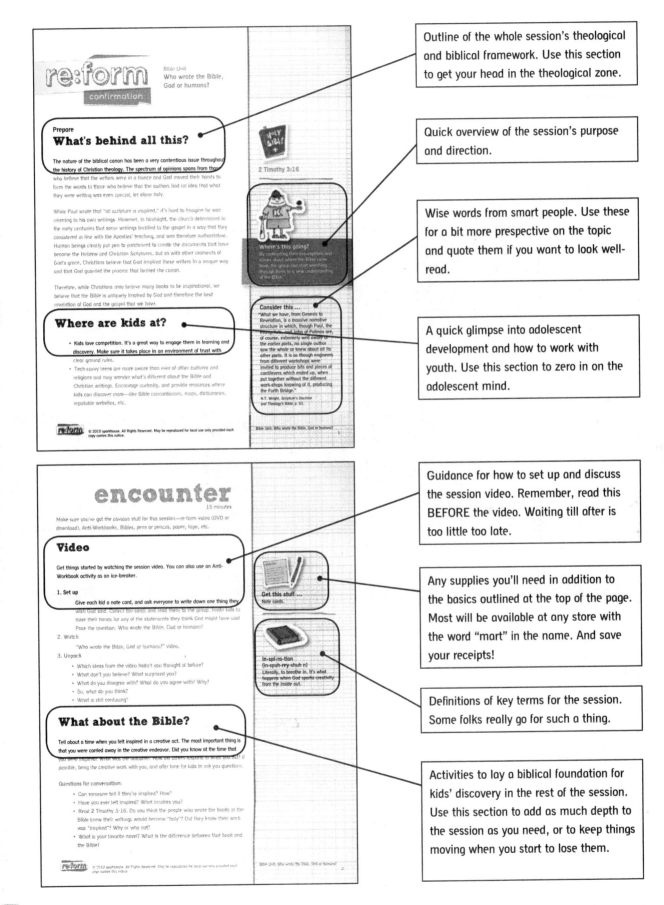

Outline of the whole session's theological and biblical framework. Use this section to get your head in the theological zone.

Quick overview of the session's purpose and direction.

Wise words from smart people. Use these for a bit more prespective on the topic and quote them if you want to look well-read.

A quick glimpse into adolescent development and how to work with youth. Use this section to zero in on the adolescent mind.

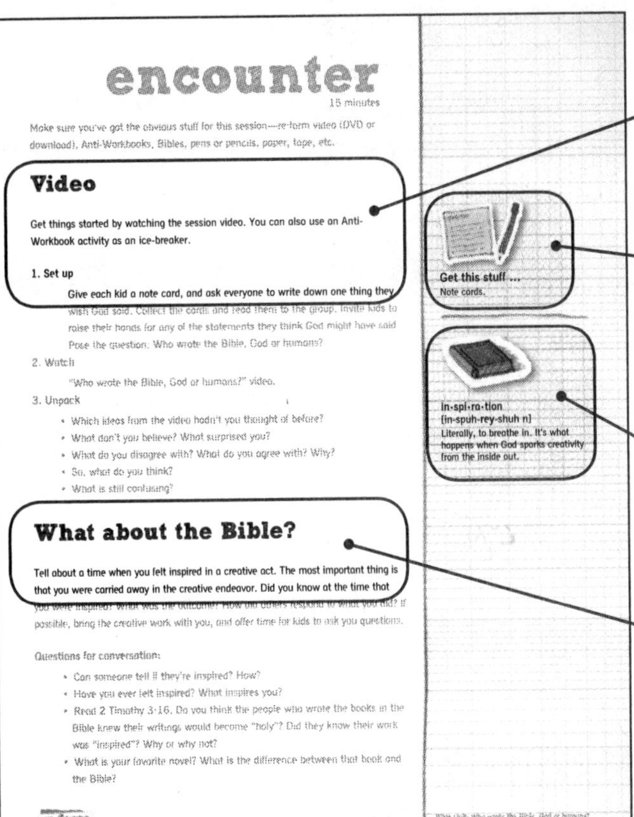

encounter

15 minutes

Make sure you've got the obvious stuff for this session—re·form video (DVD or download), Anti-Workbooks, Bibles, pens or pencils, paper, tape, etc.

Video

Get things started by watching the session video. You can also use an Anti-Workbook activity as an ice-breaker.

1. Set up
   Give each kid a note card, and ask everyone to write down one thing they wish God said. Collect the cards and read them to the group. Invite kids to raise their hands for any of the statements they think God might have said. Pose the question: Who wrote the Bible, God or humans?
2. Watch
   "Who wrote the Bible, God or humans?" video.
3. Unpack
   - Which ideas from the video hadn't you thought of before?
   - What don't you believe? What surprised you?
   - What do you disagree with? What do you agree with? Why?
   - So, what do you think?
   - What is still confusing?

What about the Bible?

Tell about a time when you felt inspired in a creative act. The most important thing is that you were carried away in the creative endeavor. Did you know at the time that you were inspired? What was the outcome? How did others respond to what you did? If possible, bring the creative work with you, and offer time for kids to ask you questions.

Questions for conversation:

- Can someone tell if they're inspired? How?
- Have you ever felt inspired? What inspires you?
- Read 2 Timothy 3:16. Do you think the people who wrote the books in the Bible knew their writings would become "holy"? Did they know their work was "inspired"? Why or why not?
- What is your favorite novel? What is the difference between that book and the Bible?

Get this stuff ...
Note cards.

in·spi·ra·tion
[in-spuh-rey-shuh n]
Literally, to breathe in. It's what happens when God sparks creativity from the inside out.

© 2010 sparkhouse. All Rights Reserved. May be reproduced for local use only provided each copy carries this notice.

Bible Unit: Who wrote the Bible, God or humans? 2

Guidance for how to set up and discuss the session video. Remember, read this BEFORE the video. Waiting till after is too little too late.

Any supplies you'll need in addition to the basics outlined at the top of the page. Most will be available at any store with the word "mart" in the name. And save your receipts!

Definitions of key terms for the session. Some folks really go for such a thing.

Activities to lay a biblical foundation for kids' discovery in the rest of the session. Use this section to add as much depth to the session as you need, or to keep things moving when you start to lose them.

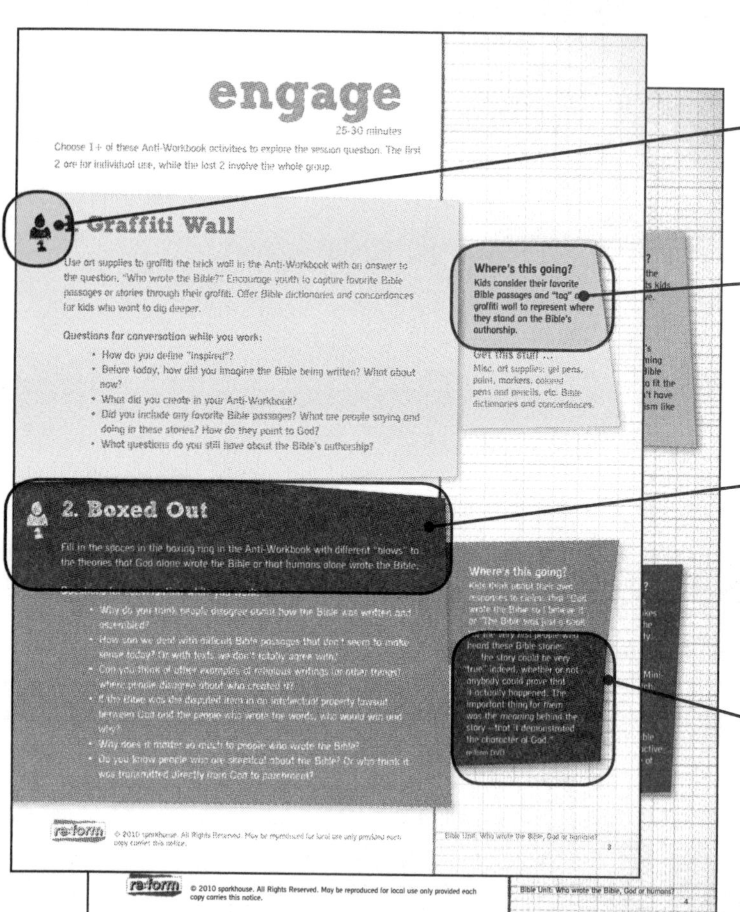

engage

25-30 minutes

Choose 1+ of these Anti-Workbook activities to explore the session question. The first 2 are for individual use, while the last 2 involve the whole group.

1. Graffiti Wall

Use art supplies to graffiti the brick wall in the Anti-Workbook with an answer to the question, "Who wrote the Bible?" Encourage youth to capture favorite Bible passages or stories through their graffiti. Offer Bible dictionaries and concordances for kids who want to dig deeper.

Questions for conversation while you work:

- How do you define "inspired"?
- Before today, how did you imagine the Bible being written? What about now?
- What did you create in your Anti-Workbook?
- Did you include any favorite Bible passages? What are people saying and doing in these stories? How do they point to God?
- What questions do you still have about the Bible's authorship?

Where's this going?
Kids consider their favorite Bible passages and "tag" a graffiti wall to represent where they stand on the Bible's authorship.

Get this stuff ...
Misc. art supplies: gel pens, paint, markers, colored pens and pencils, etc. Bible dictionaries and concordances.

2. Boxed Out

Fill in the spaces in the boxing ring in the Anti-Workbook with different "blows" to the theories that God alone wrote the Bible or that humans alone wrote the Bible.

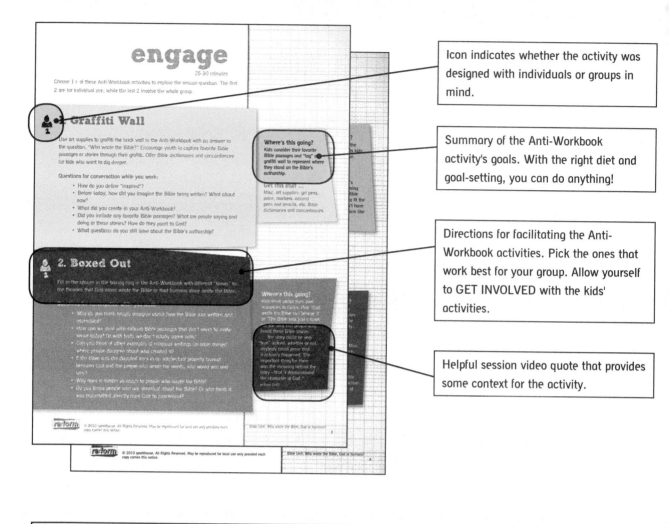

Icon indicates whether the activity was designed with individuals or groups in mind.

Summary of the Anti-Workbook activity's goals. With the right diet and goal-setting, you can do anything!

Directions for facilitating the Anti-Workbook activities. Pick the ones that work best for your group. Allow yourself to GET INVOLVED with the kids' activities.

Helpful session video quote that provides some context for the activity.

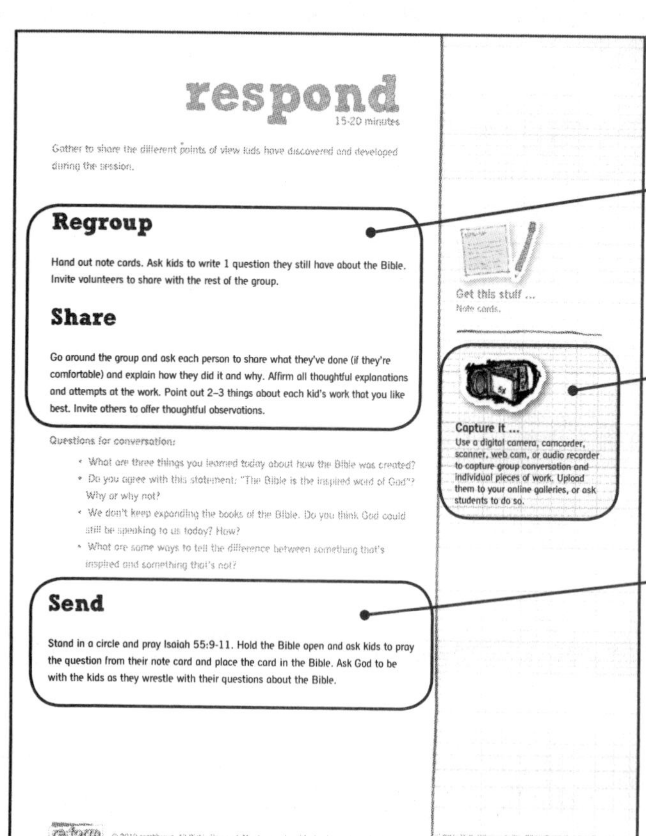

respond

15-20 minutes

Gather to share the different points of view kids have discovered and developed during the session.

Regroup

Hand out note cards. Ask kids to write 1 question they still have about the Bible. Invite volunteers to share with the rest of the group.

Share

Go around the group and ask each person to share what they've done (if they're comfortable) and explain how they did it and why. Affirm all thoughtful explanations and attempts at the work. Point out 2–3 things about each kid's work that you like best. Invite others to offer thoughtful observations.

Questions for conversation:

- What are three things you learned today about how the Bible was created?
- Do you agree with this statement: "The Bible is the inspired word of God"? Why or why not?
- We don't keep expanding the books of the Bible. Do you think God could still be speaking to us today? How?
- What are some ways to tell the difference between something that's inspired and something that's not?

Send

Stand in a circle and pray Isaiah 55:9-11. Hold the Bible open and ask kids to pray the question from their note card and place the card in the Bible. Ask God to be with the kids as they wrestle with their questions about the Bible.

Get this stuff ...
Note cards.

Capture it ...
Use a digital camera, camcorder, scanner, web cam, or audio recorder to capture group conversation and individual pieces of work. Upload them to your online galleries, or ask students to do so.

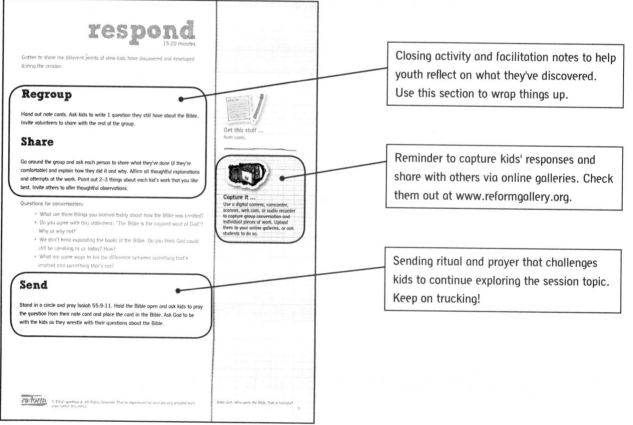

Closing activity and facilitation notes to help youth reflect on what they've discovered. Use this section to wrap things up.

Reminder to capture kids' responses and share with others via online galleries. Check them out at www.reformgallery.org.

Sending ritual and prayer that challenges kids to continue exploring the session topic. Keep on trucking!

unit No. 1
Bible

Bible Unit
Who wrote the Bible, God or humans?

Prepare

What's behind all this?

The nature of the biblical canon has been a very contentious issue throughout the history of Christian theology. The spectrum of opinions spans from those who believe that the writers were in a trance and God moved their hands to form the words to those who believe that the authors had no idea that what they were writing was even special, let alone holy.

While Paul wrote that "all scripture is inspired," it's hard to imagine he was referring to his own writings. However, in hindsight, the church determined in the early centuries that some writings testified to the gospel in a way that they considered in line with the Apostles' teaching, and was therefore authoritative. Human beings clearly put pen to parchment to create the documents that have become the Hebrew and Christian Scriptures, but as with other moments of God's grace, Christians believe that God inspired these writers in a unique way and that God guarded the process that formed the canon.

Therefore, while Christians may believe many books to be inspirational, we believe that the Bible is uniquely inspired by God and therefore the best revelation of God and the gospel that we have.

Where are kids at?

- Kids love competition. It's a great way to engage them in learning and discovery. Make sure it takes place in an environment of trust with clear ground rules.
- Tech-savvy teens are more aware than ever of other cultures and religions and may wonder what's different about the Bible and Christian writings. Encourage curiosity, and provide resources where kids can discover more—like Bible concordances, maps, dictionaries, reputable websites, etc.

2 Timothy 3:16

Where's this going?
By confronting their assumptions and biases about where the Bible came from, the group can start wrestling through them to a new understanding of the Bible.

Consider this . . .
"What we have, from Genesis to Revelation, is a massive narrative structure in which, though Paul, the evangelists, and John of Patmos are, of course, extremely well aware of the earlier parts, no single author saw the whole or knew about all its other parts. It is as though engineers from different workshops were invited to produce bits and pieces of cantilevers which ended up, when put together without the different work-shops knowing of it, producing the Forth Bridge."

N.T. Wright, *Scripture's Doctrine and Theology's Bible*, p. 61.

encounter

15 minutes

Video

Get things started by watching the session video. You can also use an Anti-Workbook activity as an ice-breaker.

1. Set up

Give each kid a note card, and ask everyone to write down one thing they wish God said. Collect the cards and read them to the group. Invite kids to raise their hands for any of the statements they think God might have said. Pose the question: Who wrote the Bible, God or humans?

2. Watch

"Who wrote the Bible, God or humans?" DVD 1, Chapter 1

3. Unpack

- Which ideas from the video hadn't you thought of before?
- What don't you believe? What surprised you?
- What do you disagree with? What do you agree with? Why?
- So, what do you think? What is still confusing?

What about the Bible?

Tell about a time when you felt inspired in a creative act. The most important thing is that you were carried away in the creative endeavor. Did you know at the time that you were inspired? What was the outcome? How did others respond to what you did? If possible, bring the creative work with you, and offer time for kids to ask you questions.

Questions for conversation:

- Can someone tell if they're inspired? How?
- Have you ever felt inspired? What inspires you?
- Read 2 Timothy 3:16. Do you think the people who wrote the books in the Bible knew their writings would become "holy"? Did they know their work was "inspired"? Why or why not?
- What is your favorite novel? What is the difference between that book and the Bible?

Make sure you've got the obvic stuff for this session—re:form video (DVD or download), Anti-Workbooks, Bibles, pens pencils, paper, tape, etc.

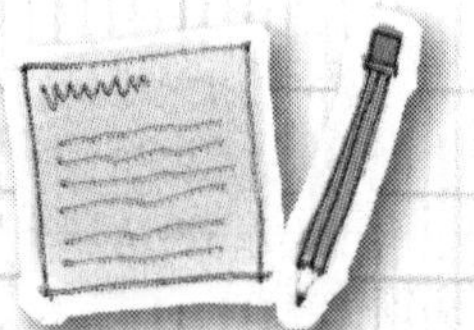

Get this stuff . . .

Note cards.

in·spi·ra·tion

[in-spuh-rey-shuh n]

Literally, to breathe in. It's what happens when God sparks creati from the inside out.

25-30 minutes

Choose 1+ Anti-Workbook (AW) activities to explore the session question. The first 2 are for individual use, while the last 2 involve the whole group.

1. Graffiti Wall, AW p. 10

Use art supplies to graffiti page 10 with an answer to the question, "Who wrote the Bible?" Encourage youth to capture favorite Bible passages or stories through their graffiti. Offer Bible dictionaries and concordances for kids who want to dig deeper.

Questions for conversation while you work:

- How do you define "inspired"?
- Before today, how did you imagine the Bible being written? What about now?
- What did you create in your Anti-Workbook?
- Did you include any favorite Bible passages? What are people saying and doing in these stories? How do they point to God?
- What questions do you still have about the Bible's authorship?

Where's this going?

Kids consider their favorite Bible passages and "tag" a graffiti wall to represent where they stand on the Bible's authorship.

Get this stuff ...

Misc. art supplies: gel pens, paint, markers, colored pens and pencils, etc. Bible dictionaries and concordances.

2. Boxed Out, AW p. 11

Fill in the spaces in the boxing ring on page 11 with different "blows" to the theories that God alone wrote the Bible or that humans alone wrote the Bible.

Questions for conversation while you work:

- Why do you think people disagree about how the Bible was written and assembled?
- How can we deal with difficult Bible passages that don't seem to make sense today? Or with texts we don't totally agree with?
- Can you think of other examples of religious writings (or other things) where people disagree about who created it?
- If the Bible was the disputed item in an intellectual property lawsuit between God and the people who wrote the words, who would win and why?
- Why does it matter so much to people who wrote the Bible?
- Do you know people who are skeptical about the Bible? Or who think it was transmitted directly from God to parchment?

Where's this going?

Kids think about their own responses to claims that "God wrote the Bible so I believe it" or "The Bible was just a book written by people."

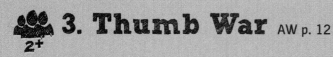

3. Thumb War AW p. 12

Hold a thumb war tournament. Punch out the thumb-wrestling mat on page P1 of the Anti-Workbooks, and fill in the tournament bracket on page 12 with your wrestlers. Each match's winner argues what they think and then progresses to the next round until you have a champion.

Questions for conversation while you work:

- Do you think this is a good way to determine who wrote the Bible? Why or why not?
- Do you think God cares about the argument over who wrote the Bible?
- Do you know what the word "plagiarism" means? Which of the four gospel writers plagiarized the others? Or could something else have been happening?
- If God wrote the gospels, why did it take four different versions to get the job done?
- Is there any way to prove conclusively who wrote the Bible? Can we prove who wrote any of the books of the Bible?
- Jesus quoted the Old Testament all the time. What does this tell you about what God thinks of the Bible?

Where's this going?
Friendly competition in th form of a thumb war gets kids sharing what they believe.

pla•gia•rism
[play-juh-riz-um]
Stealing another person's words or ideas and claimi them as your own. (In Bib times, retelling a story to the author's context woul have been considered plagiarism like it might be today.)

4. Tower Races, AW p. 13

Create teams of two or three kids. Hand out an equal number of toothpicks, gumdrops, and mini-marshmallows to each team. Give teams 132 seconds to build a free-standing tower on the yellow circle in one of their Anti-Workbooks—in silence! After time is up, use a tape measure to determine the tallest tower.

Questions for conversation while you work:

- What was your favorite part of this activity?
- What's the most challenging part of working together without being able to talk?
- Would it have been easier to build if you could talk with your team members?
- Name some of the benefits of doing this activity with others. Some difficulties?
- When you look at the Bible, what are some of the benefits of having a lot of different writings together in one book? The challenges?
- Compare the foundations of each tower. What designs worked best?
- What does a tower need to be tall and strong?
- How was the Bible designed? What kind of foundation does the Bible have?

Where's this going?
Tower-building gets kids thinking about what make a solid foundation and the importance of community.

Get this stuff...
Toothpicks. Gumdrops. Mi marshmallows. Stopwatch Tape measure.

Back it up...
"At its foundation, the Bible is a true witness to an acti moving God and the life of Jesus Christ."
re:form DVD

15-20 minutes

ather to share the different points of view kids have discovered and eveloped during the session.

Regroup

land out note cards. Ask kids to write 1 question they still have about the ible. Invite volunteers to share with the rest of the group.

hare

o around the group and ask each person to share what they've done (if ey're comfortable) and explain how they did it and why. Affirm all thoughtful xplanations and attempts at the work. Point out 2–3 things about each kid's ork that you like best. Invite others to offer thoughtful observations.

uestions for conversation:

- What are three things you learned today about how the Bible was created?
- Do you agree with this statement: "The Bible is the inspired word of God"? Why or why not?
- We don't keep expanding the books of the Bible. Do you think God could still be speaking to us today? How?
- What are some ways to tell the difference between something that's inspired and something that's not?

end

tand in a circle and pray Isaiah 55:9-11. Hold the Bible open and ask kids o pray the question from their note card and place the card in the Bible. Ask od to be with the kids as they wrestle with their questions about the Bible.

Get this stuff . . .
Note cards.

Capture it . . .
Use a digital camera, camcorder, scanner, web cam, or audio recorder to capture group conversations and individual pieces of work. Upload them to your online galleries, or ask students to do so.

Bible Unit
Is the Bible true?

Prepare

What's behind all this?

During the Enlightenment (17th–18th centuries) we entered the age of *empirical truth.* In other words, truth was measured by a statement's accuracy in relation to facts—*what really happened.* This matters a lot in a court of law, a scientific laboratory, or a newspaper article. They all try to get at empirical truth. Empirical truth is helpful, but it does not give the full picture.

In the past, many who told and wrote the stories that defined cultures were less interested in empirical truth than they were in capturing the entire scope and feel of a narrative—the whole story. The way they thought of truth versus how we do can be compared to the difference between a hand-painted canvas and a photograph: while a portrait relies upon the painter to add lines and shading that tell a fuller story about the subject—to create a rendering that is shaped by the artist's level of skill and what he or she feels is important to emphasize or de-emphasize—a photograph captures a literal moment in time that really happened.

Rather than depending primarily on the factual accuracy of eyewitness accounts (dubious at best) or scientific proofs, the truth of the Bible is corroborated by our experience of its truth, and by the longstanding testimony of the church that God's Spirit is active in the world—just as the Bible portrays it.

Where are kids at?

- Kids are trying to make sense of the world around them. They're wrestling with perception vs. reality in social, educational, and political structures.
- Kids are constantly paying attention to how people in authority function. Adolescents are in varying stages of moving from concrete to abstract thinking. Where kids are in this transition will impact their ability to distinguish between positive and negative uses of authority.

John 8:32
John 18:37-38

Where's this going?
Kids will explore various understandings of truth and their relationship to the Bible.

Consider this . . .

"What is truth? said jesting Pilate, and would not stay for an answer."
Francis Bacon, *Essays 1: Of Truth*

"You will know the truth, and the truth will make you free."
John 8:32

encounter

15 minutes

Video

1. Set up

Ask kids to find one partner each and to take turns sharing their favorite mysteries. These mysteries might come from books, movies, or television shows. Give each tandem a note card and pen. Ask each pair to make a list of steps that take place before a mystery can be solved. Pose the question: "How do people arrive at the truth?"

2. Watch

"Is the Bible true?" DVD 1, Chapter 2

3. Unpack

- Which ideas in the video hadn't you thought of before?
- What don't you believe?
- What surprised you?
- Did you see anything in the video that reminded you of something else you've experienced or felt?
- What questions do you have about the video?

What about the Bible?

As a leader, what questions do you have about figuring out what's true in your life? Help kids think about the word *truth* by sharing a time when your personal experience impacted your version of the truth. Is your true story the same as someone else's who shared that experience? Is truth always based in proven facts? Can opinion ever enter into truth? Consider sharing an experience from your childhood that kids can relate to.

Questions for conversation:

- Read John 18:37-38. What made Jesus' truth different from Pilate's truth?
- Was there common ground that could have been shared by Jesus and Pilate?
- When have you had a different version of a story than someone else?

Make sure you've got the obvi stuff for this session—re:form video (DVD or download), Anti-Workbooks, Bibles, pens pencils, paper, tape, etc.

Get this stuff . . .

Note cards.

Back it up . . .

"Their faith was never in the stor all, or in the storyteller, or even the pages of a book. Their faith in God."

re:form DVD

"A lot of times when people ask, the Bible true?' what they're rea asking is: 'Is the Bible historicall accurate?'"

re:form DVD

truth
[trooth]
a statement based in fact or reali

Truth
[Trooth]
the eternal wisdom of God which Bible helps us understand

engage

25-30 minutes

Choose 1+ Anti-Workbook (AW) activities to explore the session question. The first 2 are for individual use, while the last 2 involve the whole group.

1. How D'Ya Know? AW p. 14

Before asking kids to begin, think of people who helped you define truth in your life. Then ask kids to examine the vertical list of statements and think of the person or people who helped them arrive at the *truth* about those items. Some truths may have been influenced by multiple people. Encourage kids to talk with a partner if they have trouble coming up with additional statements at the bottom.

Questions for conversation while you work:

- Are there any statements that you disagree with? What experience has led you to believe they are untrue?
- Which statements are the most difficult to think about? Why?
- What is your primary source of information? How do you know it can be trusted?
- How can technology help you seek truth? How can technology make it more difficult to seek truth?

Where's this going?

Kids think of people who helped them arrive at diverse realizations about the world around them.

ev•o•lu•tion
[ehv-oh-**loo**-shun]
a theory stating that living things develop from earlier forms of life

2. Fact? True? AW p. 15

Begin by telling kids that there can be a difference between something you believe to be true and a fact. "It's nice outside" may be true for someone and not for someone else. "It's 59°" is a measurable fact. Write some statements you can prove in the "fact" column and statements you believe to be true in the "true" column.

Questions for conversation while you work:

- Can something in the "true" column also belong in the "fact" column?
- Is truth the opposite of fact? Is truth synonymous with opinion?
- Are there examples of Biblical writings that can be true but not fact?
- How should we view people or events in the Bible that cannot be proven as fact?
- Who decides which Biblical stories are true? Scientists? Christians? Nobody?

Where's this going?

Kids wrestle with the nuanced differences among truth, belief, and fact.

Back it up . . .

"For the *very first* people who heard these Bible stories . . . the story could be very "true" indeed, whether or not anybody could prove that it actually happened. The important thing for *them* was the *meaning* behind the story—that it demonstrated the character of God."
re:form DVD

3. A Matter of Perspective AW p. 16

Begin by asking kids to share what they think they know about "Moses and the Red Sea" (*burning bush, wilderness, plagues, 10 Commandments*). Write their comments on a sheet of poster board so everyone can see. Read Exodus 14:21-31. Form groups to examine the illustration in the Anti-Workbook and describe the scene from the perspective of a historian, a scientist, and a pastor.

Questions for conversation while you work:

- What parts of this story—if any—can be proven?
- Are some details from the Biblical text omitted from the illustration? Are other details not mentioned in the story but added by the artist?
- What are we assuming about how a pastor, historian, or scientist would examine this illustration?
- Is it possible for different people to have different understandings (truth-claims) and each of them be right? Why or why not?

Get this stuff . . .
Poster board. Markers. T

Where's this going?
Kids examine a historical event through various len

in·ter·pre·ta·tion
[in-ter-pruh-tay-shun]
explaining something bas on a particular perspectiv

4. B.S.I. AW p. 17

Talk about something that seemed miraculous in your life. What made it feel that way? Ask a volunteer to read the story (John 6:1-14) aloud while other kids follow along.

Invite kids to think of themselves as detectives trying to explain what actually happened. Punch out the Clue Cards. Clues are recorded on three cards. Ask groups of kids to identify and record three other clues on the blank cards. Fold the cards to make table tents and set them up showing the order of the clue's importance in leading to the truth. Record your "Bible Scene Investigation" on page 17. Kids may want to adopt the persona of their favorite crime drama show.

Questions for conversation while you work:

- Who would you want to interview as part of your investigation?
- What questions would you ask them?
- How would you go about making a factual case for the bread and fish miracle?
- Can you use the Bible as evidence? Why or why not?
- Should you believe the Bible as a book of historical fact?
- Is it possible that this miracle took place, even if it can't be proved? Why?
- Is there a more important truth to this story than "just the facts"?

Get this stuff . . .
Clue cards, Anti-Workbook page P2.

Where's this going?
Kids explore truth in new ways while examining a miracle through the eyes o detective.

Back it up . . .
"A whole lot of really smart people have argued about this very question for hundreds of years. And both sides have stacks of evidence."
re:form DVD

15-20 minutes

ather to share the different points of view kids have discovered and eveloped during the session.

Regroup

land out note cards. Ask each kid to write one question he or she still has bout truth as it relates to the Bible. Invite volunteers to share with the rest of he group.

nvite kids to think of an ordeal in their life. A fight with a sibling, a lisagreement with parents, the first lost tooth, the longest car trip ever, etc. How would they tell that story to a friend? Would someone who shared that xperience have a different version of the story? Which story is "most true"?

Get this stuff . . .
Note cards.

Share

nvite kids to share their work and describe how and why they did it. Affirm those things you appreciate or find interesting and ask others to offer helpful observations.

Capture it . . .
Use a digital camera, camcorder, scanner, web cam, or audio recorder to capture group conversations and individual pieces of work. Upload them to your online galleries, or ask students to do so.

Questions for conversation:

- What do you think about truth found in the Bible?
- Which people, events, or stories do you think are not factually accurate?
- How can the Bible be true if it contains inaccurate information?
- What do you think is the most important event in the Bible? Would you feel differently if that event didn't happen in the exact same way the Bible says?

So, is the Bible true?

Send

Ask kids to place their note cards in their Bibles. State today's question, "Is the Bible true?" and ask them to join you in brief silence reflecting on your time together. Then encourage kids to add questions throughout the week as they read and discuss the Bible with friends and family.

Bible Unit
Why does the Bible contradict itself at times?

Prepare

What's behind all this?

Critics of Christianity often point to the contradictions in the Bible as proof that it is inconsistent and thus unreliable and not worthy of our trust. One oft-cited example is the sign that hung over Jesus' head on the cross—each of the four Gospels has a slightly different account of what was on that sign.

However, it must be remembered that the Bible is, in fact, a collection of books (in Greek, *ta biblia* means "the books") written over the course of 2,000 years by scores of authors. With that in mind, the consistency displayed across the Biblical narrative is actually quite astounding.

The Bible's primary subject—God and God's relationship to humankind—has a singular message: God created us, loves us, and will never give up on us. That doesn't mean we should ignore the contradictions and inconsistencies in the Bible, but maybe we should think of them like this: If you listened to a 3-hour-long symphony, would you let the two missed notes by the clarinetist ruin your experience of the beauty of the overall work? Probably not.

Where are kids at?

- Kids' brains are shifting from a concrete, all-or-nothing perspective to an abstract, both/and understanding of the world. Not all kids will be able to look past Biblical contradictions without invalidating the whole of Scripture.
- Kids want to be trusted with information that might have been withheld from them in childhood. They will be curious about and excited by the possibility of unearthing new information about inconsistencies in Biblical narratives.

John 20:30-31

Where's this going?
Kids wrestle with Biblical contradictions and search for big-picture themes revealed in Scripture.

Consider this . . .

"The Bible is not simply an anthology; there is a unity which binds the whole together."
F.F. Bruce, *The Books and the Parchments*

"The Gospels are not, and never were intended to be inspected as if they were ancient photographs of Jesus taken with a high resolution, all seeing lens. On the contrary these documents are much more like portraits, and portraits always are selective, tendentious, perspectival."
Ben Witherington, beliefnet.com blog

encounter

15 minutes

Video

1. Set up

Before talking with kids, think about your kindergarten experiences. Was this a positive time? Ask kids to share a kindergarten story with a partner—first day, learning to read, favorite game, teacher, etc. Then ask: "Are you sure your story is accurate? Would someone else tell a slightly different version of this same story?"

2. Watch

"Why does the Bible contradict itself at times?" DVD 1, Chapter 3

3. Unpack

- What surprised you in the video?
- What ideas were new?
- Are details important when you tell a story? In the Bible?
- Why do you think the Bible contradicts itself?

What about the Bible?

Consider how you have come to your understanding of who God is, despite imperfections in Scripture. Ask kids to listen for the words posted on the sign over Jesus' head on the cross as volunteers read aloud Matthew 27:37, Mark 15:26, Luke 23:38, and John 19:19. Are the differences significant? Do they say anything about the historical accuracy of the story of the crucifixion?

Before reading John 20:30-31 aloud, tell kids Jesus was speaking to his disciples after his death and resurrection. He had just questioned Thomas's need for a physical sign before he would believe Jesus was alive.

Questions for conversation while you work:

- What does John say about the purpose of the Bible?
- What "other signs" might have been omitted from the Bible? Why?
- How do you react when someone keeps important information from you? Why?

Make sure you've got the obvio stuff for this session—re:form video (DVD or download), Anti-Workbooks, Bibles, pens o pencils, paper, tape, etc.

con•tra•dict
[kahn-trah-**dihkt**]
when two sets of facts are not in agreement

mes•si•ah
[mes-**sye**-uh]
one who is anointed, especially tc rescue people or set them free

Back it up . . .

"The Bible was written to help poi people toward an understanding c who God is and how God is at wo in the world."
re:form DVD

engage

25-30 minutes

Choose 1+ Anti-Workbook (AW) activities to explore the session question. The first 2 are for individual use, while the last 2 involve the whole group.

1. On the Third Day AW p. 18

Were you surprised when you first discovered there wasn't just one definitive creation story? Confused? Did it matter? Tell kids the book of Genesis contains two stories of creation. (This may surprise many!) Have them read Genesis 1 and 2 following the Anti-Workbook directions.

Questions for conversation while you work:

- What are the stories' similarities and differences?
- What is your reaction to TWO creation stories in Genesis?
- Is one story more accurate? Why? Is it possible neither story has it exactly right? Can they both be right?
- How do these "contradictions" make you feel about the Bible?
- What are some big-picture themes in both stories?
- What do these stories tell us about God?

Get this stuff . . .
Creation stickers, Anti-Workbook page S1.

Where's this going?
Kids look for meaning in the contradictions in the creation stories.

cre•a•tion
[kree-**ay**-shun]
the act of God that brought the universe and all living things into existence

2. Hear It Draw It AW p. 19

Think about a time when you imagined what something looked like based on another person's description—a car, a building, a new coat. Was it the same as you imagined when you saw it? Tell kids that they will hear a 2,500-year-old verbal description of the prophet Isaiah's dream. Encourage kids to close their eyes and imagine the temple as it is being described. Slowly read Isaiah 6:1-8 aloud. When finished, have kids draw what they think the temple looked like. As they draw, consider reading the passage again. When most people are done drawing, ask for volunteers to share what they created.

Questions for conversation while you work:

- What is challenging about drawing Isaiah's vision?
- What surprises you about someone else's work? Puzzles you?
- Do you disagree with someone else's interpretation?
- Are different interpretations contradictions? Why or why not?
- Did you hear anything differently the second time the vision was read?
- Which kid had the most accurate drawing? How do you know?

Get this stuff . . .
Colored pencils. Markers. Crayons.

Where's this going?
Kids create visual contradictions as they compare their illustrations with those of others.

proph•et
[**prahf**-it]
a person who speaks on behalf of God

Back it up . . .
"In the Bible the exact details aren't nearly as important as the overall message that is being shared."
re:form DVD

3. Ring Ring! AW p. 20

Before starting this activity with kids, think of a time when someone heard something very different than what you said. Was the outcome funny? Disastrous? Begin by telling kids how the oral tradition of Scripture impacted the early writings of Scripture. A story about a story is usually not the same word for word.

Ask a volunteer to explain the child's game of Telephone. Tell kids to follow the plan in the Anti-Workbook. TIP: It's easy to intentionally sabotage a game of Telephone by passing along an incorrect and preposterous statement. Invite everyone to help make this a meaningful activity by participating with honesty.

Questions for conversation while you work:

- What's the most difficult part of a game of Telephone?
- What words or phrases are the easiest to misunderstand? Why?
- What could prevent misunderstandings in Telephone? In life?
- What are the many ways people react to misunderstandings?
- What does this have to do with contradictions in the Bible?

Where's this going?

Kids experience the sometimes unreliable natu of word-of-mouth storytell

o•ral tra•di•tion
[aw-ruhl truh-di-shuhn]
passing along a communit cultural and historical background through spoke (or sung) stories

4. A Picture is Worth AW p. 21

Before asking kids to describe what they see in the dinner-table scene in the Anti-Workbook, think about the assumptions you make when observing people near you in a public space.

Ask kids to examine the dinner-table scene through the eyes of each person and write three sentences describing what they see. Share statements while writing and/or when finished.

Questions for conversation while you work:

- What stories were similar? What was different among the stories?
- Did someone's story directly contradict your story?
- How did situations (joys or concerns) in your life influence how you see this story?
- If the people who were actually in the dinner scene told their stories, who would decide which story was the accurate one? What about in stories in the Bible?
- How do various perspectives of an event lead to contradictions?

Where's this going?

Kids examine how each person's perspective affect his or her interpretation of events.

per•spec•tive
[pur-spek-tihv]
evaluating a situation from one person's point of view

Back it up . . .

"Each person who wrote a part of what would become the Bible had their own perspective and their own way of describing events."
re:form DVD

15-20 minutes

Gather to share the different points of view kids have discovered and developed during the session.

Regroup

Hand out note cards. Ask each kid to write one question he or she still has about how/if contradictions in stories (in the Bible or life) change the big picture of the story. Invite volunteers to share with the rest of the group.

Ask kids to help you think of a few big-picture themes, stories, or characters in the Bible that don't seem to be affected by contradictions. Help kids move from focusing on the minutiae of most Biblical contradictions to broader claims Christians agree on.

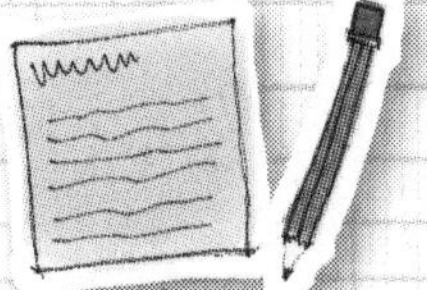

Get this stuff . . .

Note cards.

Capture it . . .

Use a digital camera, camcorder, scanner, web cam, or audio recorder to capture group conversations and individual pieces of work. Upload them to your online galleries, or ask kids to do so.

Share

Invite kids to share their work and describe how and why they did it. Affirm those things you appreciate or find interesting and ask others to offer helpful observations.

Questions for conversation:

- How do contradictions in the Bible make a story more true? Less true?
- How have your feelings changed about Biblical contradictions throughout this session?
- Are there Bible stories or themes you wonder about in light of your discussions or activities?

Send

Ask kids to place their note cards in their Bibles. State today's question, "Why does the Bible contradict itself at times?" and ask them to join you in brief silence reflecting on your time together. Then encourage kids to add questions throughout the week as they read and discuss the Bible with friends and family.

Bible Unit

Is the New Testament more important than the Old Testament?

Prepare

What's behind all this?

Most movies are made of three acts: setup, conflict, and resolution. Now think of your favorite dramatic movie. Can you imagine, the first time you saw it, skipping the first two acts, and only watching the final 30 minutes? Surely that would gut the film of its beauty and meaning.

Similarly, for Christians, the Christian Scriptures (New Testament) make no real, meaningful sense without the Hebrew Scriptures (Old Testament). The Hebrew Scriptures were Jesus' Bible. They describe the relationship God had with Israel, and the promise made in that relationship. The Christian Scriptures record the story of Jesus as the fulfillment of God's promise for all people.

Jesus himself often quoted the Hebrew Scriptures, demonstrating the unity of the narrative. The writers of the Christian Scriptures used the Hebrew Scriptures not only as illustrations, but even as citations—support for their arguments. For Christians, it is the indispensable bond between the Christian and Hebrew Scriptures that makes the narrative whole. In other words, the "movie" is only complete with both parts.

Where are kids at?

- Kids can become overwhelmed by an abundance of historical data. They often want to know what is most relevant for the here-and-now.
- From a young age, kids are most familiar with a traditional, linear flow of a story. In adolescence, they are also being exposed to different narrative sequences and unique methods of storytelling.

Matthew 5:17

Where's this going?

Kids question, discuss, and ponder the connectedness of the Old and New Testaments.

Consider this . . .

"The unity of the two Testaments proceeds from the unity of God's plan and his Revelation. The Old Testament prepares for the New and the New Testament fulfills the Old; the two shed light on each other; both are true Word of God."

Catechism of the Catholic Church, Part One: The Profession of Faith; Section One: I Believe—We Believe; Chapter Two: God Comes to Meet Man; Article 3: Sacred Scripture; 140

encounter

15 minutes

Video

1. Set up

Have kids find partners and think of their favorite movies. Give each kid 90 seconds to explain the movie's details to his or her partner. What aspects of a story are most important when sharing it with someone else?

2. Watch

"Is the NT more important than the OT?" DVD 1, Chapter 4

3. Unpack

- What can happen when you enter in the middle of something—a movie, discussion, argument, or just people hanging around?
- What can happen if you just know part of the Bible?
- How did you feel about comparing the Bible to a movie?
- What questions do you have about the video?

What about the Bible?

Help kids think about the relationship of the Old Testament and the New Testament by highlighting Jesus' understanding of the Hebrew Scriptures. Ask a volunteer to read Matthew 5:17 aloud. Translate the verse into language kids use today. How do John 13:34 and Matthew 5:38-48 reinforce or challenge what Jesus said about fulfilling the Scriptures?

Questions for conversation while you work:

- What does it mean for something to be fulfilled?
- How do you react when someone changes the rules of something that seemed to be working just fine? Why?
- What "Bible" did Jesus read?
- How do you think the crowds of people felt when Jesus added a new spin to their old way of doing things (Matthew 5:38-48)?
- Does the New Commandment (John 13:34) undo or add to the other commandments found in the Old Testament? How?

Make sure you've got the obv stuff for this session—re:form video (DVD or download), Anti-Workbooks, Bibles, pens pencils, paper, tape, etc.

smite
[smyt]
to punish someone by inflicting disaster on them

blas•phe•my
[**blass**-fuh-mee]
disrespect for God and other ho things

Ho•mer
[**hoh**-mur]
an ancient poet who wrote *The Iliad* and *The Odyssey:* not to b confused with Bart Simpson's d (d'oh!)

ful•fill
[fuhl-**fihl**]
to complete or carry out what is expected

Back it up . . .

"For Christians the whole story f its ultimate completion in the p of Jesus Christ."
re:form DVD

engage

25-30 minutes

Choose 1+ Anti-Workbook (AW) activities to explore the session question. The first 2 are for individual use, while the last 2 involve the whole group.

1. Better Together AW p. 22

Have you ever thought, "If only _____ were here"? But when you tell that person it's just not the same. Ask kids to think of things, places, people, events that go together. Write their ideas on the whiteboard. Distribute supplies and invite kids to make collages—pairs or trios or many objects all together. Encourage kids to talk with one another and as a group as they work. Invite kids to add new pairings to the list.

Questions for conversation while you work:

- Which groupings give a whole new purpose to both items?
- Which groupings enhance but don't change the purpose of the items?
- Are there things you prefer by themselves and not paired with other things?
- Do some groupings make one of the items less important?
- What might this tell you about pairing the Old and New Testaments?

Get this stuff . . .

Old magazines. Scissors. Glue. Whiteboard. Dry-erase markers.

Where's this going?

Kids compare the independent and interdependent natures of people and things and of the OT and NT.

2. Hammer Time AW p. 23

Have you ever panicked when you couldn't find an important part of something you wanted to use? What might happen if you focused on the remaining part and figured out what to do with that? Invite kids to spend a few minutes examining the "half-hammer" picture and write some creative uses for this tool in the space provided in the Anti-Workbook. Additionally, write the things this tool is unable to do. As kids talk while working they'll have more—and likely unique—ideas. Encourage kids to share ideas with the whole group.

Questions for conversation while you work:

- Are there things the half-hammer would no longer be able to do if the other half were present?
- What important tasks did you think the half-hammer could accomplish that you wouldn't normally think of as tasks for a whole hammer?
- How have you used broken or incomplete things for a good purpose?
- What if all OT references were removed from the NT? In what way is the OT incomplete without the NT?

Where's this going?

Kids wrestle with the important, but ultimately incomplete, nature of the Old Testament.

Back it up . . .

"The arc of the story holds together, from the Old Testament to the New Testament to now: God is constantly seeking us out, constantly seeking *everyone* out, in love."

re:form DVD

3. Cell Phone Ancestors AW p. 24

Begin by talking about the evolution of communication in the last 20 years. How has the shift from pencil-and-paper communication to wireless gadgets changed people's behavior? Encourage kids to think back to a time when even writing utensils were unheard of—when oral traditions were the only ways of communicating important truths. What difference might that have made for the crowds of people who saw and heard Jesus? Does it change how you think about the connection between the Old and New Testaments? Keep talking as you recreate the cell phone's ancestry.

Questions for conversation while you work:

- What stories have your parents, grandparents, or other people told you to help you know more about yourself?
- Why is it important to know the origin and evolution of people or things?
- How can history help you imagine the future?
- What would it feel like to live in a world with no digital technology?
- How would Jesus' story be different if we didn't know the Old Testament story?

Where's this going?
Kids reflect on the importance of ancestral milestones.

an•ces•tor
[ann-sehs-ter]
somebody or something from which another perso or thing is descended; predecessor

4. Create-A-Comic AW p. 25

Before asking kids to begin, try to remember a time when you saw the ending of a happening before learning the beginning—maybe a broken window or an unhappy kid standing apart from a group of kids. What story did you imagine? Did it match the real beginning?

Invite kids to use their creativity to imagine what happened in the six panels before the final three. Encourage kids to work independently for a bit, creating a lively conversation by comparing stories. Are there other characters, locations, and events that might have led to the fence being broken? Allow time for everyone to share drawings and ideas.

Questions for conversation while you work:

- What is/was the most difficult part of this activity?
- Did anyone write a story based on personal experience?
- What similarities did people write? Differences?
- Think of the last three panels as the New Testament and the first six as the Old Testament. What information was added in the beginning that clarified the ending? How would more background information be helpful?

Get this stuff . . .
Colored pencils.

Where's this going?
Kids consider how differe beginnings of a story can lead to a known ending.

chro•nol•o•gy
[kruh-nahl-uh-gee]
the order in which events occur

Back it up . . .
"As any good storyteller knows, hearing about the beginning and the middle makes all the difference when you get to the end.
re:form DVD

respond

15-20 minutes

Gather to share the different points of view kids have discovered and developed during the session.

Regroup

Hand out note cards. Ask each kid to write one question he or she still has about the how the Old and New Testaments are connected. Invite volunteers to share with the rest of the group.

Both parts of Scripture point to God's loving relationship with God's people. Give each kid a chance to talk about an important relationship he or she has with another person. What makes this relationship so special? How do you see God's love through the other person?

Share

Invite kids to share their work and describe how and why they did it. Affirm those things you appreciate or find interesting and ask others to offer helpful observations.

Questions for conversation:

- What do you think about the role and purpose of the Old Testament?
- Which part of the Old Testament are you most curious about?
- Does the story of the Bible have an end? Why or why not?
- How are you involved in this continuing story of God's love?

Send

Ask kids to place their note cards in their Bibles. State today's question, "Is the New Testament more important than the Old Testament?" and ask them to join you in brief silence reflecting on your time together. Then encourage kids to add questions throughout the week as they read and discuss the Bible with friends and family.

Get this stuff . . .
Note cards.

Capture it . . .
Use a digital camera, camcorder, scanner, web cam, or audio recorder to capture group conversations and individual pieces of work. Upload them to your online galleries, or ask kids to do so.

Back it up . . .
"The "after" picture without the "before" picture is just a snapshot. It's only when you see the pictures side-by-side that you know what happened."
re:form DVD

Bible Unit
Why are there so many versions of the Bible?

Prepare
What's behind all this?

There's a story about a missionary who was translating the Bible for the Eskimos, whom he realized had never seen sheep, a common word in the Bible. So, instead of trying to describe a sheep, he simply substituted seal for sheep in his translation. Translating a text from one language to another is as much an art as it is a science. Some Christians would say the translator was untrue to the Bible by doing this; others would say he performed a great service to it.

While translation challenges and differing viewpoints can crop up in any text, they are particularly common when it comes to the Bible, a sacred and inspired text for billions of people. The many versions of the Bible we have today are the result of the many cultural differences among people—around the world and through the years—for whom the Bible is the most important text of all.

In addition, arguments over how the Bible *should* be translated have spawned more versions, as have advances in publishing technology, making it easy to produce new versions. And since the Bible is a perennial best seller, there's always a market for a new and improved translation.

Often, different church communities use different translations based on their particular cultural contexts. So in the end, unless you can read ancient Hebrew or Koine Greek, you will have to rely on a translation of the Bible that you *can* read to know what it says.

Where are kids at?

- Kids spend much of their school day searching for one correct answer to questions about math, history, or literature. The notion of hundreds of Bible translations may be difficult for them to grasp at first.
- As kids begin to question authority, they become intrigued by conspiracy theories. Use this curiosity to engage them in conversations about the reasons behind multiple versions of Scripture.

John 8:31-32
2 Peter 3:14-16

Where's this going?
Kids consider how history, culture, language, and human behavior create the need for many translations of Scripture.

Consider this . . .

"That God's Word is accessible to all people in a language that speaks to their heart."
The Vision of the Wycliffe Bible Translators

"If you continue in my word, you are truly my disciples; and you will know the truth, and the truth will make you free."
Jesus, speaking to the disciples (John 8:31-32)

encounter

15 minutes

Make sure you've got the obvi stuff for this session—re:form video (DVD or download), Anti-Workbooks, Bibles, pens pencils, paper, tape, etc.

Video

1. Set up

Translating words from one language to another is tricky. There are at least four Greek words for the English word *love* (*eros, agape, philia,* and *storge*). Have kids find partners and look in the two-language dictionaries for words with more than one meaning. How would people who speak different languages be able to communicate if not all words have one meaning?

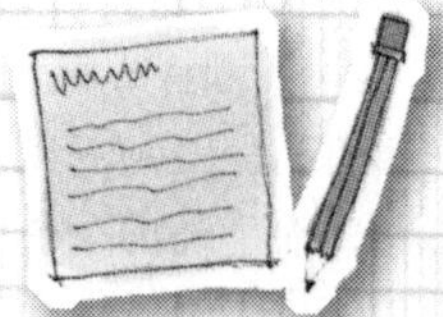

Get this stuff . . .

Two-language dictionaries (Engli Spanish, English-German, etc.). Whiteboard. Dry erase markers. Bibles (different translations).

2. Watch

"Why are there so many versions of the Bible?" DVD 1, Chapter 5

3. Unpack

- Which ideas from the video hadn't you thought of before?
- What does it feel like when you're trying to say something and the other person doesn't understand what you're saying?
- Does it really matter which translation you read?
- What questions do you have about the video?

trans·la·tion
[trans-**lay**-shun]
the rendering of a word, phrase, or text in a second language

con·demn
[kun-**dehm**]
to state that someone is wrong o guilty

What about the Bible?

Write a feeling word (e.g., *love, hate, good, bad*) on the whiteboard. Give kids 60 seconds to add as many synonyms as possible. Which synonym has the closest meaning to the original? Which is most accurate? Would every generation know what the word means? Ask kids to find Mark 16:16 in the Bibles provided and write each translation on the board.

Questions for conversation while you work:

- What similarities do you see? What differences?
- Why do you think so many translations exist?
- Do you have a favorite translation? Why?
- Can you tell which translations are older? How?
- How would your group translate this verse?

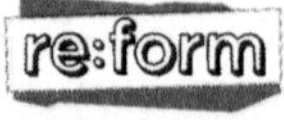

engage

25-30 minutes

Choose 1+ Anti-Workbook (AW) activities to explore the session question. The first 2 are for individual use, while the last 2 involve the whole group.

1. Tricky Translating AW p. 26

Peculiar has a very different meaning in "How peculiar!" than in Exodus 19:5, "Ye shall be a peculiar treasure to me." Ask kids for examples of words used today that people might not understand even 10 years from now. Ancient texts are hard to understand because they contain dead words or are written in dead languages. Finding a new word for a common word can be just as tricky. Time kids as they write as many names (words or phrases) as possible for *money* in their Anti-Workbooks. Write a master list on the whiteboard.

Questions for conversation while you work:

- Who would—or would not—know some of these money words?
- Are the words okay in every context? Why or why not?
- What can you learn from dead languages? Why did people quit using them?
- How do you react when an adult tries to use "your" language?
- Is it a problem if there is not a good English equivalent for some of the words in the original Biblical texts? Why?

Get this stuff . . .
Stopwatch. Whiteboard. Dry erase markers.

Where's this going?
Kids discover the challenges of translation.

dead lan·guage
[ded **lang**-gwij]
a language no longer used in conversation

Back it up . . .
"Once the Bible was translated people could encounter God's word directly."
re:form DVD

2. The Year is 3011 AW p. 27

Hey, leader. Do you remember the Jetsons? What did George, Jane, Elroy, Judy, Rosie, and Astro have right about the future? What hasn't happened yet? Write several well-known Bible stories kids suggest on the board. Do kids know why they thought of these stories? The characters? The outcome? A holiday? Invite them to pick one story and write it for the year 3011. Encourage kids to share ideas for translations while working and when finished.

Questions for conversation while you work:

- What could you tell about 3011 through the story you wrote? Dress? Work? Transportation? Families?
- Can you be sure that your translation will make sense in 1,000 years? Why or why not?
- What might this activity show about how we read and understand the Bible translations we use?
- What won't change about the Bible story you selected?

Get this stuff . . .
Colored pencils. Markers. Whiteboard. Dry erase markers.

Where's this going?
Kids reflect on how cultural changes impact our ability to understand the Bible by predicting the culture 1000 years from now.

Jet·sons
[Jet-suhnz]
a 1960s Hanna-Barbera animated sitcom predicting life in 2062

3. Diaper Dash AW p. 28

"Do you remember when. . .?" Responses to this question have the benefit of hindsight. Our experiences change the way we see the world. Help kids think "way back" to when their perspective was mostly from the floor looking up. Determine how you'll play the Diaper Dash with your group. If you think some people may be embarrassed wearing an adult diaper, a towel and clothespin or white boxer shorts may be more appropriate. You know your kids.

Questions for conversation while you work:

- What do you remember about your childhood?
- How have you changed over the last year? The last 5 years? 10 years?
- Think of a country on another continent. What childhood experiences are probably similar/different for kids in that country?
- How do culture, language, and location make a difference in the way you understand the world?
- What does this have to do with how you understand the Bible?

Get this stuff . . .
Diaper (towel, white boxe shorts, or adult diaper). Stacking items (blocks, boxes, etc.).

Where's this going?
Kids reenact prior experie to recognize changes in th worldview.

4. The Great Debate AW p. 29

Imagine people writing ancient Biblical texts. Is the scene serene and calm? Are there people with opposing views? Ask kids to imagine the conversations and debates that probably occurred while the words we read in the Bible were written. What languages are they hearing? What's the attitude?

Prepare for The Great Debate. Select people for the roles or ask for volunteers. Divide into groups, if needed, so everyone can participate actively. Brainstorm possible topics important to your group. Pick one. Proceed as described in the Anti-Workbook.

Questions for conversation while you work:

- What was surprising as you prepared and debated? Puzzling? Affirming?
- Did you come to a compromise? Would that be possible?
- What emotions pop up in debates? Is civil debate possible?
- How can people "agree to disagree" in matters of faith and Scripture?
- What kinds of things might be debated by people who are translating the Bible?

Where's this going?
Kids clarify their position c an issue by debating peopl with a different interpretat

Back it up . . .
"The argument over which is best has often divided communities, congregatior and even families."
re:form DVD

respond

15-20 minutes

Gather to share the different points of view kids have discovered and developed during the session.

Regroup

Hand out note cards. Ask each kid to write one question he or she still has about whether it matters which version of the Bible we read. Invite volunteers to share with the rest of the group.

Encourage kids go to a local bookstore or library (or plan to meet there as a group) to check out different Bible translations. Is the language very formal (usually long sentences) or informal (shorter sentences)? Is there additional information on the pages (footnotes, questions, illustrations, titles)? Be sure to talk about their findings (and preferences) the next time you meet.

Share

Invite kids to share their work and describe how and why they did it. Affirm those things you appreciate or find interesting and ask others to offer helpful observations.

Questions for conversation:

- What criteria will you use to choose your preferred translation? Why?
- Bible paraphrases are not translated verse-by-verse but tell a story or groups of stories, often taking liberties with the original texts. Would you consider paraphrases of Scripture?
- What concerns, curiosity, or questions do you still have about different versions of the Bible?

Send

Ask kids to place their note cards in their Bibles. State today's question, "Why are there so many versions of the Bible?" and ask them to join you in brief silence reflecting on your time together. Then encourage kids to add questions throughout the week as they read and discuss the Bible with friends and family.

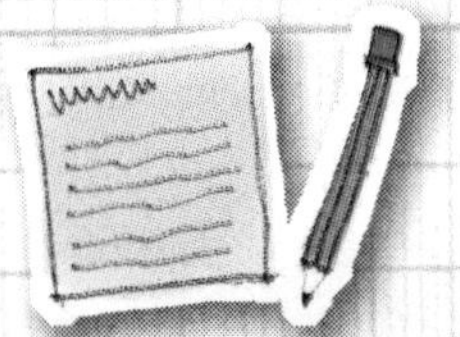

Get this stuff . . .
Note cards.

Capture it . . .
Use a digital camera, camcorder, scanner, web cam, or audio recorder to capture group conversations and individual pieces of work. Upload them to your online galleries, or ask kids to do so.

par•a•phrase
[pare-uh-frayze]
to restate something using simpler or shorter words

Back it up . . .
"Some translations focus on making it as easy as possible to read and to understand the main ideas in the Bible so they'll often paraphrase a text. While others focus on trying to get as close to a word for word translation as possible."
re:form DVD

UNIT No. 2
CREED

re:form

Creed Unit
Can it be proven that God exists?

Prepare

What's behind all this?

From time immemorial, human beings have attempted to prove there is a God (or gods), and we've never quite succeeded. In the past, proofs of God's existence were made primarily using philosophical arguments, the most famous being Thomas Aquinas's Five Proofs (e.g., everything that moves is moved by something, except the first mover, and that is God, the Unmoved Mover).

More recently, as our world has become more technical and scientific, people have looked for empirical, scientific proofs of God. Some argue, for instance, that the finely tuned nature of the universe suggests the hand of a divine Creator—the analogy being that a watch or a 747 airplane could not come into existence by random chance.

The fact remains: the concept of God's existence is not something that can ultimately be proved—or disproved. The vast majority of people—both those living and those who are no longer alive—believe God exists. Most believe because they have experienced God's divine love; they can attribute that to no other cause than God. And of course, if God were provable, that proof would negate the need for faith.

Where are kids at?

- Kids this age are beginning to question things they had easily accepted when they were younger, which often leads them to wonder about God's existence. Don't feel like you need to find ways to prove to kids that God exists. They'll likely continue to wonder about this question for much of their faith journey. Focus on using re:form and your own exploration and stories to provide them the tools to wrestle with this important question.

Matthew 18:20
1 John 4:7

Where's this going?
Kids play with the differences between knowing and believing.

Consider this . . .
"Consider, anatomize the eye; survey its structure and contrivance; and tell me, from your own feeling, if the idea of a contriver does not immediately flow in upon you with a force like that of sensation. The most obvious conclusion, surely, is in favour of design; and it requires time, reflection, and study, to summon up those frivolous, though abstruse objections which can support Infidelity."
David Hume, *Dialogues*

encounter

15 minutes

Video

1. Set up

Designate one wall in your meeting space as "I believe" and the opposite wall as "I don't believe." The space between the walls is a spectrum between total belief and total disbelief. Make the following statements and ask kids to stand at one wall or the other, or somewhere between the two, in response. "Bigfoot." "UFOs." "Humans have landed on the moon." For each statement, ask, "Why doesn't everyone believe this?"

2. Watch

"Can it be proven that God exists?" DVD 1; Chapter 6

3. Unpack

- Which would be more difficult—to prove that God does exist, or that God does not exist?
- Do you think not *knowing* something is true, such as God's existence, necessarily means that it isn't so?
- Which is more important to you—to *believe* something, or to *know* something? Or can they both be important?

What about the Bible?

Have kids pair up. Give a blindfold to one kid in each pair. The "seeing" kid must promise out loud to lead the blindfolded kid safely around. Let kids lead their partners for a bit. Switch blindfolds and repeat.

Questions for conversation while you work:

- How did it feel to rely on your partner's promise?
- What is the last promise someone made to you? What's the last promise you made to someone?
- Did you know or believe your partner would keep their promise? Why?
- In Matthew 18:20, Jesus makes a promise. How would he have had to say this line in a way that gives proof instead of promise?

Make sure you've got the obvi stuff for this session—re:form video (DVD or download), Anti-Workbooks, Bibles, pens pencils, paper, tape, etc.

em•pir•i•cal
[em-pir-ih-kuhl]
proven by evidence that can be seen, heard, felt, smelled, and/o tasted; can be proven by scienti experimentation

be•lief
[bih-leef]
confidence in the truth, the existence, or the reliability of something, even though there is absolute proof that you are right

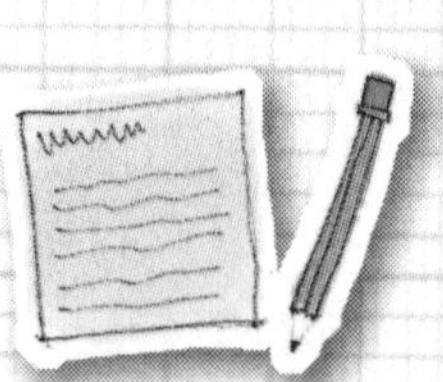

Get this stuff . . .
Blindfolds.

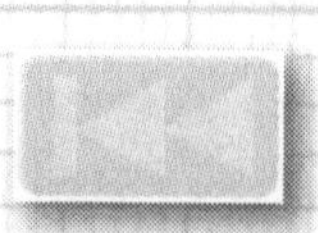

Back it up . . .
"But what *can* we prove? I mean, empirically, undeniably *prove?* Nothing, really. Think about it. Y can't even prove to me that *you* exist."
re:form DVD

25-30 minutes

Choose 1+ Anti-Workbook (AW) activities to explore the session question. The first 2 are for individual use, while the last 2 involve the whole group.

1. Knowing & Believing AW p. 34

Review the definitions of *empirical* and *belief*. Guide kids to complete the two lists in their AW. Remind them that others will see their lists so they don't need to get too personal with their items. Have kids swap AWs to compare lists. Have them circle things they agree with in the AWs of other kids.

Questions for conversation while you work:

- Which list is longer—things you know, or things you believe? Why?
- Not everyone believes the same things. How does it feel when people don't believe things you believe?
- How do people end up with certain beliefs?
- Why doesn't everybody believe the same stuff?
- Can you prove that your favorite food is the best food in the world? Why or why not?
- If other people don't believe that pizza is the best food in the world, can it still be your favorite?

Where's this going?

Kids play around with the differences between knowing and believing by creating lists of things they believe to be true and things they know to be true.

Back It Up

"If you used all five of your senses to detect your youth leader . . . that still wouldn't prove he exists. What if you're dreaming? Right now? . . . But my point is . . . even your 5 senses aren't PROOF of existence. So . . . we can't PROVE . . . anything."
re:form DVD

2. Weigh the Facts AW p. 35

Before beginning this activity with kids, consider what experiences you have had that support or go against your belief in God. What has made you feel certain God exists? What has made you question or wonder? How are your feelings now different from when you were a teenager?

Remind kids they can include any evidence they deem worthy, whether it's empirical or experiential. Sunrises, best friends, family, and tragedies all count.

Questions for conversation while you work:

- What's in your lists? Is it possible to agree with stuff in both lists?
- Which list is longer? Why do you think that is?
- Do you think it's possible to agree totally with the list against God's existence and still believe in God? Why or why not?

Where's this going?

Kids consider experiences they have had that show evidence for or against God's existence.

3. That's Beauty AW p. 36

Give kids time to work alone and create their single, absolute definition of beauty. Create boundaries and send kids to find examples that represent beauty. (Be sure kids attach them to their Anti-Workbooks with supplies provided.) Make sure they look for beauty itself, not just beautiful things.

Then divide into groups of 3 or 4 to debate who has achieved a definition and example of beauty. Pay attention to how kids act and react when arguments are made about why each definition and item is or is not beauty. Point these reactions out during your discussion.

Questions for conversation while you work:

- How do your definition and item show true beauty?
- How does it feel when someone argues that your item is not beauty?
- Why do you think the group can't decide on one definition or one object that is beauty?
- How is our debate similar to or different from the debate about the existence of God?
- If you can't prove your belief to others, does that mean your beliefs are wrong?

Get this stuff . . .
Stapler. Tape. Glue. Strin

Where's this going?
Kids define beauty and search out physical exam of beauty to explore how empirical evidence doesn' always prove that someth is true.

4. The Scientific Method AW p. 37

Use this activity to get your community involved. Set up a "lab" in your meeting space. Recruit volunteers who show different kinds of love. Get an older couple, a young couple, a mom and baby, two siblings, a person and their pet, etc. Give each love pair a separate space for this activity.

Let kids get into lab groups of 2 or 3 to work through the activity. They can choose as many or as few of the love pairs to "experiment" on as they'd like. Be present throughout to give guidance and ask questions!

Questions for conversation while you work:

- Do people generally believe in the existence of love? Why or why not?
- What's your group's hypothesis about love?
- Do you need to prove love exists in order to be loved or to love?
- Has your group proved that love exists? Why or why not?
- How is trying to prove that love exists like or unlike trying to prove God exists?

Where's this going?
Kids take the concept of l which is generally accepte to exist, and investigate it within the rigors of the scientific method.

love
[luhv]
a feeling of warm persona attachment or deep affect for another person

respond

15-20 minutes

ather to share the different points of view kids have discovered and veloped during the session.

Regroup

you have a toy UFO or space alien, pull it out. Announce to kids that a UFO s landed outside your building and space aliens are coming in to learn the fferences between knowledge and belief. Quick! How will you teach them? xplain to kids that, in order for the aliens to understand them, they must en their Anti-Workbooks and hold them directly in front of their mouths henever they speak. Encourage them to use words, props, and motions as ey teach the aliens.

Get this stuff . . .

Toy UFO or toy space alien (optional).

Capture it . . .

Use a digital camera, camcorder, scanner, web cam, or audio recorder to capture group conversations and individual pieces of work. Upload them to your online galleries, or ask kids to do so.

Share

vite kids to share their work and describe how and why they did it. Affirm ose things you appreciate or find interesting and ask others to offer helpful bservations.

uestions for conversation:

- What empirical knowledge have you gained today?
- What beliefs of yours have been strengthened today?
- Which would you rather do—use logic to explain to someone that God exists, or tell someone why you believe in God? Give an example of how you would do this.
- How does not being able to prove God's existence affect your faith?

Send

ave kids stand in a circle with you. Turn to the person on your left and make sign of the cross on their forehead as you say, "God knows you and believes you." Have that kid do the same for the next kid and so on, until everyone the circle has received this promise.

Creed Unit
Is God male?

Prepare

What's behind all this?

Throughout history, there have been many schools of thought about the nature of God. For example, in ancient Greece, the common people believed the gods to be a quarrelsome lot who lived on Mt. Olympus. But the philosophers taught that god was an all-knowing, immaterial, and impersonal Mind (*Nous*).

The Abrahamic faiths (Judaism, Christianity, and Islam) teach that God is one and all-knowing, and that God is personally involved with the creation. Since God is personal, we desire to refer to God not with impersonal pronouns ("It"), but personal ones ("He" or "She").

Our language is limited, however, because our personal pronouns are gender-specific. So even though we do not believe God is male or female, we are often forced to choose a gender-specific pronoun when referring to God. The Bible, written in a male-dominated culture, most often refers to God as "He," but there are Biblical feminine images of God, as well.

We must hold these two ideas in tension—God as personal, yet not gendered—as we talk about God.

Where are kids at?

- Kids this age are developing their own sense of gender identity. Keep in mind that kids are bombarded daily with society's and the media's stereotypes of gender and sexuality. While the attitudes of your kids may vary, many will likely follow the traditional roles of male and female. This tendency toward conformity will also shape their image of God. Be sensitive to kids' feelings about the subject as you explore together the idea that God goes beyond gender.

Genesis 1:26a, 27
Isaiah 66:13
Matthew 23:37

Where's this going?
Kids explore biblical images for a God who is beyond the limitations of language and human gender.

Consider this . . .

"Even though monotheists would insist that their God transcended gender, he would remain essentially male."
Karen Armstrong, *A History of God*, 50

"If God is male, then male is God."
Mary Daly, *The Church and the Second Sex*, 38

encounter

15 minutes

Video

1. Set up

Get everyone in place to watch the video. Announce to kids that [name of currently famous male whose picture you are cleverly hiding behind your back] is going to join you today. Reveal the picture. Speak to the picture like it's a person. "Thanks for taking time out of your busy schedule to be here with us. I'm excited to hear your ideas about our question, 'Is God male?'" Keep up the charade no matter how the kids react. Place the photo in a spot where it can "see" the video.

2. Watch

"Is God Male?" DVD 1, Chapter 7

3. Unpack

- Besides your name, what positive words do people call you?
- What feelings or emotions do you have about those names?
- What three things did the video ask you to consider? Why do you think those are important?

What about the Bible?

Tell kids about the first time someone addressed you as "ma'am" or "sir." What was the situation? Did it feel good? Did it feel awkward? Why did they address you this way?

Questions for conversation while you work:

- Why do we use certain words, such as "sir," "ma'am," "him," and "her," to talk to and about other people?
- Read Isaiah 66:13 and Matthew 23:37. Why do you think we don't call God "Mother" or a chicken, even though they're both in the Bible? What do those two images tell us about God?
- Read Genesis 1:26a and 27. Why did God create both males and females in his image?

Make sure you've got the obvi
stuff for this session—re:form
video (DVD or download),
Anti-Workbooks, Bibles, pens
pencils, paper, tape, etc.

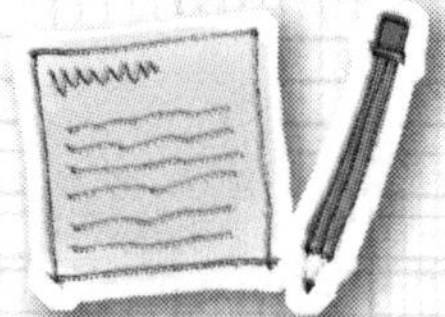

Get this stuff . . .

Picture of a currently famous male cut out of a teen heartthro magazine.

met·a·phor
[met–uh–for]

a figure of speech in which one t is used to describe something els Examples: It's raining cats and d He looks mean but he's really a teddy bear.

Back it up . . .

"Of course, we're not God. We're made in the image of God. That' important distinction. The same a photograph of you isn't you. N even close."

re:form DVD

25-30 minutes

Choose 1+ Anti-Workbook (AW) activities to explore the session question. The first 2 are for individual use, while the last 2 involve the whole group.

1. Hello. My Name is . . . AW p. 38

Set the picture from Encounter at the front of the room. As a group, brainstorm some labels for whoever is in the picture and write them on the picture. Tape the picture to your copy of the Anti-Workbook and display it while the kids work individually on the activity. Challenge kids to come back next time with a picture of their person covered in the labels.

Questions for conversation while you work:

- How would you label yourself? How might others label you?
- How do your labels for people you know differ from the labels we used for the famous guy?
- Why can't one of these labels completely describe the person you chose?
- What labels would you make for God?
- Think about the phrase "Actions speak louder than words." How do your actions speak louder than the words people might use to describe you? How do God's actions speak louder than the words we use to describe God?

Get this stuff . . .

Digital camera. Photo printer. Photo from Encounter. Blank stickers from page S2 of the Anti-Workbook.

Where's this going?

Kids create labels for someone they know to demonstrate how single words aren't able to fully describe a person.

Back It Up

"So . . . our word, "Father," can be a great image of a loving God . . . But it's also completely inadequate. It can't possibly define or contain all of who God is. And it can't possibly reveal all of God's attributes."

re:form DVD

2. Language Limits AW p. 39

Explain this activity to kids without using any of these words or phrases: "Anti-Workbook," "page 39," "kids," "partner," "write," "describe," "backwords," or any of the words forbidden by the Anti-Workbook. Work alongside kids as they work through the activity. Give it a try yourself!

Questions for conversation while you work:

- What words do you have to rely on to do this activity?
- On a scale of 1 (Super Easy) to 6 (Super Hard), how hard is it to write this description?
- On the same scale, how difficult is it to write the description backwards?
- What kind of limits do we have when we try to describe God?
- Make up some Dr. Seuss-style nonsensical words for God. Why did you create the words you did? How do they describe the God you believe in?

Where's this going?

Kids examine limits of language to get a better glimpse of the limits we face when talking about God.

3. Is God A . . . ? AW p. 40

Have kids attach the punch-out arrows to the game board with paper fasteners. Split your group into teams of three or four and allow the teams to devise their own way to play the game. Give them two rules: 1. You must spin the arrow and do what the arrow tells you each turn. 2. You must write down the name of the image you find each time.

Remind kids that if the arrow lands on "Bible Roulette!" all kids in the group must follow the instructions and all images must be written down. If the arrow lands on "Your Turn!" the kid who spun it must describe how he or she sees God or invent a new metaphor for God. Whichever group finds all of the images the fastest wins!

Questions for conversation while you work:

- What do you think of these images? What's your favorite? What's your least favorite?
- How does your idea of God change knowing that God could be all of these things?
- Why do you think we don't hear these images for God very much?

Get this stuff . . .

Punch-out arrow from pa
P9 of the Anti-Workbook.
Paper fasteners.

Where's this going?

Kids play with their Bibles in order to discover a vari of non-masculine Biblical references for God.

Back It Up

"We create, we nurture, w sacrifice, we love . . . just like . . . our Father. But n just Father. Which brings to thing number three. Th Bible gives lots of images God other than just father ones."

re:form DVD

4. Guess Who AW p. 41

Prior to starting this activity, come up with a description for yourself that follows the instructions given on page 41 of the Anti-Workbook.

"A person who is in charge of this class wishes you to complete the activity on page 41 of the Anti-Workbook. This person is tall, smells like roses, and has long brown hair. If you know who it is, you can get to work."

After a minute, have kids pass their Anti-Workbooks to someone sitting a few people away and give the drawers 3 minutes to draw. Pass the Anti-Workbooks back and allow kids to rate the accuracy of the drawings.

Questions for conversation while you work:

- What if you had to talk like this whenever you talked about people?
- What if you could use only actions—not words—to describe someone? Would that be harder or easier?
- How does language help you understand God, even if you know language can't fully describe God?

Where's this going?

Kids describe a family member without using personal or relational worc in order to experience our reliance on these words to describe others.

15-20 minutes

ather to share the different points of view kids have discovered and eveloped during the session.

Regroup

ive each kid a picture of a currently famous person. Have them dream up ays to attempt to interact with their pictures using the props you have on and. They could play Frisbee, discuss global warming, help clean up the eeting space, etc. Give each kid two sticky notes to attach to his or her icture. On one sticky note, have kids write down ways that metaphors for od help us understand God. On the other sticky note, have them write down ays that metaphors limit our understanding of God.

Get this stuff . . .
Pictures of currently famous men and women cut out of a teen heartthrob magazine. Sticky notes. Props such as a Frisbee or a deck of cards.

Share

nvite kids to share their work and describe how and why they did it. Affirm hose things you appreciate or find interesting and ask others to offer helpful bservations.

Capture it . . .
Use a digital camera, camcorder, scanner, web cam, or audio recorder to capture group conversations and individual pieces of work. Upload them to your online galleries, or ask kids to do so.

uestions for conversation:

- What is your favorite metaphor for God we discovered today? What is your least favorite? Why?
- How can you use some of these metaphors in your daily faith life?
- What do you picture when you think of God? How is that different from how you pictured God at the beginning of class? How is it different from how you pictured God when you were little?
- Why is language important for our relationship with God?

Send

Have kids take turns giving brief prayers of praise, or thanks to God, or asking God to respond to some need. Here's the catch: have them use the spinning game from today's lesson to give them a way to address God. For instance, if a kid spins and lands on the mother bear metaphor, he or she would address God as "Mother Bear." "Mother Bear, please protect us all this week."

Creed Unit
How can God be "three-in-one"?

'repare

What's behind all this?

Vhile not explicitly spelled out in the Bible, the early church combined wo words—*tri-* ("threeness'") and *–unitas* ("oneness")—to describe the novements of Father, Son, and Spirit that they found in Scripture. The :ouncil of Nicaea in 325 C.E. wrote that God is constituted by three persons, ut by one substance. This concept explained how Jesus of Nazareth could oth be God incarnate and be in a prayer-relationship with God.

nother way to understand the Trinity is to focus not so much on the three 'persons," but on the relationship that binds the three. That eternal, divine elationship can be understood as a mutual indwelling or as a reciprocal nveloping, each of the other two. When this understanding is applied, the ncarnation of Jesus is seen as the invitation by God for human beings to nter this relationship, and the crucifixion is God's own experience of broken elationship and godforsakenness.

Where are kids at?

- For kids this age, emotional memory trumps all other kinds of memory. Remember to ask lots of questions about how kids are feeling throughout the lesson. You may hear responses ranging from frustration about not understanding, to excitement that they're finally beginning to grasp this tough subject.

John 14:11a

Where's this going?

Kids wrestle with the mystery of the Trinity and confront the idea that we can never fully understand all the mysteries of God.

Consider this . . .

Each member of the Trinity "reciprocally contains the others, so that one permanently envelops, and is permanently enveloped by, the other whom he yet envelops."

Hilary of Poitiers, *Concerning the Trinity,* 3:1, qtd. in *The Reason for God: Belief in the Age of Skepticism* by Timothy Keller, 280.

encounter

15 minutes

Video

1. Set up

Describe the family you grew up in; show the photo. Tell kids a fun memory about your family. Ask for volunteers to share memories about their families, too. Family relationships can be one way for us to think about God the Father, Son, and Holy Spirit. But they don't totally explain the Trinity. How can God be "three-in-one"?

2. Watch

"How can God be 'three-in-one'?" DVD 1, Chapter 8

3. Unpack

- How would you describe love?
- What are some things family members do for one another simply because they love one another?
- What are some things the Trinity does for us simply out of love?
- Do people love you the exact same way? Look at the Apostle's Creed. In what unique ways does each person of the Trinity love you?

What about the Bible?

Tell kids about a time when you had to believe something you were being told, even though it may have been difficult to do so. Perhaps someone was making a promise to you that seemed too good to be true, or that seemed too difficult to carry out. Why did you believe them? Did your belief prove to be correct?

Questions for conversation while you work:

- Tell about a time when you had to believe something that a trusted person was saying to you, even though it may have been difficult to do so. What made you believe them?
- How did it turn out for you?
- Read John 14:11a. Here Jesus is making some big claims about his relationship with God. What is it in the second half of this verse (11b) that helps us trust what Jesus says in the first half (11a)?

Make sure you've got the obvi stuff for this session—re:form video (DVD or download), Anti-Workbooks, Bibles, pens pencils, paper, tape, etc.

Get this stuff . . .
A photograph of your family fron when you were a kid. A copy of the Apostles' Creed to hand out project.

Back it up . . .
"Trying to draw or describe God as a physical being is like trying to describe or draw what love lo like. You can try but ultimately anything you come up with will only symbolic of what love is to
re:form DVD

25-30 minutes

Choose 1+ Anti-Workbook (AW) activities to explore the session question. The first 2 are for individual use, while the last 2 involve the whole group.

1. Tag! AW p. 42

What things work even though you don't understand how? How is your understanding different now from when you were a kid? Are you the type of person who wants to know how everything works, or someone who accepts things as they are? Keep your thoughts about this in mind as you work through this activity with kids.

Questions for conversation while you work:

- When you look in the mirror, what works even though you don't understand how? How about when you look outside or in your garage?
- Who could you go to to get an explanation of how these things work?
- How is it that these things can work or do what they're supposed to do even if we don't understand them?
- Why might it not be such a bad thing that we don't understand everything about God?
- According to the creed, what does each person of the Trinity *do?*

Get this stuff . . .

String or yarn. Digital camera. Photo printer. Punch-out tags from page P4 of the Anti-Workbook. A copy of the Apostles' Creed to hand out or project.

Where's this going?

Kids tag things in the world that work even though they don't understand how, in order to help them explore the idea that we can't completely understand all the mysteries of God.

mys·ter·y
[mis-tuhr-ee]
an event or concept that cannot be fully understood or that baffles or eludes the understanding

2. Relationships AW p. 43

Before class, familiarize yourself with genograms. You can do a search on the Internet or practice creating one using the key on page 43 of the Anti-Workbook. Some kids will grasp this activity quickly. Others might need a little more guidance as they create their own genograms. Consider what a genogram of your closest family and friends might look like. Are there lots of connections among the people you know?

Questions for conversation while you work:

- How hard is it to create your genogram?
- How might genograms be helpful for understanding relationships?
- What would a genogram of all your online friends look like?
- What sort of symbols would you add to the key for this activity?
- Review the Hilary of Poitiers quote from the Prepare section with kids. What symbols would we have to add in order to make a genogram for the Trinity? Add a genogram of the trinity to your Anti-Workbook.

Where's this going?

Kids consider human relationships as context for understanding the relationships of the Father, Son, and Holy Spirit.

gen·o·gram
[jeen-uh-gram]
a visual model of a family tree or set of relationships that provides information about the interactions of several individuals

3. Poetic Analogy AW p. 44

Split your group into pairs or threes, and allow enough time for groups to come up with analogies for each of the items on page 44 of their Anti-Workbooks. Let them know ahead of time that each group will be reading their analogies poem-style for the entire group.

When all groups have completed their Poetic Analogies, give each group a chance to perform their poem. Let each performer choose a hat to wear as a costume. After a poem is read, respond as a group with a round of finger snaps.

Questions for conversation while you work:

- Which of these things was the easiest to create an analogy for? Why?
- Which was most difficult? Why?
- No analogy totally describes its object; why is that?
- Where does each of the analogies we created fall apart?
- What analogies have you heard for the Trinity? Why don't any of those fully describe the Trinity?

Get this stuff . . .

Assortment of hats.

Where's this going?

Kids will create analogies to explore the language limitations we face in tryi to describe and understan the Trinity.

a·nal·o·gy
[uh-nal-uh-jee]
a comparison between tw things that are different fr each other but have some similarities. Usually, one simple idea is used to exp another, more complicate idea. For example, "A fam is like a chair; they both h you up and support you."

4. Multi-Taskers AW p. 45

Do some thinking beforehand about where kids might go for this activity. Will there be other groups of people in your meeting space whom kids could interview? Is there a grocery store or library within walking distance of your building? Consider different places you could visit so kids will have lots of variety for this activity.

Before setting kids free to explore, have them teach you how to do the activity. Then send them out, armed with cameras, to find some three-in-ones.

Questions for conversation while you work:

- What are some things that have three (or more) functions?
- When have you done three things at one time?
- What was it about some of these items that required you to be extra creative?
- How do your examples help you understand the Trinity a little better?
- How are we still limited in our understanding?
- How does it make you feel that even your best three-in-one example isn't a true representation of the Trinity?

Get this stuff . . .

Digital cameras. Photo printer.

Where's this going?

Kids will toy with the idea the Trinity by searching ou things or people who have least three functions.

Back it up . . .

"The Trinity is really just a symbolic way to describe how the Father, the Son, a the Holy Spirit relate to or another and us. Because its important to understan that they are all different; they weren't different, the wouldn't have different names in the Bible. But th are all a part of one anoth They are all in a Holy relationship with one anot and with the world."
re:form DVD

respond

15-20 minutes

Gather to share the different points of view kids have discovered and developed during the session.

Regroup

If the weather permits, go outside and use chalk to draw on the sidewalk or parking lot. Ask kids to write or draw analogies for the Trinity. If the weather doesn't permit, do the same activity inside using the chalk on sandpaper.

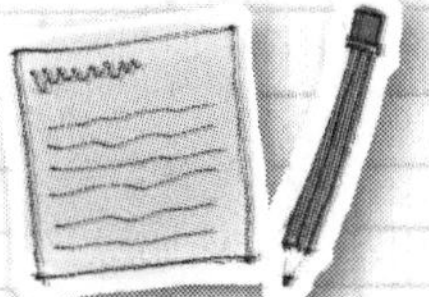

Get this stuff . . .
Sidewalk chalk. Sandpaper (if needed).

Share

Invite kids to share their work and describe how and why they did it. Affirm those things you appreciate or find interesting and ask others to offer helpful observations.

Capture it . . .
Use a digital camera, camcorder, scanner, web cam, or audio recorder to capture group conversations and individual pieces of work. Upload them to your online galleries, or ask kids to do so.

Questions for conversation:

- What are some new things you understand about the Trinity?
- What are some things you still don't understand about the Trinity?
- How does it make you feel that you can't ever fully understand the Trinity?
- How would you explain to someone why it's okay that we can't fully understand the Trinity?

Send

Stand in a circle for a sending prayer. Invite kids to say a prayer of praise to God for things we can't understand. You can begin the prayer in this way: "Dear God, we are glad that you are so big and wonderful that we cannot fully understand you. So we praise you for your mysteries and the things we don't fully understand."

Creed Unit
Does God still create stuff today?

Prepare
What's behind all this?

The "first person" of the Trinitarian God is known primarily as Creator. Indeed, the entire biblical narrative begins with two accounts God's creation of the cosmos and of humankind—both of which served to set the monotheism of the Israelites apart from the polytheistic creation stories of their neighbors. No matter how one reads the creation accounts in Genesis—be it more literally or more figuratively—the message is clear: God and God alone is the author of everything that exists. When God rests on the seventh day, according to the first narrative, it suggests that a particular mode of God's creative activity has ceased.

However, the second narrative suggests that when Adam and Eve are banished from the Garden of Eden, a new mode of creative activity begins; Adam is to work to cultivate crops, and Eve will bring forth new life from her body. In each case the creative act is made possible by God, but human beings are now called upon to cooperate with God in God's creativity. This being the case, the Christian witness testifies to a God who relies upon human participation in the creation of new things, be they works of art, medical advances, the birth of a child, or even the emerging kingdom of God's grace in Christ.

Where are kids at?

- Youth are moving from concrete to abstract thinking. They probably picture God in human terms and may struggle reconciling the creation story with evolution and other scientific topics. Instead of arguing for one understanding of creation, focus on exploration, wonder, and questions so that kids reach their own conclusions.
- Kids may suppress their personal beliefs so they don't contradict their peers. Create an environment of openness where youth can share their thoughts and beliefs without judgment or criticism.

Genesis 2:1-3

Where's this going?
Kids have an opportunity to consider God's presence in creation and re-creation and discover what it might mean for them to be co-creators.

Consider this . . .
"Understood as imago Dei, human beings are...God's proxy in the community of creation. They represent his glory and his will. They intercede for God before the community of creation. In this sense they are God's representatives on earth."
Jürgen Moltmann, *God in Creation*, p. 190.

encounter

15 minutes

Make sure you've got the obvi
stuff for this session—re:form
video (DVD or download),
Anti-Workbooks, Bibles, pens
pencils, paper, tape, etc.

Video

1. Set up

Post the signs around the room. Pose the question: Does God still create stuff today? Give kids a minute to think about their answer. Ask them to stand by the sign they agree with most (Yes, No, or I Don't Know). Invite volunteers to share why they chose their answer.

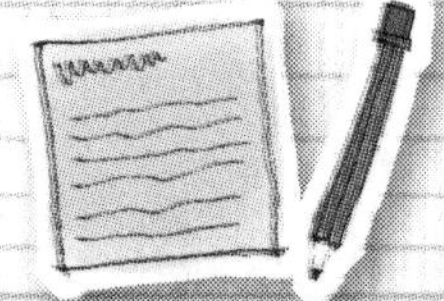

Get this stuff . . .

Sheets of paper with "Yes," "No
"I Don't Know" written on them
erase board and marker. Kids' s
Bibles (optional).

2. Watch

"Does God still create stuff today?" DVD 1, Chapter 9

3. Unpack

- Which ideas from the video hadn't you thought of before?
- What do you disagree with? What do you agree with? Why?
- What is still confusing?
- So, what do you think? Does God still create stuff today?

Im·a·go Dei
[ee-MAH-go Day]
Latin, *the image of God*. Genesi
1:26-27 reveals that God inten
human beings to be a reflection
divine creativity and care.

What about the Bible?

Break into 5 groups. Assign 1 of the following passages to each group: Genesis 1:1–2:3 (Creation), Exodus 16:1–18 (Manna and Quail in the Wilderness), 1 Kings 6 (Solomon's Temple), Matthew 14:13–20 (Jesus Feeds 5,000), John 11:32–44 (Jesus Raises Lazarus to Life). Ask kids to skim or read their passage from a Bible or story Bible and recreate the story for the group. (Act it out, pantomime, recite a poem, sing a song, perform a skit, read aloud, or any other creative way to share the story with the group.) Capture thoughtful responses to the conversation questions on a dry-erase board.

Questions for conversation while you work:

- Name 3 ways the Bible tells us about how God was involved in creation at the very beginning.
- What are a few ways the Bible tells us about how God continued to be involved in creation and re-creation, even after "the beginning"?
- Name 3 ways people are involved in God's ongoing creation today.
- So what? Why would this make any difference for your life today?

engage

25-30 minutes

Choose 1+ Anti-Workbook (AW) activities to explore the session question. The first 2 are for individual use, while the last 2 involve the whole group.

1. Dripping with Creativity AW p. 46

Place water, bowls, food coloring, markers, and towels on a table.

Following the instructions on page 46, have everyone drip water on their Anti-Workbooks and create designs from the water drops.

Questions for conversation while you work:

- How do you define creation? How do you define creative?
- Do you think of yourself as a creative person?
- Tell about the most creative person you know. What makes them creative, in your eyes?
- What did you create in your Anti-Workbook?
- What's the weirdest creation you've ever seen, either God-made or human-made?
- What makes a creation valuable?
- What's the best thing you've ever created? Why is it your favorite?

Where's this going?
Kids play around with their own creativity.

Get this stuff ...
Water. Bowls. Food coloring (5 colors). Markers. Towels or paper towels.

2. Creation Walk & Talk About AW p. 47

Go for a walk—outside or inside—to find things God made both long ago and very recently, as indicated on page 47.

Questions for conversation while you work:

- What's the newest creation you found? The oldest?
- What's the oldest thing God ever created?
- What do you think about this phrase: "God is still creating today."
- How do you know if something is God-created versus human-created?
- When does something go from being created by God to created by human beings? Paper, for example, made from trees? Or iron made from taconite? Or a shirt made from cotton?
- What's some human-created stuff that's good? Have people ever created stuff that messes with God's creation?

Where's this going?
Kids search for created things, old and new, to consider how God may be at work creating today.

3. The Joy of Re-creating AW p. 48

In groups, build something new using "found" objects lying around outside (or inside, if the weather is bad). If you have a digital camera or camera phone, snap photos of the new creations. Share them on the re:form online gallery.

Questions for conversation while you work:

- What do you wish God had created?
- If you could create anything, what would it be?
- What's the difference between making something and creating something?
- What's the best part of creation? What's your least favorite?

Where's this going

Kids experience the difference between crea and re-creation, making something new out of something else.

4. Teach Your Church! AW p. 49

Mark a section of sidewalk or parking lot where kids will create chalk retellings of the Creation Story. Using pictures and numbers, use colorful sidewalk chalk to depict Genesis 1. Try to illustrate it somewhere people will see it when they go to worship. Get everyone working together—including you!

Questions for conversation while you work:

- Why do you think the creation story is in the Bible?
- What does the creation story show us about God?
- If God created human beings last, does that mean things like snails and mosquitoes and elephants and parakeets are more important, since God made them first?
- What's the easiest thing for you to believe about the creation story? The most difficult?
- If a day is like a thousand years for God, and 1,000 years is like a day, did God really create everything in 7 solar days? Does it really matter how long it took?

Where's this going

Kids create a retelling o creation story to share w their church.

Get this stuff...

Sidewalk chalk.

respond

15-20 minutes

Gather to share the different points of view kids have discovered and developed during the session.

Regroup

Share a brief story about the first time you made something you were proud of. Did it work? Do you still have it? What did you learn about yourself through that experience? Or, tell a story about the biggest creative failure of your life; a pot roast gone horribly wrong, or a knitting project that unraveled. What did that teach you about creating? What did that teach you about creation?

Get this stuff . . .
Play-Doh or Silly Putty.

Capture it . . .
Use a digital camera, camcorder, scanner, web cam, or audio recorder to capture group conversations and individual pieces of work. Upload them to your online galleries, or ask kids to do so.

Share

Go around the group and ask each person to share what they've done (if they're comfortable) and explain how they did it and why. Affirm all thoughtful explanations and attempts at the work. Point out two or three things about each kid's work that you like best. Invite others to offer thoughtful observations.

Questions for conversation:

- What are three things you learned about God as the Creator today?
- When Christians say the Apostles' Creed in worship, they say, "We believe in God the Father, Almighty, Creator of heaven and earth." What do you think of when you hear or say that?
- If God is responsible for all creation and creative activity, what do you think God's objective might be? What is God trying to do with all that creating?
- What are some ways you participate with God in creation every day?

Send

Give kids a piece of Play-Doh or Silly Putty and have them create whatever they want. Gather in a circle with the creations and invite kids to say a one-line prayer for creation. Ask kids to place their creations on a tray or table as they exit.

Creed Unit
Am I really supposed to believe Mary was a virgin?

'repare

What's behind all this?

Miraculous births are an important part of the Biblical narrative, most notably the birth of Isaac to the aged Sarah, and the birth of John (the Baptizer) to the aged Elizabeth. This trajectory culminates with the birth of Jesus.

The Gospels of Matthew and Luke recount that Mary was a virgin when she became pregnant with Jesus, the conception being the result of impregnation by the Holy Spirit. The church has held this as a core component of orthodoxy since. Some branches of the Christian church have added the beliefs that Mary was still a virgin when Jesus was born (Virgin Birth), that Mary remained a virgin her entire life (Perpetual Virginity), and that Mary herself was born without sin (Immaculate Conception), but none of these is mentioned in the Bible.

In every miraculous birth in the Bible, and most significantly in the birth of Jesus, the theological point is that God's Spirit has been involved in human affairs—actually in the biology of a woman—in order to precipitate the birth of a special, anointed, and holy person. And the virginal conception of Jesus signals that his direct progenitor is God's Spirit, and we have since worshipped Jesus as the incarnation of *Logos* (the second person of the Trinity).

Where are kids at?

- Kids' ability to reason varies at this age. Some won't think of Mary's virginity as a logical problem. Others will find it a hard concept to reconcile. Rather than spending time arguing for the possibility of her virginity, focus on the way in which this notion links Jesus directly to God and lifts up his divinity.
- Be prepared for some giggling when the ideas of virginity and intimacy are mentioned. Allow for this natural reaction, then direct conversation back to the topic at hand.

Isaiah 7:14

Where's this going?
Kids move past the possibility of Mary's virginity and consider what it means that God is the Father of Jesus of Nazareth.

Consider this . . .

"Ms. Tickle, I believe in the virgin birth, because the story is too beautiful not to be true."
Fourteen-year-old boy to the author Phyllis Tickle

Mary is the "highest woman and the noblest gem in Christianity after Christ . . . She is nobility, wisdom, and holiness personified. We can never honor her enough. Still honor and praise must be given to her in such a way as to injure neither Christ nor the Scriptures."
Martin Luther, Christmas Sermon, 1531

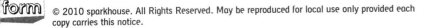

encounter

15 minutes

Video

1. Set up

Take turns telling each other something wonderful about your moms, grandmas, or other female role models in your lives. Kids can share a skill this person has, a time she did something surprising, or other stories. Moms, grandmas, and important women in our lives play a big role in how we grow up. Jesus' mom played a big role in his life, too.

2. Watch

"Am I really supposed to believe Mary was a virgin?", DVD 1, Chapter 10

3. Unpack

- What characteristics do you share with your parents and family?
- What characteristics do you think Jesus shared with Mary?
- Why do you think the *theology* of Jesus' birth is more important than the *biology*?
- If you could confront Mary in person, would you try to get her to tell you the truth? Why or why not?

What about the Bible?

Have kids brainstorm a list of words that have more than one meaning. Write them on chart paper and talk about the definitions for each. Ideas may include: ball—a round object or a fancy dance; bat—a flying mammal or a wooden rod; bank—the side of a river or a place for money.

Questions for conversation while you work:

- Grab a partner and take turns using words from our list in a sentence. How do you know which meaning your partner intends?
- Read Isaiah 7:14 in an NRSV Bible and then in an NIV Bible. What is different between these two passages? What is the same?
- If you were going to sum up the message of this verse, what would you say? Is your message different between the translations? Why or why not?

Make sure you've got the obvi stuff for this session—re:form video (DVD or download), Anti-Workbooks, Bibles, pens pencils, paper, tape, etc.

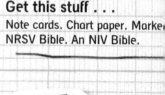

Get this stuff . . .

Note cards. Chart paper. Marke NRSV Bible. An NIV Bible.

the·ol·o·gy
[thee-**ahl**-oh-jee]
the study of the nature of God a how God is involved in our worl

Back it up . . .

"According to the Bible God was involved when Mary conceived J because God decided that Jesus God's son, should go to Earth an live among us. And so God sent Jesus by way of the Holy Spirit b way of Mary to the world."
re:form DVD

engage

25-30 minutes

Choose 1+ Anti-Workbook (AW) activities to explore the session question. The first 2 are for individual use, while the last 2 involve the whole group.

1. The Fam AW p. 50

Think through some of the influences in your life, including your parents, mentors, friends, and family members. Use your insights to help kids think about the traits (physical, emotional, behavioral, and even spiritual) they have and why. For kids who aren't being raised by a mom and dad, suggest re-labeling the stick figures as appropriate, and let those kids focus on emotional, behavioral, and spiritual traits. Give kids the opportunity to draw in other stick-figure influences in their lives. Perhaps they learned to be organized from a grade-school teacher. Perhaps they learned about how to pray from you! Open this activity up to the many ways we come to be who we are.

Questions for conversation while you work:

- If you have siblings, what do you have in common with them? How are you different from them?
- What about you is different from everyone else in your family?
- What traits do you think Jesus may have gotten from Mary? From God? What about from Joseph?

Get this stuff . . .
Scissors. Clear tape.

Where's this going?
Kids think about the traits they have gotten from their parents and consider what traits Mary and God the Father handed to Jesus.

2. Birth Certificate AW p. 51

Think back on the details of your birth. Could you fill out all of the information on this birth certificate for yourself? How is your experience different than Jesus' and his parents' experience? Use this reflection to guide your discussion as you and the kids wrestle with the tough parts of this activity.

Questions for conversation while you work:

- What stories have you heard about the day you were born?
- How can you account for both God *and* Joseph in the birth certificate?
- Are the date and place of Mary's birth important? Why or why not?
- What can you learn about yourself from your birth certificate?

Where's this going?
Kids will take a closer look at details of Jesus' birth and wonder about his divine and human traits.

Back It Up
"The only problem is there's no way to prove by scientific or any other methods whether Mary was indeed a virgin in the anatomical, biological, medical sense. The only person who know's that for sure is Mary. And she's not talking."
re:form DVD

3. The Magnificat AW p. 52

Split your group into teams of four for today's activity. If needed, groups can have more than one reporter, or they can assign someone to be solely in charge of all the recording equipment.

While kids get organized, reflect on what you would ask these characters about their experience. Listen to the questions kids come up with as they work. How are yours different? Pop in periodically throughout the radio interview to share questions of your own.

Questions for conversation while you work:

- What sorts of hopes, dreams, or plans does your family have for your future?
- Do you think you're a part of your parents' or guardians' calling? Why or why not?
- How do you think Mary was feeling during the Magnificat? How would you have been feeling?
- Do you think Mary was brave? Crazy? A really good storyteller? Or something else? Explain your response.
- How do we see some of the stuff from the Magnificat coming true in our world?

Get this stuff . . .
Audio recorder or a compu with microphone.

Where's this going?
Kids will act out Mary's response to Gabriel's announcement that she would give birth to God's Son, and will unpack its meaning.

Mag•nif•i•cat
[mag-**nif**-ih-cot]
The song of praise that M sang after the angel Gabri told her that she would giv birth to God's Son. The na comes from a Latin word which means to magnify, praise.

4. Family Tree AW p. 53

The traits we got from our immediate family members are pretty obvious, but what about the traits we got from our grandparents and great-grandparents and great-great-grandparents? Again, remind any kids who aren't living with their biological parents that there are lots of emotional, habitual, and spiritual traits we can inherit from the people whom we live with and who love us. If kids don't know much about their family trees, have them text or call family members for more information.

Questions for conversation while you work:

- What sorts of patterns show up in your family tree? Any long lines of circus performers, for example?
- What predictions could you make about your future after studying your family tree?
- Is Jesus or God in your family tree? Why or why not?
- Where should Joseph be included in Jesus' family tree?
- What does Jesus' family tree (Matthew 1:1-17) tell us about him?

Where's this going?
While climbing their own family trees, kids will consider Jesus' family tree and wonder what it says about him.

ge•ne•al•o•gy
[jee-nee-**ahl**-oh-jee]
a record of a person's ancestry or family tree

respond

15-20 minutes

Gather to share the different points of view kids have discovered and developed during the session.

Regroup

Have kids write letters to an ancestor telling them some of the things that happened after that person's time. Take some time to share the letters with one another. Staple them to this lesson in their Anti-Workbooks.

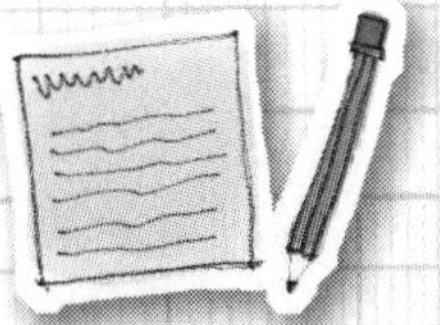

Get this stuff . . .
Blank paper. Audio recorder or computer with a microphone.

Share

Invite kids to share their work and describe how and why they did it. Affirm those things you appreciate or find interesting and ask others to offer helpful observations.

Questions for conversation:

- How is your family tree important to you?
- How is Jesus' family tree important to him? What important roles did Mary play in Jesus' life?
- How is having God as a Father significant in Jesus' life? How is this significant in our lives?
- Why are you who you are? Who made you this way?
- Why was Jesus who he was? What does this mean for you and me?

Capture it . . .
Use a digital camera, camcorder, scanner, web cam, or audio recorder to capture group conversations and individual pieces of work. Upload them to your online galleries, or ask kids to do so.

Send

Have kids open their Anti-Workbooks to the family tree. If your group didn't complete this activity today, give kids two minutes to write down as many names as they can think of from their family history. Tell them that when you begin praying, they should begin quietly reading the names on their family tree or list. Wait until all names are said before praying the last line of the prayer. Pray: Heavenly Father, thank you for using Mary to bring your Son to us and our world. Thank you for using Joseph to raise him up. Thank you for all the people in his family tree. Most of all we thank you for giving him to us so that we can be included in your family.

Please use us and our families to carry Christ's love into our world. Amen.

Back it up . . .
"So the reason the virgin birth is so important to Christians is less about the biology of it and more about the *theo*logy, that is, what it *means*. Because it demonstrates God did something really amazing. For Christians, it shows that Jesus of Nazareth truly is God's son, God's loving gift to bless and save the world."
re:form DVD

Creed Unit
Why did Jesus go to hell?

'repare

What's behind all this?

urely the most vexing line in the Apostles' Creed is, "He descended into hell." ome churches have changed it to, "He descended to the dead," and others ave excised it altogether.

he Hebrew Scriptures do not have a developed doctrine of the afterlife, much ess one for heaven and hell. Instead, it was believed that all persons go to *heol* (*Hades* in Greek), which is the place of the dead. This particular line in he Creed is based on a passage from 1 Peter, in which it is written that Jesus escended to the place of the dead and preached the good news to the people athered there.

heologically, the importance is twofold. First, that God in Jesus really xperienced the totality of human death—not just the crucifixion, but also the escent to Sheol. And second, that even the place that seems most removed rom God is, in fact, not beyond the good news of Jesus Christ. Sometimes ell is experienced on earth, and Jesus shows up there too.

Where are kids at?

- Some kids in your group will still think of Heaven and Hell as concrete, real places—one up and one down. Others will be starting to wonder what it more broadly means for something to be heavenly or to be hellish. Keep this in mind as you discuss hell as "the place of the dead." Help the concrete thinkers begin to see that this doesn't necessarily have to be a physical place, but rather a state of being—with or without God.

1 Peter 3:18-20
Romans 8:38-39

Where's this going?
Kids experiment with the definition of hell and what that says about God.

Consider this . . .
"Today a great silence reigns on earth, a great silence and a great stillness. A great silence because the King is asleep. The earth trembled and is still because God has fallen asleep in the flesh . . . Greatly desiring to visit those who live in darkness and in the shadow of death, he has gone to free from sorrow Adam in his bonds and Eve, captive with him—He who is both their God and the son of Eve . . . 'I order you, O sleeper, to awake. I did not create you to be a prisoner in hell. Rise from the dead, for I am the life of the dead.'"
Ancient Christian Liturgy, quoted in the Catechism of the Catholic Church, 635

encounter

15 minutes

Make sure you've got the obvi-
stuff for this session—re:form video (DVD or download), Anti-Workbooks, Bibles, pens
pencils, paper, tape, etc.

Video

1. Set up

As a group, brainstorm a list of words your group would use to describe hell. With that list in mind, ask kids to tell about the worst things that have happened to them in the last month. Do they use any of the words from the list when they describe how those events made them feel? Let kids know that, in many ways, these experiences are pieces of hell on earth. If hell is so rotten, why did Jesus go to hell?

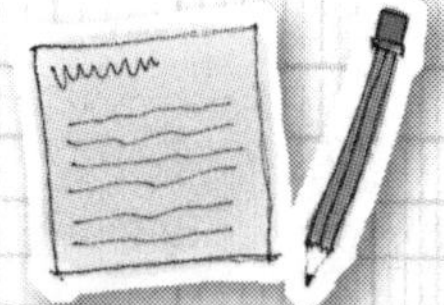

Get this stuff . . .
Chart paper. Marker.

2. Watch

"Why did Jesus go to hell?" DVD 1, Chapter 11

3. Unpack

- What is the nastiest, grossest thing you've ever had to clean up?
- Tell about a time when you were really sick; who took care of you and cleaned up after you?
- How did it feel to have someone caring for you?
- When you are sick or experiencing something really awful, what do you think about to give yourself hope?

proc·la·ma·tion
[prok-luh-**may**-shun]
an official, formal announcemen-
about something that has happe-
or will happen

What about the Bible?

Tell kids about a time when you were separated from the people you love, or from a group you were supposed to be with. What caused the separation? How did you find each other again? What did separation feel like for you?

Questions for conversation while you work:

- Read 1 Peter 3:18-20. Who did Jesus make a proclamation to?
- Considering that Jesus had just died on the cross and was about to be resurrected, what do you suppose he said in his proclamation?
- Read Romans 8:38-39. How does this verse make you feel? How might it make you feel if you heard it when you were lost?
- Where do you think God is when you are feeling rejected, sick, frightened, or downright hellacious?

25-30 minutes

Choose 1+ Anti-Workbook (AW) activities to explore the session question. The first 2 are for individual use, while the last 2 involve the whole group.

1. Bad News AW p. 54

As you prepare yourself for this activity, think about the last tragedy you heard about in the news. How did those involved in the tragedy react? Were they angry? Terrified? Worried? Or were they hopeful? Prayerful? Determined to go on? Where was God working in the tragedy? Keep in mind that you might need to help out your concrete thinkers in today's activity. God's presence isn't always obvious, so be prepared to offer some guidance as kids search for the places where God was present in their Bad News situations.

Questions for conversation while you work:

- How might these news stories be reporting about hell on earth?
- What does the Psalm writer seem to be feeling?
- How do you feel about the promise that God is always with you?
- What examples of God's presence do you see in these stories?
- What are some ways that we could help people in these stories?

Get this stuff . . .

Assorted newspapers and news magazines.

Where's this going?

Kids search for reports of hell on earth as well as for indications that God is present there.

2. God Is Here AW p. 55

Before this session, arrange to go somewhere away from your regular meeting place, such as a mall, park, downtown city block, or some other public setting. Set some ground rules for places kids are and aren't allowed to go, and then set them loose for 10 minutes to complete the activity. Come back together to discuss findings and print photographs. If you aren't able to transport your group to another place, spend time talking about places in your community that would be good spots to place the stickers. Challenge kids to complete this activity throughout the week. Remind them to take pictures and to email or text message the photos to you during the week. Then spend some time during the next session discussing the places kids found God in your community.

Questions for conversation while you work:

- What is the best news you've ever been able to tell someone?
- Do you know anyone who is experiencing hell in this world? Who?
- How could you let them know about God's presence?

Get this stuff . . .

Digital cameras or cell phone cameras. Photo printer. Stapler. Transportation.

Where's this going?

Kids go out and find the places where God is present in their community and discover that God isn't just in the nice and happy places.

3. Like A Spirit Outta Hell AW p. 56

Before this activity, consider how Jesus would find you if you were lost. What part of your spirit reflects Jesus within you?

Allow kids enough time to decorate their punch-out dolls. Set boundaries and rules before setting your group free to hide the dolls. Have a couple of extra volunteers shoot video of the hide-and-seek activity. Post it to the re:form online library.

Questions for conversation while you work:

- What makes your paper doll yours?
- What makes you belong to Jesus?
- How did you find and rescue your paper doll?
- What might have kept you from finding and rescuing your paper doll?
- How did Jesus find and rescue "the spirits in prison"? (1 Peter 3:19)

Get this stuff . . .

Punch-out doll from page
Art materials for decoratin
paper doll.

Where's this going?

Kids search out paper doll
and explore what Jesus
accomplished by descendi
into hell.

4. Hell Mixture AW p. 57

While kids are working on their nasty mixture, challenge them to create a "HELL" cheer that represents what their Hell Mixture is made of. They can use their cheer as they mix, stir, and paint. Be sure they add their cheer to their Anti-Workbook.

Questions for conversation while you work:

- What kinds of sounds are you making as you mix up your ingredients?
- Do any physical reflexes come to mind?
- How is your mixture a good representation of hell?
- What is it about God that makes it possible to have God by your side in even the messiest, nastiest, grossest mixture of ingredients?

Get this stuff . . .

Assorted ingredients like
those suggested on page 5
of the Anti-Workbook. Bow
Mixing utensils. Sponge
brushes. Mess-proof zone.

Where's this going?

Kids create a nasty mixtur
of materials as a tool for
considering the lengths to
which God will go to save
and care for us.

15-20 minutes

Gather to share the different points of view kids have discovered and developed during the session.

Regroup

Hand out index cards and ask kids to write down any questions they still have about hell and about Jesus going to hell. Invite them to share their questions. Don't feel the need to offer answers. Rather, discuss the questions and see what your group can discover.

Get this stuff . . .
Index cards.

Share

Invite kids to share their work and describe how and why they did it. Affirm those things you appreciate or find interesting and ask others to offer helpful observations.

Questions for conversation:

- What are your feelings about hell?
- What are some situations that are hellish in our world today?
- Why do you think Jesus went to hell?
- What are some clues that show you Jesus is present in your life?
- How can Jesus use you to reach out to places of hell on earth?

Capture it . . .
Use a digital camera, camcorder, scanner, web cam, or audio recorder to capture group conversations and individual pieces of work. Upload them to your online galleries, or ask kids to do so.

Send

Teach kids the response, "There is nowhere that God is not present." Have kids take turns naming some places or people who are experiencing hell on earth. After each kid names a situation, respond together, "There is nowhere that God is not present." Close the prayer time by praying something like this: "God, please be more than present, but show your face and love to people who feel a million miles away from you. Amen."

Creed Unit

Is the Holy Spirit a person or wind or fire or what?

'repare

What's behind all this?

rom the beginning of the Bible, God's Spirit (*ruach* in Hebrew) is present, overing over the face of the primordial waters. In the Christian Scriptures, it the Holy Spirit (*pneuma* in Greek) that gives Jesus his powers to heal. And, ltimately, it is the Spirit that Jesus promises and then delivers to the early hurch after his resurrection.

o the Holy Spirit—also known as the third person of the Trinity—is present iroughout the Biblical narrative, and throughout history. In fact, that is ie best way to understand the Holy Spirit, as God's *presence* (*shekinah* in lebrew) in history and in our world today.

he Biblical writers used various metaphors to describe God's Spirit, including ind, fire, breath, and water—each an attempt to give us some sense of what ultimately a mystery. It is notable that several of the Biblical words for the loly Spirit are feminine.

Where are kids at?

Kids in your group are becoming more and more independent. They desire more control over their own lives, yet they still need the guidance of their parents and other adults. This lesson can touch on both of those aspects: The Holy Spirit leads and guides us. At the same time, the Spirit equips us and uses us to do God's work in the world.

Genesis 1:1
John 3:8

Where's this going?
Kids explore what the Holy Spirit is and does.

Consider this . . .

"I believe that I cannot by my own reason or strength believe in Jesus Christ, my Lord, or come to Him; but the Holy Spirit has called me by the Gospel, enlightened me with His gifts, sanctified and kept me in the true faith; even as He calls, gathers, enlightens, and sanctifies the whole Christian Church on earth, and keeps it with Jesus Christ in the one true faith."

Martin Luther, *Small Catechism*

encounter

15 minutes

Video

1. Set up

Have kids draw pictures of or write stories about themselves doing impossible things. Have each kid describe his or her impossible feat. The Holy Spirit can be the most mysterious and confusing part of the Trinity. As a matter of fact, we'll see that it is pretty much impossible to describe the Holy Spirit. So, is the Holy Spirit a person or wind or fire or what?

2. Watch

"Is the Holy Spirit a person or wind or fire or what?" DVD 1, Chapter 12

3. Unpack

- What are some things in this world that you can't fully understand?
- If describing the Holy Spirit is impossible, then why do you think people try so hard to do it?
- The video said that the Holy Spirit is known through the work it does. What work do you think it is doing when it's represented by fire or rushing wind?

What about the Bible?

Tell kids about a time when you have been or felt out of control of a particular situation. Since this lesson focuses on the Holy Spirit's life-giving (Genesis 1:1) and attentive (John 3:8) presence, reflect on how the Spirit was at work even when you felt like you weren't in control.

Questions for conversation while you work: (bulleted list)

- When is a time when you've felt you weren't in control?
- When have you tried to be in control of something but have had to have someone else help you?
- When are you happy to have someone else in control?
- Read Genesis 1:1 and John 3:8. What do these passages tell us about the Holy Spirit?

Make sure you've got the obv stuff for this session—re:form video (DVD or download), Anti-Workbooks, Bibles, pens pencils, paper, tape, etc.

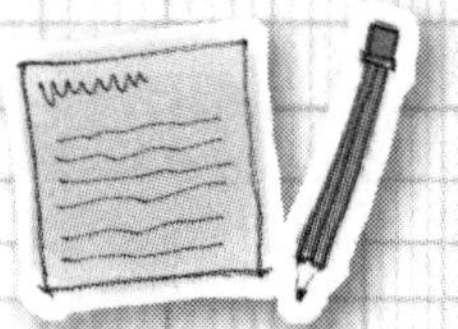

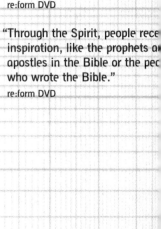

Get this stuff . . .
Blank paper.

ho•ly
[hoh-lee]
something or someone who ha given the purpose of doing God work

Back it up . . .

"Christians believe the Holy Spi how God takes action in our w In fact, the Holy Spirit seems t all about action, about making things happen."
re:form DVD

"Through the Spirit, people rece inspiration, like the prophets a apostles in the Bible or the pec who wrote the Bible."
re:form DVD

25-30 minutes

Choose 1+ Anti-Workbook (AW) activities to explore the session question. The first 2 are for individual use, while the last 2 involve the whole group.

1. Bond. Agent Bond. AW p. 58

Before kids have a chance to open their Anti-Workbooks to page 58, sit extra-close to one of the kids so your arm is pressed up against his or hers. If the kid tries to move away, move too so you stay stuck together. Talk about the different kinds of closeness we can experience—physical, emotional, experiential. Let kids offer examples during this opening chat. Then reveal the materials they'll be using in this activity and let them dive in.

Questions for conversation while you work:

- Which stuff works best for sticking the toothpicks to the page?
- Which doesn't work so well?
- What are some real-world reasons to use fasteners or bonding agents?
- In what ways does the Holy Spirit binds us together as Christians?
- What does it mean to you to be connected with Christians around the world, or even from the past or future?

Get this stuff . . .

Toothpicks. Digital camera. Assorted sticky stuff like what's listed on page 58 of the Anti-Workbook.

Where's this going?

Kids will experiment with different fasteners and bonding agents to consider how the Holy Spirit binds us together.

Back It Up

"Christ Jesus, God the Father, and the Holy Spirit are bonded together like glue in a holy relationship which is the Trinity. Father, Son, and the Holy Spirit."
re:form DVD

2. Wind AW p. 59

Plug in and turn on several fans as near to kids as possible—the louder the fan noise, the better. Turn on the ocean recording and set the volume as loud as will be tolerable. Let kids soak in the noise for awhile, then open up your copy of the Anti-Workbook and point to the first part of the activity on page 59. Signal kids to go outside and collect evidence of wind.

Once kids return with their wind evidence, turn off the fans and ocean recording, dim the lights, light a couple of candles, and sit in silence for a moment. Again, open your Anti-Workbook and point to part 2 of the activity. Signal kids to go out into your building and collect evidence of the Holy Spirit.

Questions for conversation while you work:

- What was all of the fan noise and ocean noise like at the beginning of the activity?
- What's it like outside on a really windy day?
- What evidence is there that the Holy Spirit is working in our church?
- How do you know the wind is powerful? How about the Holy Spirit?

Get this stuff . . .

Digital camera. Photo printer. Assortment of fans. Recording of the ocean. Candles. *Be careful with fire!*

Where's this going?

Kids explore the work of the unseen Holy Spirit by finding evidence of the unseen wind and its power.

3. Holy Spirit Postcards AW p. 60

Before meeting, think about what kids in your group might need to hear—about their lives, faith, family, friends, or calling. Write a postcard to your group from the Holy Spirit. Read it aloud to help kids start thinking about the kinds of things the Holy Spirit might say through them to help others.

Questions for conversation while you work:

- How did you choose whom to write your postcard to?
- How do you think your postcard will affect the person who receives it?
- What sorts of things are you good at? How do you know you're good at them?
- What is your greatest need right now?
- What sorts of things help you feel good about yourself?
- When in your life might the Holy Spirit have been using you to do work in the world?
- On a scale of 19 to 25, with 19 being not so good and 25 being super-duper, how would you rate your faith today?

Where's this going?

Kids fill out and deliver postcards from the Holy Spirit to their friends to discover how the Holy Sp uses them to bring love i the world.

Back It Up

"Some Christians say the Spirit is like a radio signa signal from God that cove the whole world. And whe our hearts are tuned in to the Holy Spirit then we're grooving with God."

re:form DVD

4. Blow, Spirit, Blow AW p. 61

Set up a wind experimentation lab complete with various wind-makers such as fans, hair dryers, straws, megaphones, balloons, and paper-towel tubes. Once dry, scan the results and upload them to the re:form gallery!

Questions for conversation while you work:

- What are two or three things that happened when your wind blew the food coloring droplets?
- Could you have predicted the directions or patterns that resulted?
- How did the different kinds of wind-makers affect the droplets differently?
- If you left the water droplets for a week, what would they look like?
- In what ways does the Holy Spirit move Christians and the church?
- What does the Holy Spirit do for you? What does the Holy Spirit do for the church?
- What would happen to the church if the Holy Spirit just left it alone?

Get this stuff . . .

Several different colors of liquid food coloring. Items with nonporous surfaces, such as plates or cookie sheets. Assortment of fans, hair dryers, straws, megaphones, balloons, and paper-towel tubes. Blank paper (if needed).

Where's this going?

Kids use wind to move liq and wonder how the Holy Spirit moves Christians an the church.

15-20 minutes

ather to share the different points of view kids have discovered and eveloped during the session.

Regroup

sk kids to write any questions they still have about the Holy Spirit in the orm of a prayer around the lines and patterns of their picture from today's Blow, Spirit, Blow" activity. If you didn't do that activity today, have kids write their questions on note cards.

Share

nvite kids to share their work and describe how and why they did it. Affirm hose things you appreciate or find interesting and ask others to offer helpful bservations.

Questions for conversation:

- What surprised you in today's lesson?
- How has the Holy Spirit moved you or used you in your life?
- How does it feel to know that the Holy Spirit works in unpredictable and uncontrollable ways?

Send

Ask kids to take turns praying by reading the questions they've written for the Holy Spirit. Then recite the third portion of the Apostles' Creed together. If your kids wrote their questions on note cards, have them staple them into their Anti-Workbooks.

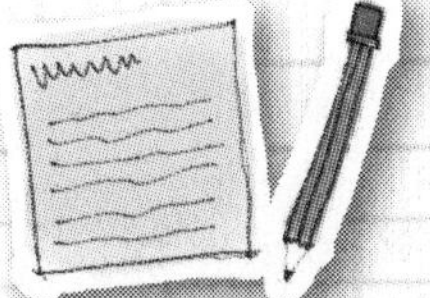

Get this stuff . . .
Note cards (optional). Stapler (if needed).

Capture it . . .
Use a digital camera, camcorder, scanner, web cam, or audio recorder to capture group conversations and individual pieces of work. Upload them to your online galleries, or ask kids to do so.

Creed Unit

Why do we say we believe in "the holy catholic church" if we're not Catholic?

Prepare

What's behind all this?

When the Apostles' Creed was first used in the early church, there was only one Christian church. Although there were theological disagreements, there was no such thing as "Catholic" and "Protestant," not to mention thousands of denominations. So when people confessed "one holy, catholic, and apostolic church," they were actually stating their own experience.

Today, when we proclaim that the church is one (meaning unified) and catholic (meaning universal) we are as much praying for the overcoming of our differences as we are professing that, in God's eyes, we are all one.

This confession about the church occurs in the third part of the Creed in a discussion about the Holy Spirit—the Spirit that descended upon the disciples at Pentecost (Acts 2). This same Spirit binds the whole global church together as unified, even though we are still divided.

Where are kids at?

- Kids' opinions are strongly influenced by what they hear at home, in the media, and from their friends. Depending on where your kids are coming from and what the latest Catholic news headline is, your group may come to this discussion with some pretty well ingrained stereotypes. Don't feel like you have to raise up or shoot down these stereotypes. Stay focused on "catholic" rather than "Catholic." Kids will draw their own conclusions, and that's okay!

John 17:20-23

Where's this going?

Kids investigate what binds the church together across time and space, despite differences.

encounter

15 minutes

Video

1. Set up

Ask kids to name as many different Christian denominations as they can think of. Look in the Yellow Pages and/or newspaper to see if you can find any more. There are so many different sorts of churches in the world that your list probably doesn't even begin to scratch the surface. Ask kids, so why do we say we believe in "the holy catholic church" if we're not Catholic?

2. Watch

"Why do we say we believe in 'the holy catholic church' if we're not Catholic?" DVD 1, Chapter 13

3. Unpack

- If you've ever been part of a congregation of a different denomination, which denomination was it?
- What are the different denominations in our community?
- How are they different? How are they the same?

What about the Bible?

Ask kids to share where they would go in history if they could travel back in time, and why they would go there. Ask the same question about traveling into the future. Ask them to spot how Jesus talks about time travel in John 17:20-23. Read the passage out loud for them.

Questions for conversation while you work:

- So, where did Jesus talk about time travel here?
- What is the last argument you've had with a sibling or someone else in your family?
- What makes you a family even when you disagree with each other?
- How is it possible for all Christians to be the holy catholic church when we are divided by time and disagreements?

Make sure you've got the obv
stuff for this session—re:form
video (DVD or download),
Anti-Workbooks, Bibles, pens
pencils, paper, tape, etc.

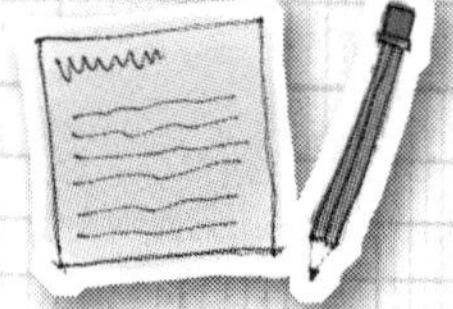

Get this stuff . . .

Yellow Pages phone book and/o
worship schedule from a newsp

u·ni·ver·sal
[yoo-nih-**vur**-suhl]
present everywhere in the world

de·nom·i·na·tion
[dih-nom-ih-**nay**-shuhn]
Specific groups of congregations within the one holy catholic chu are called denominations. For instance, the United Methodist denomination has many congregations throughout the Ur States and Canada.

Back it up . . .

"The word "catholic" means "universal." Or "universal in exten involving all; of interest to all." A "pertaining to the whole Christian body or church." All of us. Every who believes in Jesus."
re:form DVD

25-30 minutes

Choose 1+ Anti-Workbook (AW) activities to explore the session question. The first 2 are for individual use, while the last 2 involve the whole group.

1. Draw Yer Family AW p. 62

Bring in a photo of your family for this activity and share a couple of stories about how the members of your immediate and extended family are very different from one another. Also share any common themes that tie your family together. Maybe there are a lot of teachers in your family. Maybe everyone is a fan of the Pittsburgh Penguins. Encourage kids to a take a similar look at the people in their families.

Questions for conversation while you work:

- Do you have any extended family members (aunts, uncles, cousins) in other countries?
- How is it that you are one family even though you are different from one another?
- What makes you one family with your ancestors from 100 years ago? How about 100 years in the future?
- What makes different congregations of different denominations all part of one holy catholic church?

Get this stuff . . .
Family photo.

Where's this going?
Kids examine family differences to explore the idea that different Christian denominations are part of one holy catholic church.

Back It Up
"Jesus' gospel transcends race, nationality, ethnicity, and societal norms. So people with widely different ways all live in this catholic, this *universal* church."
re:form DVD

2. Time Machine AW p. 63

Spend some time before meeting thinking about how you imagine the future. Are there flying cars? Superheroes? Robots? How do you think faith might change in the next 500 years? Do you feel connected to those changes?

Provide a variety of craft items for your visual thinkers today. Kids can feel free to write about their future worship or they can use the supplies to create a picture of the future worship space and share what they created.

Questions for conversation while you work:

- What parts of your future worship are the same as worship today?
- What parts of your future worship are different from worship today?
- What might be some totally new things that happen?
- Which seems more interesting—worship now or worship in the future?
- How are we connected to the people who will be worshiping more than 500 years from now?

Get this stuff . . .
Assorted craft items, such as sequins, stick-on gems, and glitter. Glue. Markers.

Where's this going?
Kids expand their imagination and consideration of the one holy catholic church by imagining a worship service 500 or more years in the future.

3. Make a Video AW p. 64

Are there times in your life when you weren't able to do something until you accepted that you needed the help of the Holy Spirit? Kids probably haven't thought of this, so encourage them to try some Holy Spirit™ Gloo® as they try to make it through these challenging challenges.

Questions for conversation while you work:

- What is most difficult about each challenge?
- What could make each challenge easier?
- When have you felt like you had an impossible task to do? How did you get through it?
- If we can't build a model of the holy catholic church using boxes and our teeth, how does it exist?

Get this stuff . . .
Video camera. Several bo

Where's this going?
Kids take on some challenging and impossibl challenges and consider h the Holy Spirit can make t holy catholic church possi

4. Field Trip! AW p. 65

Make arrangements to take your group to visit a church of a different denomination. If you plan this event before this lesson, make some time to talk about the field trip during today's activity. If you plan the trip for after this lesson occurs, make time to debrief during the lesson following the field trip.

Questions for conversation while you work:

- What was the biggest difference between worship at our congregation and worship at this congregation?
- What was most familiar to you?
- How did it feel to you?
- What new insight about worship did you gain here?
- What evidence did you discover that our congregation and this one are both part of the holy catholic church?

Where's this going?
Kids visit a church of anot denomination to explore th similarities and differences between their church and another.

respond

15-20 minutes

Gather to share the different points of view kids have discovered and developed during the session.

Regroup

As a group, make a list of what makes up the holy catholic church. Challenge the kids in your group: If it were possible to create a single building for the holy catholic church, what would it look like? Draw a model.

Get this stuff . . .
Blank paper.

Share

Invite kids to share their work and describe how and why they did it. Affirm those things you appreciate or find interesting and ask others to offer helpful observations.

Questions for conversation:

- Are Catholics a part of the holy catholic church? Are you a part of the holy catholic church? How do you know this?
- What was your biggest surprise about the holy catholic church?
- What are possible difficulties with the existence of the holy catholic church?
- How do you think members of the holy catholic church can settle their differences?

Capture it . . .
Use a digital camera, camcorder, scanner, web cam, or audio recorder to capture group conversations and individual pieces of work. Upload them to your online galleries, or ask kids to do so.

Send

Ask kids to think of difficult things they can do, such as solving algebraic equations, mastering certain video games, riding a unicycle, etc. Teach them this response: "Only the Holy Sprit can create the holy catholic church."

Have kids take turns saying, "I can do difficult things like [the difficult thing they can do]." Each time, have the entire group respond with, "Only the Holy Sprit can create the holy catholic church."

Creed Unit
Do cremated people go to heaven?

Prepare

What's behind all this?

It's a common misconception that God cares a lot about the soul of a person, and very little about the body. In fact, disdain for the body comes more from the philosophy of Plato than it does from Christianity. In the Hebrew Scriptures, God cares very much about the body; thus, there are numerous laws that dictate how Jews are to eat and bathe and live. And in the Christian Scriptures, the very incarnation (literally, "enfleshment") of the Logos in Jesus of Nazareth shows the importance of the body.

Both Jesus and Paul make it clear that at the end of time, all humankind will be resurrected in the body. Jesus' own resurrection was a foreshadowing of this. The early church affirmed this, opting for bodily burial rather than cremation, since they believed Jesus would return before their corpses decayed.

However, all corpses decay into dust, whether it happens immediately by cremation, or gradually via the ravages of time. And God's promise of our resurrection is not contingent upon the state of our bodies at the time of Christ's return. When God's kingdom comes again, sorrow, death, pain, and suffering will be no more.

John 5:28-29
1 Corinthians 15:20-25

Where's this going?
Kids navigate through biblical ideas of bodily death and resurrection.

Where are kids at?

- Kids in your group will have had different experiences with death. Be sensitive to both those who have and those who haven't experienced the death of a close family member or friend.
- Keep in mind that there may be some kids in your group who are suffering from depression. Remember that if you hear anyone mention thoughts of suicide, report those comments to a church staff member immediately. Remember to surround each member of your group with a net of support and love. Being a teenager is tough!

encounter

15 minutes

Video

1. Set up

Have kids draw pictures of what heaven will look like for them. Encourage conversation about what inspires their visions of heaven.

2. Watch

"Do cremated people go to heaven?" DVD 1, Chapter 14

3. Unpack

- How does the stuff the video said about life after death compare with the picture of heaven you drew? How do you feel about that?
- If you got to pick at what age your body was resurrected, what would you pick?
- Is it good news or bad news that there's no such thing as zombies?
- Why do people seem to be so eager to make lists of who will be in heaven and who won't?

What about the Bible?

Have kids close their eyes tightly. Tell them that you are going to silently tap someone on the shoulder. The person whose shoulder is tapped should say, "Hello." Keeping their eyes closed, everyone else must guess who it was that just spoke. Play a few rounds of this game.

Questions for conversation while you work:

- How hard was it to figure out who was speaking without being able to see them?
- How did God create the world in the first chapter of Genesis?
- Read John 5:28-29. According to this passage, how will the dead be raised at the resurrection?
- How powerful are words?
- Read 1 Corinthians 15:20-25. According to Paul, who was the one person who brought sin into the world?
- How is Jesus like that person? How is he different?

Make sure you've got the obvi[ous] stuff for this session—re:form video (DVD or download), Anti-Workbooks, Bibles, pens [or] pencils, paper, tape, etc.

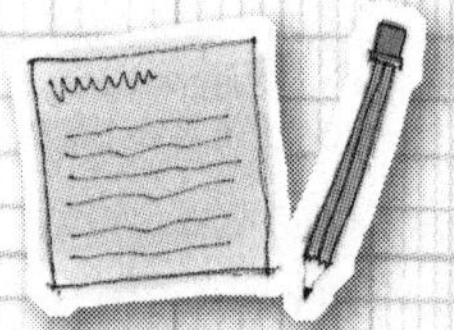

Get this stuff . . .
Blank paper.

in·car·na·tion
[in-car-**nay**-shun]
the taking on of flesh; for Christi[ans] incarnation means that God bec[ame] human in the birth of Jesus

Back it up . . .
"In fact studies have shown that m[ore] than 9 out of 10 people eventua[lly] die. *Now* turn that frown upside down, it's not the end of the wor[ld]. In fact, according to the Bible, it [can] be the beginning of a new and be[tter] one. I'm talking of course about y[our] resurrection."
re:form DVD

25-30 minutes

Choose 1+ Anti-Workbook (AW) activities to explore the session question. The first 2 are for individual use, while the last 2 involve the whole group.

1. Now & Later AW p. 66

Where are you currently in the scope of this photo strip? Near 32? Near 75? Somewhere in the middle? How would you have pictured yourself at 32 when you were a teenager? Think about how God has worked throughout your life to change you. Share some of your thoughts with kids as they work.

Begin this activity with a photo shoot. Catch the kids in your group in action, jumping, dancing, laughing, or playing a game. Print the pictures for kids to attach to their Anti-Workbooks in the "what you look like today" rectangle.

Questions for conversation while you work:

- What do you think you'll be doing when you're 32? How about 75?
- Who will you be eager to see again after you die?
- What do you think you'll look like at the resurrection if you die old and wrinkly?
- What do you think babies who die will look like at the resurrection?

Get this stuff . . .
Digital camera. Photo printer.

Where's this going?
Kids imagine the lifetime and decay of their physical bodies and consider God's power and promise for a physical resurrection that won't be limited by our former, perishable bodies.

res•ur•rec•tion
[rez-er-**reck**-shun]
the raising of the dead to new life, never to die again

2. Dust to Dust AW p. 67

Bring in a bag of dust and dirt from your home. Hold it up and introduce it to your group as your new friend, Roger. Tell the kids about what Roger likes to do, his favorite foods and music, and how excited Roger is to be joining your confirmation group. Ask a volunteer to bring Roger along as they work on the next Anti-Workbook activity. If your group is unable to go outside for this activity, make sure you have some potting soil and water on hand.

Questions for conversation while you work:

- Why do you think Roger is still just a bag of dust even though I decided to make him a person?
- What are some of the best places to find dust?
- What do you think dust is made out of?
- According to the Bible, what is your connection with dust?
- Why do you think this activity has you writing your name with dirt?

Get this stuff . . .
Zip-lock bag of dust and dirt. Potting soil and water (optional).

Where's this going?
Kids consider God's power to create "from dust" and God's power in our resurrection.

Back It Up
"The Bible, however, says that, in the same way Jesus was resurrected, those who have received the gospel will be physically resurrected right here, to walk in what is termed the "New Jerusalem," a physical heaven on earth. So your body is madefully alive."
re:form DVD

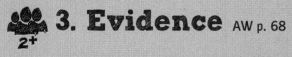

3. Evidence AW p. 68

Hold up the mirror and greet your reflection, but give him or her a different name from you. Tell your group about all of the things that are the same between you and your reflection, like your hair color, smile, ears, nose, and teeth. Then start comparing your reflection to the kids in the group. Find people with similar hair color, eye color, ear shape, and smile. After you find each similarity, also point out something unique about each of those kids. Then pair the kids up and let them get to work collecting evidence.

Questions for conversation while you work:

- What are some similarities between you and other kids in the group?
- What are some things about yourself that make you absolutely different from other people?
- Why do you suppose God makes us so unique?
- If God has paid this much attention in creating you, how much attention to detail do you think God will give to your resurrection?

Get this stuff . . .

Mirror. Digital cameras. Photo printer. Staplers. In pads. Hand wipes. Scisso Tape.

Where's this going?

Kids find evidence of the details of their uniquenes and ponder how God mig approach our resurrection

Back It Up

"We are always a part of creation and creation is p of us through God for all eternity. And yes all creat would include puppies an rainbows. But no zombies

re:form DVD

4. Design Your Own Gravestone! AW p. 69

What kinds of gravestones do you know about? Are there any creative gravestone stories you know? What will you put on your own gravestone? What do you want to be remembered for? When have you felt particularly mortal?

Use your reflections to guide your discussion about this activity with your kids.

Questions for conversation while you work:

- How does it feel to be designing your own gravestone?
- Why does thinking about death sometimes really bother people?
- What do you want to be remembered for in life?
- According to the Bible and the Creed, who gets the last word with you—death or Jesus?
- What will you want to do first at the resurrection?

Where's this going?

Kids design their own gravestones and plan thei own resurrection parties a a way to think about deat as a beginning of somethi new.

respond

15-20 minutes

ather to share the different points of view kids have discovered and eveloped during the session.

Regroup

ave kids write down or draw on three different note cards the first three ings they will do or say at the resurrection.

Share

nvite kids to share their work and describe how and why they did it. Affirm ose things you appreciate or find interesting and ask others to offer helpful bservations.

uestions for conversation:

How is resurrection different from reincarnation?
What effect do the things you do on earth have on your resurrection?
How is the resurrection similar to or different from your ideas of heaven?
How do you feel about God being in charge of your resurrection?

Send

ave everyone lie down on the floor with eyes closed and recite together the ird part of the Apostles' Creed. When you get to the word "resurrection," veryone jump up while finishing the Creed.

Get this stuff . . .
Note cards.

Capture it . . .
Use a digital camera, camcorder, scanner, web cam, or audio recorder to capture group conversations and individual pieces of work. Upload them to your online galleries, or ask kids to do so.

UNIT
No. 3
DISCIPLESHIP

Discipleship Unit
Why should I follow Jesus; can't I just say I believe in him?

Prepare

What's behind all this?

When Jesus approached his first disciples—fishermen on the beach—he did not ask them to believe in him. He asked them to follow him, and they did. In fact, they didn't really believe in him until much later. Instead, they spent three years of their lives following Jesus from town to town, listening to him and watching him work miracles. They had momentary expressions of belief, but just as many moments of doubt. But they followed.

Sometimes religion in general—and Christianity in particular—is criticized for just being lists of rights and wrongs, things you can do and things you can't do. Indeed, there is a Christian way to live. It's centered on following Jesus—loving God and loving others. That, to Jesus, was essential.

Where are kids at?

- Kids love competition. Allowing them to compare and compete helps them remain engaged. Keep the competitions fair and the environment safe by emphasizing the competition itself over the winners or losers.
- Kids this age are identifying role models in their lives. But their ability to make fully reasoned choices of whom to follow is not yet fully formed.

Matthew 4:18-20

Where's this going?
Kids distinguish believing from doing when it comes to following Jesus.

Consider this . . .

"We come to know by doing."
Unknown

"In golf as in life it is the follow-through that makes the difference."
Unknown

"I will act as if what I do makes a difference."
William James

encounter

15 minutes

Video

1. Set up

Okay, leader! What do you follow? The news? Your favorite sports team? Directions? *Follow* has many meanings. The Greek word *akoloutheo* used in the Bible translates literally as "taking the same road." Your role is to think with kids about *following* Jesus. Pick one kid to lead a game of follow-the-leader. Play for 2-3 minutes so kids experience following's plusses and minuses. Ask: What does it mean to follow Jesus?

2. Watch

"Why should I follow Jesus; can't I just say I believe in him?" DVD 1, Chapter 15

3. Unpack

- What surprised you in this video?
- What is still confusing?
- Share a time when it felt like the right thing to follow someone. Was there ever a time you felt regret for following?

What about the Bible?

Have one kid read Matthew 4:18-20 out loud. Ask if kids have questions about the text. Have kids pair up or work in groups to create a set of interview questions Jesus could have asked people before picking them to be disciples.

Questions for conversation while you work:

- What do you want to know about someone you follow?
- What might that person want to know about you?
- The video's narrator said that in order to follow Jesus we have to "get over ourselves." What does that mean?
- What would come first for you—following and then believing, or believing and then following?

Make sure you've got the obvic stuff for this session—re:form video (DVD or download), Anti-Workbooks, Bibles, pens c pencils, paper, tape, etc.

doc·trine
[dok-trin]
a belief or set of beliefs the churc teaches

quo·ta
[kwoh-tuh]
a fixed or required number

Back it up . . .

"And the moment things start bei all about God, then following and believing just come naturally because God is working in you."
re:form DVD

engage

25-30 minutes

Choose 1+ Anti-Workbook (AW) activities to explore the session question. The first 2 are for individual use, while the last 2 involve the whole group.

1. Imitate AW p. 74

Before asking kids to think about improving by doing, think of something you've become better at—but not perfect—through practice. What changed in you as you practiced? Talk about your experience and invite kids to think about the progress they've made in writing or drawing since they were 5 years old. Help them recognize that it's not about how well they write or draw, but about the practice itself and how it shapes us: we are writers because we write.

Questions for conversation while you work:

- What makes you a writer? What makes you an artist? Do you have to be good at something to be that thing? Or does it just matter that you do it?
- How did you express your faith as a 3-year-old Christian? How about when you were 8 years old? 10?
- If we make the things we practice in life—like writing or drawing or tuba playing or praying—about God, what changes? Anything?

Where's this going?

Kids consider how practice leads to improvement and how doing something makes you that thing (artist, musician, etc.).

Back it up . . .

"Being a faithful Christian is not about what *you* think of do. It's about what *God* has done for you and does through you."
re:form DVD

2. Paper Airplanes AW p. 75

Before having kids make paper airplanes, try to remember who taught you how to make a paper airplane. What else did this person teach you? Talk about your experiences learning how to do things from someone else. As you make paper airplanes together, consider both the distinctions and the connections between believing and doing.

Questions for conversation while you work:

- How did you learn how to make a paper airplane?
- Do you have to believe everything about someone to follow his or her advice?
- Does it matter what we believe? Or only what we do?
- If you didn't believe making paper airplanes was fun, would you still make them? How else do our beliefs influence our actions?
- Do you have to believe everything about Jesus before following him?

Where's this going?

Kids differentiate between thinking/believing something and doing/experiencing something.

3. Community Needs AW p. 76

What are the images you, as a leader, associate with following Jesus? How has this understanding changed over the years? Can you just make a list of Jesus' actions to check off when completed? How does following Jesus today look different than it did when Jesus was alive?

Invite kids to read Matthew 25:34-40. Ask kids what images came into their mind as Jesus spoke of hunger, thirst, the concern for the stranger, and sickness. Use the Bible story, Anti-Workbook, and newspapers to imagine together what following Jesus looks like in your community today.

Questions for conversation while you work:

- What needs do you see in your school?
- Do you know—or know of—people who are working to meet the needs of others (e.g., people in the church, historical figures, people we've learned about in school, friends)?
- Whom haven't we thought of who might require God's help through us?
- What keeps us from doing things to help more often?
- Does what you believe about following Jesus influence what you do?

Get this stuff . . .
Newspapers. Scissors. Glu
or tape.

Where's this going?
Kids create images of wha
following Jesus looks like
today's world.

Back it up . . .
"Christians that say they *follow* Jesus are saying th they try to adhere to Jesus teachings and example fro the Bible, to actually beha as he did."
re:form DVD

4. Sandwich AW p. 77

Be sure to ask kids about food allergies. As a leader, consider how challenging it is to try to teach someone something using words only, especially if it is something physical in nature. Kids may be frustrated as they try to work together to build a sandwich. Encourage them to have fun with it. Discover how our beliefs (brains) and our actions (hands) work together, both to make a sandwich and to follow Jesus.

Questions for conversation while you work:

- For the sandwich makers: what's it like not to be able to use your hands/eyes?
- For the watchers: what's it like to watch others try to make a sandwich and not be able to help?
- What would happen if one of the sandwich makers just quit?
- What does this have to do with following Jesus?
- What experience have you had of your brain believing something that consequently led you to do something?

Get this stuff . . .
Bread. Plastic knife. Peanu
butter. Marshmallow fluff.
Bandana.

Where's this going?
Kids discover the importan
of both brains (beliefs)
and actions as they work
together.

respond

15-20 minutes

Gather to share the different points of view kids have discovered and developed during the session.

Regroup

Place a large piece of newsprint on a wall with the question "What could God accomplish through you?" on the top. Invite kids to use markers or crayons to draw or write ideas for how they could follow Jesus in their daily lives.

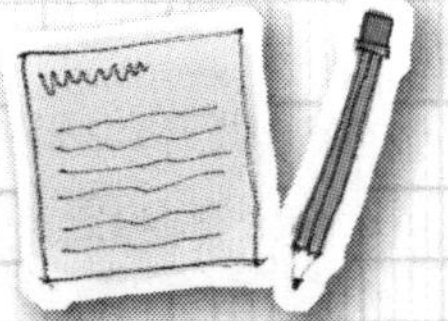

Get this stuff . . .
Large piece of newsprint. Tape. Markers or crayons.

Share

Invite kids to share their work and describe how and why they did it. Affirm those things you appreciate or find interesting and ask others to offer helpful observations.

Capture it . . .
Use a digital camera, camcorder, scanner, web cam, or audio recorder to capture group conversations and individual pieces of work. Upload them to your online galleries, or ask kids to do so.

Questions for conversation:

- What was new for you today?
- What might you want to think more about?
- How do beliefs impact or influence actions?
- How might your actions influence your beliefs?
- Who do you know who follows Jesus? What evidence can you name?

Send

Gather in a circle to reflect on your time together and bless kids on their way. Offer a prayer of thanksgiving for people who show us how to follow Jesus. Invite each kid to name someone they know who shows them how to follow Jesus. Close with a blessing that sends your group out to notice people following Jesus in their daily lives.

Discipleship Unit
Why should I pray when God doesn't answer all my prayers?

'repare

What's behind all this?

ccording to the Bible, prayer changes God. Abraham negotiated with God on ehalf of people. Moses did the same. We are to pray without timidity or fear. 'he Psalms are excellent examples for us, showing us ways to reveal our full motions. Jesus taught us that when we pray with persistence, God—like a nan holding tightly to his loaf of bread—will eventually relent.

nd Jesus himself prayed in the Garden of Gethsemane, asking that God vould let him avoid suffering. But God didn't respond to that prayer the way hat Jesus wanted, nor does God always respond to our prayers the way that ve would like.

o the other thing to keep in mind is that prayer changes *us*. By being in egular contact with God, we are constantly made aware of how God sees the vorld.

n the end, with Jesus as our example, prayer should be our way of life—less ıbout making requests of God, and more about engaging God with the stuff of ɔur lives.

Where are kids at?

- Kids this age are beginning to explore their sense of identity and how they present themselves to the world. The concept of masks and true selves presented in the video will be something many of them can relate to.
- Adolescents are becoming more and more aware of their bodies and how their bodies are changing. Considering a variety of physical prayer postures helps them stay active and engages all their senses through prayer.

1 Thessalonians 5:17

Where's this going?
Kids define prayer in their own terms and explore its possibilities for their lives.

Consider this . . .
"To be a Christian without prayer is no more possible than to be alive without breathing."
Martin Luther

encounter

15 minutes

Video

1. Set up

What prayer postures are you most comfortable with? Do you always pray in the same position? What does praying feel like in a different position (head up, eyes open, on the ground, arms spread, etc.)? Invite kids to find an open space and show a posture that symbolizes prayer for them, then one showing how they feel when God doesn't answer their prayers, and one representing when prayers are answered.

2. Watch

"Why should I pray when God doesn't answer all my prayers?" DVD 1, Chapter 16

3. Unpack

- What surprised you in this video?
- What do you agree with? What do you disagree with? Why?
- How have you responded when it feels like God hasn't heard you? When God answered the way you hoped?

What about the Bible?

How or from whom did you learn to pray? Many of us learned by watching others, but the Bible also tells us about prayer. Have kids read 1 Thessalonians 5:17 and then work in groups looking through the Bible for references to different kinds of prayer (corporate, solo, lament, praise, bodily, etc.). For various prayers and prayer postures check out: Exodus 12:27; Exodus 15:20-21; Deuteronomy 9:18; Job 1:20; Psalm 47:1; Psalm 95:6; Psalm 123:1; Daniel 6:10; Luke 22:40-41; 1 Timothy 2:8. Create a group statue or posture showing what they find.

Questions for conversation while you work:

- What does prayer look like?
- What does it feel like if God is with you all the time?
- Is praying easy? Hard? Comforting? Awkward?
- Does God hear hypocrites when they pray?

Make sure you've got the obvi stuff for this session—re:form video (DVD or download), Anti-Workbooks, Bibles, pens pencils, paper, tape, etc.

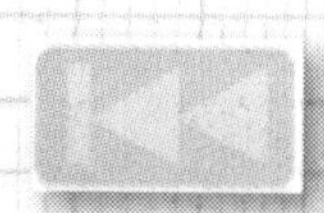

Back it up . . .

"Talk to God, as though God is w you all the time."
re:form DVD

"Prayer puts us in the right postu see God working in our lives."
re:form DVD

Get this stuff . . .

Bible concordances.

hyp·o·crite
[hip-uh-krit]

1. someone who pretends to be moral or holy than they actually (modern)
2. someone who wore a dramati mask, hiding their true self behin false identity (Greek)

25-30 minutes

Choose 1+ Anti-Workbook (AW) activities to explore the session question. The first 2 are for individual use, while the last 2 involve the whole group.

1. Don't Speak AW p. 78

How did you react the last time a problem was created when someone misunderstood something you were saying or doing? How did this affect your relationship? Ask kids to join you in a communication experiment. Tell them to follow the directions at the top of page 78 on the count of 3. Then try the experiment at the bottom of the page.

Questions for conversation while you work:

- Is it hard to be silent? Why? How was this silence a form of prayer?
- How do you react when someone misunderstands something you say or do?
- How do you communicate to people feelings of being lonely, upset, happy, or surprised?
- How do you communicate those feelings with God?
- How do your friends or family or God communicate in return?
- Is it easier or harder to talk about your feelings with your friends, family, or God? Why?

Where's this going?
Kids experience the importance of communication as they practice silence.

Back it up . . .
"So, when you pray from the inside, when your prayer is not a show, when your prayer reflects how you genuinely feel, would the results be different?"
re:form DVD

2. Wordless Prayer AW p. 79

Make a prayer collage using drawings, magazine cutouts, or other items representing prayer, to show as an example of wordless prayer. Invite kids to be creative as they think of prayer requests (joys and concerns). Tell them you'll talk about their wordless prayer experiences the next time you meet. Work on today's prayer using the stuff you assembled.

Questions for conversation while you work:

- What might praying without words look like?
- What might church be like if everyone prayed with their bodies instead of using words?
- How is the ability to communicate a gift?
- What's the value of communicating with God? Is prayer just about getting God to give us what we want?
- Have you experienced an unexpected answer to prayer like the girl in the video whose grandma got potassium from the banana?

Get this stuff . . .
Crayons. Markers. Scissors. Magazines. Tape. Glue. Other artistic stuff.

Where's this going?
Kids illustrate creative and expressive ways to pray and practice them for a week.

3. Prayer Launcher AW p. 80

As a leader, which of the five kinds of prayer on page 80 do you gravitate toward? Which do you rarely engage in? Share your experiences and encourage kids to consider their own. Some prayers follow a specific formula. Others pray in their own unique way. We all are more comfortable with some kinds of prayer than we are with others. Use this activity to encourage your group (and yourself) to branch out and incorporate other types of prayers into daily life.

Questions for conversation while you work:

- Can you think of prayer that doesn't fit confess, tell, praise, thanks, or ask?
- Which kind is usually easiest? Hardest? Does the Prayer Launcher change your answer?
- What does it feel like when you pray? Awkward? Easy? Is it harder sometimes than it is at other times? How come?
- Sometimes sports teams pray before a game. Does God choose sides based on the best prayer? What are some things we pray for that might be silly? Is it still okay to pray for them? Why or why not?

Get this stuff . . .
Scissors. Markers. Colore
pencils.

Where's this going?
Kids practice common kin
of prayer in not-so-typical
ways.

4. Stick-People Prayer AW p. 81

Before meeting with kids, think of a time when a sign or sound or image invoked a particular prayer. Perhaps it was a hospital sign, or the siren of an emergency vehicle passing. What if we thought of life as a scavenger hunt for symbols reminding us to pray for different things? Share an experience of this and invite kids to think and pray "inside the sign."

Questions for conversation while you work:

- Does God have a sense of humor? What's the funniest thing we could pray about or for? The most serious?
- What "normal" stuff calls us to prayer each day? Sights? Sounds? Actions? People?
- Do you think there's anything we shouldn't pray for? Why?
- What prayer sign would you pick to hang on your bedroom wall or door? Why?

Get this stuff . . .
Markers. Colored pencils.

Where's this going?
Kids consider nontradition
ways to pray.

in·voke
[in-vohk]
to call upon a greater pow
such as God, for help

Back it up . . .
"God is in a relationship wi
us. There is communicatio
Back and forth."
re:form DVD

15-20 minutes

ather to share the different points of view kids have discovered and eveloped during the session.

Regroup

ive each kid a sheet of construction paper. Spread the scrap paper shapes in common area. Ask kids to make visual images of prayer as they experienced in your time together. Invite them to talk while working.

Get this stuff . . .
Construction paper. Scrap paper (various shapes, colors, and sizes). Glue sticks.

Share

nvite kids to share their work and describe how and why they did it. Affirm hose things you appreciate or find interesting and ask others to offer helpful bservations.

uestions for conversation:

What was new for you today?
What might you want to think more about?
Where might you look for signs of God's communication this week?
Is there a new way of prayer you might try?
In what way has your response to today's session question changed?

Capture it . . .
Use a digital camera, camcorder, scanner, web cam, or audio recorder to capture group conversations and individual pieces of work. Upload them to your online galleries, or ask kids to do so.

Send

ather kids in a circle to reflect on your time together and bless kids on their vay. Invite each person to think of a movement, word, sound, or symbol hat expresses his or her prayer to God for this moment. When everyone as an opportunity to communicate their chosen action or word, end with benediction charging the group to go into the week looking for new pportunities and ways to carry on their conversation with God.

ben·e·dic·tion
[ben-ih-**dik**-shuhn]
bestowing of a blessing and charge

charge
[charj]
to entrust someone with the responsibility for a particular action or actions

Discipleship Unit
Why should I pray the Lord's Prayer when it feels like I'm just going through the motions?

repare

What's behind all this?

ne Bible is full of prayers—both in the Hebrew Scriptures (Old Testament) nd the Christian Scriptures (New Testament). But the Gospels record only ne prayer of Jesus. Known as the "Lord's Prayer," it was delivered by Jesus the Sermon on the Mount (Matthew) and the Sermon on the Plain (Luke). sus introduced the prayer with these words, "Pray then in this way: . . ."

), when we pray the Lord's Prayer, we are actually following Jesus' advice. sus calls upon his followers to pray boldly, without timidity. The Lord's rayer does ask for specific things —that God's kingdom will come soon, that od's will might prevail, for daily bread and forgiveness, avoidance of trial, nd rescue from evil. We also need to be careful to follow another bit of Jesus' dvice: "When you are praying, do not heap up empty phrases as the Gentiles); for they think that they will be heard because of their many words." In ther words, think about what you're saying when you pray.

Where are kids at?

While some kids know the Lord's Prayer by heart, others may be less familiar. Approach your time together as an opportunity for deeper engagement for all kids.

Repeating something at regular intervals places it in our long-term memory. Once we know something by heart, it can shape us from the inside out.

Matthew 6:9-13
Matthew 6:7

Where's this going?
Kids explore the value of the Lord's Prayer, both in itself and as a model for all prayer.

Consider this . . .

"Repetition of the same thought or physical action develops into a habit which, repeated frequently enough, becomes an automatic reflex."
Norman Vincent Peale

"The capacity of memory is initially less than 30 seconds. If we don't repeat the information, it disappears."
Brain Rules, John Medina

encounter

15 minutes

Make sure you've got the obvi stuff for this session—re:form video (DVD or download), Anti-Workbooks, Bibles, pens pencils, paper, tape, etc.

Video

1. Set up

Okay, leader, what's your first memory of the Lord's Prayer? Where were you? Your strongest memory? Most meaningful? Most difficult to pray? Find out if anyone knows the Lord's Prayer by heart and is willing stand up and recite it. How about the Pledge of Allegiance? What does the Pledge mean? Ask kids what other things they know by heart (Christmas carols, nursery rhymes, etc.). Pose the question: Do you ever feel like you're just going through the motions when you pray the Lord's Prayer?

2. Watch

"Why should I pray the Lord's prayer when it feels like I'm just going through the motions?" DVD 1, Chapter 17

3. Unpack

- Which ideas from the video hadn't you thought of before?
- Can you remember a time when the words to something you knew by heart came to you unexpectedly? What was that like?
- So, what do you think the video is saying?

hal•lowed
[hal-lohd]
holy, revered, respected

a•lign
[uh-**line**]
to put into correct or appropriat relative positions; to give suppo

What about the Bible?

What language do you find archaic or old-fashioned in the Lord's Prayer? Do you like the more formal language, or does formal language make it harder for you to connect with the prayer? Have pairs of kids read Matthew 6:9-13 and then rewrite the Lord's Prayer in their own words. Pressed for time? Assign 1-2 petitions to each pair. Share their translations.

Questions for conversation while you work:

- Is God's Kingdom in the future? Could it be here now?
- Is it important to know the Lord's Prayer by heart? Why? Why not?
- Why do people say they know something "by heart" when they're talking about memorization?

Back it up . . .
"Another reason we pray is to a our hearts with God."
re:form DVD

engage

25-30 minutes

Choose 1+ Anti-Workbook (AW) activities to explore the session question. The first 2 are for individual use, while the last 2 involve the whole group.

1. Model Behavior AW p. 82

Think of an important role model in your life—perhaps someone who influenced you to be a leader for kids. What is (or was) it about them (words, actions, presence, accomplishments, etc.) that made them important to you? How have they affected you? Share this example with kids before asking them to identify and reflect on role models in their lives.

Questions for conversation while you work:

- Who is one of your role models? Why? Share a memory of something important they have said or done.
- How are you different than your role model? How are you the same?
- Why can someone be a role model for one person but not for another?
- How was Jesus a role model for the disciples? For you?
- How does the Lord's Prayer work as a model for prayer? Is anything missing from the model?

Get this stuff . . .
Letter-quality paper. Video camera (optional).

Where's this going?
Kids identify and value the people who serve as role models in their lives.

Back it up . . .
"The Lord's Prayer works as a model for all other prayers."
re:form DVD

2. Origami AW p. 83

When you know something by heart it can have the ability to shape you from the inside out. What is one thing that you, the leader of this group, know by heart (a Psalm, a prayer, song lyrics, etc.)? How has it shaped you over the years? What value do you find in knowing something by heart? Share an experience with the kids before inviting them to begin their origami projects.

Questions for conversation while you work:

- How long does it take before you can do something by heart?
- What non-verbal things can you do "by heart"—that is, you don't have to think before you do them (ride a bicycle, text, play an instrument, etc.)?
- What disciplines do you practice every day?
- What situations can you imagine in which knowing the Lord's Prayer by heart might be helpful or beneficial?

Get this stuff . . .
Paper squares of various sizes.

Where's this going?
Kids look for value in practice and repetition.

dis•ci•pline
[dis-suh-plin]
a practice—activity, exercise, or regimen—that develops or improves a skill; training

3. Your Turn to Teach AW p. 84

What do you do to prepare to lead your group of kids? How does leading the conversation help you learn the material in a new way? What makes you feel like you have succeeded? What other experiences do you have of trying to teach people something? Share a teaching experience before inviting kids to make and execute their teaching plan on page 84.

Questions for conversation while you work:

- Can you teach a skill (playing piano, throwing a football, etc.) using words only?
- What is the role of practice and repetition in learning something new?
- What was challenging about teaching something new? What was fun? Did you learn anything by teaching?
- Can prayer be taught? Why or why not?

Where's this going?
Kids analyze the steps required to master somethi well enough to teach it.

Back it up . . .
"It's a discipline, like a pra workout. The more you pra it, and the more you think about each part of it, the better and better you you'll become at forming your ow personal prayers."
re:form DVD

4. Teach Me to Pray AW p. 85

As a leader, can you remember who taught you how to pray? What's your first memory of prayer? How has your experience of prayer changed over the years? Share one of your memories about learning to pray with the group as an example to help them start thinking about how we learn to pray. Have kids begin by talking with a partner about the steps for teaching a prayer, and then have them move into the activity itself.

Questions for conversation while you work:

- Who taught you how to pray? Did they teach you with words? With actions? What did you figure out for yourself?
- What can we pray for? Is there anything we can't pray for?
- Does prayer look the same in everyone's life? Why or why not?
- If prayer looks different for each person, how do you teach it to someone else?
- What does prayer have to include/be in order to be prayer?
- What's your first memory of prayer?
- What did you consider putting in your movie but decide to leave out? Why?

Get this stuff . . .
Markers. Crayons. Video camera (optional).

Where's this going?
Kids unpack the elements of prayer as they make a teaching plan.

15-20 minutes

ather to share the different points of view kids have discovered and eveloped during the session.

Regroup

lave kids pantomime a silent movie showing how to pray. They might adapt heir movie storyboard on page 85, or they could come up with a new plan. ive them a short timeframe and celebrate what they come up with.

Share

nvite kids to share their work and describe how and why they did it. Affirm hose things you appreciate or find interesting and ask others to offer helpful bservations.

uestions for conversation:

What was new for you today?
What might you want to think more about?
The video said the Lord's Prayer is like training wheels on a bike. Can you think of another description?
In what way has your response to today's session question changed?

Send

Gather kids in a circle to reflect on your time together and bless kids on their way. Offer a prayer of thanksgiving for people who show us how to follow esus. Invite each person to say a petition of the Lord's Prayer that best epresents his or her prayers today. When everyone has had an opportunity, close the prayer by offering a prayer for the group as a whole.

Capture it . . .
Use a digital camera, camcorder, scanner, web cam, or audio recorder to capture group conversations and individual pieces of work. Upload them to your online galleries, or ask kids to do so.

Discipleship Unit
Can someone lose their salvation?

Prepare

What's behind all this?

"Perseverance of the saints" is how theologians sometimes speak of this question of whether a person can lose their faith. There are really two schools of thought: some think that a person can, indeed, lose their faith; others think that if someone seems to lose their faith, they were never really a believer to begin with.

In the end, even Jesus makes it clear that only God knows who is saved and who isn't, and it's not really worth our time to worry about something that we can know so little about. God is the one who saves, and, like the father in the parable of the prodigal son, God's love is always pining for us, aching for us, even if we've turned away for a time.

Where are kids at?

- Kids this age love competition, even if it is competing against a clock. When you're timing them for an activity, use countdowns and warnings to spark their interest and keep them focused on their timing.
- Kids' association with salvation may center on heaven and hell. Considering salvation as an ongoing relationship will be new to most kids.

Romans 8:38-39

Where's this going?
Kids find the tension between God's action in our salvation and the limitations of free will.

Consider this . . .
"Let not men say, then, that perseverance is given to any one to the end, except when the end itself has come, and he to whom it has been given has been found to have persevered unto the end. . . . But since no one has perseverance to the end except he who does persevere to the end, many people may have it, but none can lose it."
Augustine, *Of the Gift of Perseverance, http://www.logoslibrary.org/augustine/perseverance/06.html*

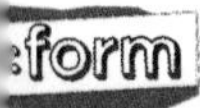

encounter

15 minutes

Make sure you've got the obv stuff for this session—re:form video (DVD or download), Anti-Workbooks, Bibles, pens pencils, paper, tape, etc.

Video

1. Set up

Hey leader, what images, feelings, or memories does the word salvation evoke for you? Give every kid paper, crayons, and 5 minutes to draw a picture of salvation. If they don't know what it means, have them guess or ask a neighbor. Ask each kid to say three words about his or her picture.

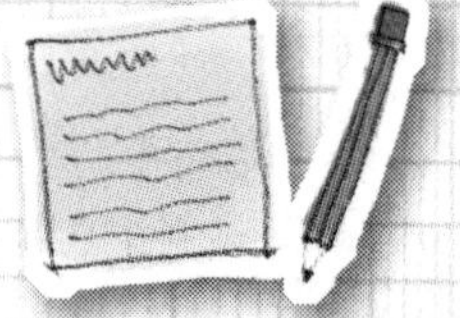

Get this stuff . . .

Paper. Crayons. Paper bags. 7–random items per bag.

2. Watch

"Can someone lose their salvation?" DVD 1, Chapter 18

3. Unpack

- What do you want to think more about?
- What is still confusing?
- Can you think of someone in your life who loves you the way the father in the video loved the prodigal son? What does that feel like? Or what does it feel like if you are not sure there's someone like that?
- So, what do you think the video is saying?

per·se·ver·ance
[per-suh-**vir**-en(t)s]
remaining in a state of grace; steadfastness in doing somethin despite difficulty

sin
[sin]
to offend or turn away from God

prod·i·gal
[**prahd**-ih-gull]
wastefully extravagant

What about the Bible?

Do you respond to Romans 8:38-39 with confidence? Is it comforting? Can you think of a time this passage would have been helpful? Create groups of four or five. Give each group a paper bag with 7–10 random items. Ask them to read Romans 8:38-39 and use all items in the bag (nothing else) to create a short skit about the verses' message.

Questions for conversation while you work:

- Is there anything not included in the verses that you think should be?
- What kinds of things feel like they get between you and God? Could we add them to this list?
- Can you think of anything else we can't be separated from?
- The video said that Kevin could never lose his relationship with his dad. How is that like our relationship with God?

engage

25-30 minutes

Choose 1+ Anti-Workbook (AW) activities to explore the session question. The first 2 are for individual use, while the last 2 involve the whole group.

1. Passport AW p. 86

Before asking kids to begin, think of something you've done that you wish you could take back. How does it feel to know that even this does not affect God's love for you? Share one of these moments with your group to help them feel comfortable naming their own worst moments or qualities.

Questions for conversation while you work:

- Why does this passport only ask for things we might not want to admit? How does it feel to have to write them down? Is it hard to be honest? Why or why not?
- Is it easy or hard to imagine someone loving you just for who you are, even with all of your mistakes? Why?
- If none of these things can destroy your relationship with God, can you think of anything that can? Does this mean we can do anything we want?
- If you were to imagine your relationship with God as a bridge, what would it be made out of? Or would it not even look like a bridge?

Get this stuff . . .
Camera. Glue stick.

Where's this going?
Kids consider how even their worst moments can't destroy their relationship with God.

Back it up . . .
"And he might lose his cell phone privileges. But he won't lose his relationship with his Dad . . . no matter how lost he was."
re:form DVD

2. Bumper Stickers AW p. 87

As a leader, can you remember where you first heard the term *salvation*? What was the context for learning this strange word/concept? What feelings does the idea of salvation evoke in you? Share some of this with your group as kids begin crafting their own bumper stickers.

Questions for conversation while you work:

- What are the funniest, weirdest, best, and worst bumper stickers you have seen? Can you change them to make them about salvation?
- What if you had to create a bumper sticker expressing the opposite of salvation? What would it look like?
- In the video you heard, "Salvation is a relationship." That's a good bumper-sticker slogan. What other bumper-sticker ideas did you hear?
- Do you think it matters what colors you use for your bumper sticker? Do colors signify anything? If salvation or your relationship with God were a color, what color would it be?
- How might your friends define salvation? Family? Your pastor?

Get this stuff . . .
Markers. Colored pens.

Where's this going?
Kids create bumper stickers with slogans reflecting their understanding of salvation.

Back it up . . .
"Salvation isn't something you possess. Salvation is a relationship."
re:form DVD

3. Prodigal Son Video AW p. 88

Before having kids create this video, consider your own reaction to the story of the prodigal son. Whom do you relate to the most? The least? If you had to retell the story so that you were the prodigal son, what would it look like? Has there been a low point in your life when it was hard to believe God still loved you?

Questions for conversation while you work:

- If you had a role in this story, who would you be? Why? Who is God? Are there characters that are hard to identify with? Why?
- What do you think led to the prodigal son's decision to go home? Should he have gone home sooner? Why or why not? Why didn't he?
- How do you think the father felt during this story? The older brother? The prodigal son?
- What's the worst thing the younger son could have done? Would his father accept him then?

Get this stuff . . .

Aluminum foil. Baseball c
Empty plastic water bottl
Toy pig. Video camera.

Where's this going?

Kids illustrate God's love for all as they dramatize t story of the prodigal son i the future.

Back it up . . .

"We may miss out on a lot of good things when we're not in fellowship with God . . . including time with Go But nothing in heaven or earth can separate us from the love of God."
re:form DVD

4. Project Protect AW p. 89

Before engaging kids in this activity, consider your own assumptions about salvation. When is it challenging to remember that your well-being and future are in God's hands? When is it easy to remember that? Ask kids to cut out the Doohicky (AW p. P9) when you meet and protect it for your entire time together, or ask them to take it home and report back the next time you meet. Kids may wreck their Doohickey when they cut it out. It's designed that way.

Questions for conversation while you work:

- What would it take to permanently protect your Doohickey?
- In the video, Kevin messed up. Are there times when you've messed up without meaning to? Who reacted? How? How did you feel?
- Who would you rather have in charge of your salvation: you or God? How does it feel to know God always loves you?
- If God's responsible for our salvation, do we get to do whatever we want? Why or why not? *(Check 1 Corinthians 6:12, Romans 6:1-11, and Romans 7:21-25.)*

Get this stuff . . .

Scissors. Glue sticks. Doohicky (AW p. P9).

Where's this going?

Kids compare the impossibility of human responsibility for salvation the permanent protection c fragile object.

15-20 minutes

ather to share the different points of view kids have discovered and eveloped during the session.

Regroup

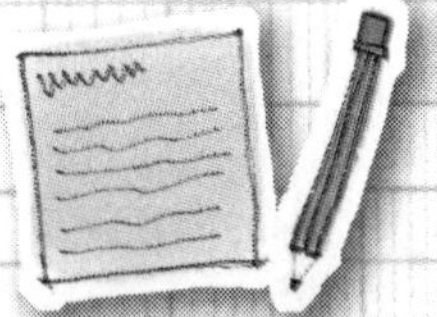

sk kids to look again at the illustrations of salvation they made earlier. What ould they change? What would they keep the same? How would they do it ifferently now? Ask them to turn their drawings over and draw new pictures represent their understanding of salvation now.

Get this stuff . . .
Drawings made in Engage. Crayons. Markers. Colored pens.

hare

nvite kids to share their work and describe how and why they did it. Affirm hose things you appreciate or find interesting and ask others to offer helpful bservations.

uestions for conversation:

- What was new for you today?
- What might you want to think more about?
- If someone asked you to talk about salvation, what would you say?

Capture it . . .
Use a digital camera, camcorder, scanner, web cam, or audio recorder to capture group conversations and individual pieces of work. Upload them to your online galleries, or ask kids to do so.

Send

ather kids in a circle to reflect on your time together and bless kids on their ay. Have kids clench their fists and hold their arms toward the center of the ircle. Thank God that we don't have to clench and cling to our salvation but ave salvation through God's love. Invite kids to open their hands. Notice how their hands can now support and care for one another. Have the group join ands as you offer a benediction, charging the group to go out into the world to love God and neighbor.

ben·e·dic·tion
[ben-ih-dik-shuhn]
bestowing of a blessing and charge

charge
[charj]
to entrust someone with the responsibility for a particular action or actions

Discipleship Unit
Can I be a Christian without going to church?

Prepare
What's behind all this?

It's interesting to note that every book of the Bible was written to communities of people. The Hebrew Scriptures (Old Testament) were written to the people of Israel, and the Christian Scriptures (New Testament) to the early church. And all of the books were meant to be read in public when these communities gathered. Thus, it is counter to the entire history of Judaism and Christianity to attempt to read and interpret these scriptures alone.

In other words, while it may be possible to have a relationship with Christ without being part of a Christian community, it's not a good idea. The Holy Spirit is active in community, and works through the church. The Holy Spirit gathers the body of Christ to pray for one another and for the world. The Holy Spirit gathers us together so that we might be given courage in faith and strengthened to go out and serve our neighbor in need. We don't come to church because we feel like it. We come to be the body of Christ to worship with our neighbor who needs us to be there. The Holy Spirit gathers us together as church because we need to be there for one another in sadness and in joy!

Where are kids at?

- Kids this age are struggling with their own senses of identity. Low self-esteem with high expectations is not uncommon. Affirm the gifts each kid brings, while highlighting the benefits of community.
- Kids today are very technologically literate. Their understanding of community is shaped not only by face-to-face groups, but also by digital and virtual communities, such as Facebook™ and MySpace™.

Acts 2:43-47

Where's this going?
Kids consider the nature of communities and what that means for Christianity.

Consider this . . .
"Living together in one place is safer than living alone. The sacred words of Jesus our God bear witness to the necessity of living together; for He says, 'Where two or three are gathered together in My name, I am in the midst of them.'" (Matthew 18:20)
Nikitas Stithatos (11th century), *Philokalia*, Vol. 4

encounter

15 minutes

Video

1. Set up

Why do you go to church? Thinking carefully about your response will help as you engage in conversation with kids about the church as community. Ask kids to get in a "team" huddle, then scatter to a space where they can't touch anyone else and play tag by themselves for a minute. Shout FREEZE and ask how it's going. Try tag as a group. FREEZE again. Talk with kids about how it's hard to play tag by yourself. Ask: Can you be a Christian by yourself?

2. Watch

"Can I be a Christian without going to church?" DVD 1, Chapter 19

3. Unpack

- What don't you believe?
- What does it mean to say the church is the body of Christ?
- So, what do you think the video is saying?

What about the Bible?

What feelings or emotions do you associate with the word *church*, the people, or the building? How is your experience different from, or similar to, the description of the church described in Acts? Read Acts 2:43-47. Have groups of three prepare dramatizations of the text—one person reads in a dramatic voice as the others act. When all are ready, groups present their interpretations individually or simultaneously.

Questions for conversation while you work:

- How was the church community in Acts similar to or different from your church community?
- What can you tell about their church attendance?
- Does it make any difference if you're in church on Sunday? Why? Why not? Does it matter to other people if you're there? Why or why not?
- What's your first memory of church?

Make sure you've got the obvi stuff for this session—re:form video (DVD or download), Anti-Workbooks, Bibles, pens pencils, paper, tape, etc.

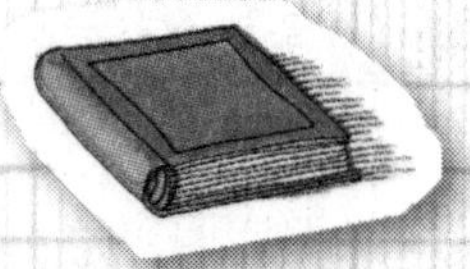

per•se•cute
[per-suh-kyoot]
subject someone to hostile treat because of his or her identity (ra religion, political beliefs, etc.)

Church
[cherch]
the people of God as a whole

church
[cherch]
individual communities that gath together; a building

25-30 minutes

Choose 1+ Anti-Workbook (AW) activities to explore the session question. The first 2 are for individual use, while the last 2 involve the whole group.

1. Deserted Island AW p. 90

Have you ever felt like you were stranded on a desert island—thinking there was no one to turn to? Take a moment to consider the people in your church community. What do they bring to the island (skills, personalities, gifts, relationships, etc.)? Who can you, and the kids in your group, turn to?

Questions for conversation while you work:

- Who is the first person you want on this island with you? Why?
- Is it different if you're stuck for a specific period of time?
- How do we benefit from community? What do we contribute to it?
- In the video, you heard that people formed communities to increase their chances of survival. Do you think the church helps you survive or live better? How? If not, why not? Do you help the church survive?
- Does participating in church or in Christian community affect or change who you are as a Christian? Why or why not?

Where's this going?
Kids consider the benefits of community and the challenges of doing some things alone.

Back it up . . .
"Now it's important to say that community doesn't mean that people all look the same or even believe the exact same things. In fact, it's vital for a community to embrace diversity and different perspectives to learn and grow together."
re:form DVD

2. On My Own AW p. 91

As a leader, what activities do you regularly engage in that require two or more people? What would it be like if you had to do these things on your own? Talk about an experience when community allowed you to do something you might not have been able to do otherwise.

Questions for conversation while you work:

- What feeling words describe trying to do community activities on your own?
- What do you do every day that would be really hard to do without other people?
- What do you help people do that they might not be able to do on their own?
- If the Church is the body of Christ, which body part do you think you are? How come? What would the church be lacking if you weren't part of it?
- What did the video mean when it stated that Christianity is all about relationships with one another and with God?

Get this stuff . . .
Camera or video camera.

Where's this going?
Kids have fun while experiencing the benefits of community.

Back it up . . .
"Christians believe that Christianity is all about relationships, with each other and with God. That God intended for us to be in community. That we can learn about God and follow Jesus far better together than by ourselves."
re:form DVD

3. Master-Pieces AW p. 92

As a leader, how have you benefited from the church community? What have you learned about God or what it means to be Christian from the people in your church? How has your understanding of what is holy grown because of the people you are in community with? Share one of these experiences with kids.

Questions for conversation while you work:

- What were the joys of working with others and with more shapes?
- What was challenging? What did you do about that?
- How did the people you worked with help you understand or see things differently?
- If we can create bigger and bigger creations by combining paper shapes, what else could we create if we worked together?
- How is the church like a bunch of people bringing together all their unique shapes?

Get this stuff . . .

Scissors. Construction pap
Camera.

Where's this going?

Kids build on the work of others to create something bigger and more diverse.

Back it up . . .

"People have always neede other people in their lives to help them understand how life works and how Gc works."
re:form DVD

4. Church Spies AW p. 93

Where do you see evidence of God at work in the church? How have you benefitted from the community? How have you contributed? What does the work of the church convey about its understanding of God? Invite kids to search for the joys and concerns of your church community.

Questions for conversation while you work:

- What do you like about your church? What do you not always like but think is a good thing? What do we think isn't so good?
- What would God like about our church? Why? What might God not like about our church? Why?
- Can we create Christian community in places other than church (friends, family)? What would it look like?
- What does it feel like when people in church don't "act like Christians"? How can we respond?

Where's this going?

Kids seek out concrete, real-world evidence of the benefits of faith communit while being honest about t Church's periodic failures.

respond

15-20 minutes

ther to share the different points of view kids have discovered and veloped during the session.

legroup

ay tag again. What benefits of community have they discovered? Sometimes s more fun doing things (like tag) together. Talk about things your group uld work on together that might benefit others (in the church, in your town, the world, etc.).

hare

vite kids to share their work and describe how and why they did it. Affirm ose things you appreciate or find interesting and ask others to offer helpful servations.

iestions for conversation:

What was new for you today?
What might you want to think more about?
How do you think beliefs impact or influence actions?
Where have you experienced God acting through our community? What did it feel like?
What consequences do you see in trying to be a Christian by yourself?

end

ather kids in a circle to reflect on your time together and bless kids on their ay. Hold on to the loose end of a ball of yarn and toss the ball to someone se in the circle as you say his or her name. The kid who catches it holds the w "end," and tosses the ball to someone else, naming that person. Continue til everyone has received the ball of yarn. Say a brief prayer thanking od for the ways in which communities connect and support us. Send kids t with a charge to be a blessing to the communities in which they find emselves.

Get this stuff . . .
Ball of yarn.

Capture it . . .
Use a digital camera, camcorder, scanner, web cam, or audio recorder to capture group conversations and individual pieces of work. Upload them to your online galleries, or ask kids to do so.

Back it up . . .
"Everyone needs love and support sometimes, even Christians."
re:form DVD

UNIT No. 4
JESUS

Jesus Unit

Was Jesus of Nazareth God?

Prepare

What's behind all this?

As young children, we're taught that Jesus of Nazareth was God. But then, at some point, we ask, "Then who was Jesus praying to? Himself?"

Let's clear up a common misconception. In Jesus' day, to call someone "Messiah" or "Son of God" or "Son of Man" did not necessarily imply divinity. In fact, theologians hotly debate whether or not Jesus really understood his own divinity.

However, after Jesus' resurrection, the disciples-turned-apostles knew Jesus was, indeed, divine. The way the church understands this is that God—being a Trinity of Father, Son, and Holy Spirit—sent the Son to Earth, and the Son was incarnated (literally, "enfleshed") in the person of Jesus of Nazareth.

This does not mean Jesus was only one-third of God. Jesus of Nazareth was and is fully God. Since his death and resurrection, we have called this Son "Jesus Christ."

Where are kids at?

- Kids at this age are encountering the reality of Jesus' work on Earth. Moving from the concrete actions of Jesus to an understanding that God, Jesus, and Holy Spirit are one will be a new and challenging concept for some kids. Start with a review of Jesus' teachings and miracles to explore if kids are seeing Jesus as human, seeing Jesus as God, or both.

John 14:7
Colossians 1:15a

Where's this going?

Kids grapple with how Jesus of Nazareth could be both God and human.

Consider this . . .

"In short, his [Jesus'] early followers experienced the risen Christ and addressed the risen Christ as the functional equivalent of God, as 'one with God.'"

Marcus J. Borg, *Meeting Jesus for the First Time: The Historical Jesus & The Heart of Contemporary Faith* (New York: Harper Collins Publishers, 1995), 16

encounter

15 minutes

Video

1. Set up

Make three columns on a piece of chart paper, labeled "Human," "Human & God," and "God." Have kids brainstorm to make three lists: things humans can do, things God can do, and things a being who was both God and human might be able to do. Record their responses on the chart paper.

2. Watch

"Was Jesus of Nazareth God?" DVD 2, Chapter 1

3. Unpack

- Do you think it was important for God to take human form? Why?
- What words would you use to describe Jesus to someone who has never heard of him before?
- Who do you look up to in your life?
- What's important to you about Jesus' humanity and divinity?

What about the Bible?

Read John 11:1-44 together. Split into teams of three or four and give 3 minutes for each team to use their Bible and write down all the things they can find that Jesus did on Earth. (Hint: Take a look at the subtitles throughout the Gospels.) Label pieces of chart paper with the categories of his actions, including the following: "Physical Healing," "Spiritual and Emotional Healing," "Teaching," "Helping Others," and "Standing Up For His Beliefs." As kids share their lists, divide their findings into these categories.

Questions for conversation while you work:

- What action of Jesus is your favorite and why?
- How do our lists compare to our lists from Set Up?
- What kinds of paradoxes did you find? Why are these important?
- What things did Jesus do on Earth that we can also do?

Make sure you've got the obvi stuff for this session—re:form video (DVD or download), Anti-Workbooks, Bibles, pens pencils, paper, tape, etc.

Get this stuff . . .

Sticky notes. Paper. Chart pape Marker.

Trin·i·ty
(trihn-uh-tee)
the three-in-one God; Father, So and Holy Spirit united

Back it up . . .

"It's important to understand that, because . . . ONE: Through Jesus' humanity, God completely understands what we're going through, no matter the situation. Jesus lived out the entire human experience. And TWO: Through Jesus' divinity, God completely redeems all our failings, sins, an even our death.
All human. Finite. Just exactly li us. And all God. Infinite."
re:form DVD

25-30 minutes

Choose 1+ Anti-Workbook (AW) activities to explore the session question. The first 2 are for individual use, while the last 2 involve the whole group.

1. HELP! AW p. 98

Use this activity to get your group up and serving in your congregation. Have a member of your grounds crew or maintenance committee come lead the group in an impromptu service project during today's meeting. There's always something to do around your church or meeting space! Kids could rake leaves, organize kitchen cupboards, sweep floors, or tidy up the Sunday school meeting spaces. Use the time together to plan a bigger service project your group can do in the near future.

Questions for conversation while you work:

- What kinds of work did Jesus do in his community?
- What kinds of service experiences have you had?
- How do your service experiences reflect the things that Jesus did? How are they different?
- How does it feel to know you're helping others out?
- What challenges did Jesus face as he tried to help others? What challenges do we face as we try to help others?
- What are some bigger service projects we could do to help our community? To help the world?

Get this stuff . . .

Video recorder. Blank paper. Drawing materials.

Where's this going?

Kids get up and serve others to connect with how Jesus served others as both human and God.

Back It Up . . .

"[Jesus] lived with, taught, ministered to, and healed society's downtrodden outcasts. Prostitutes, lepers, tax collectors, the lame, and the blind."

re:form DVD

2. Totally! Paradoxical! AW p. 99

Before this activity, think of a paradox that exists in your own life. What kind of paradox is it? How is it useful? Why do these two opposite things work together so well? Share your example with your group to get them started thinking.

Questions for conversation while you work:

- What were the benefits of Jesus being fully human and fully God?
- For Jesus, what parts of being fully human and fully God do you think may have been difficult?
- How would Jesus' work have been different if he was only human?

Get this stuff . . .

Markers. Colored pencils. Small items to create collages, such as torn paper, feathers, string, seeds, etc.

Where's this going?

Kids explore the meaning of paradox to assist them in understanding that Jesus was fully human and fully God.

Back It Up . . .

"When somebody says something seems like two opposite things . . . or two things that can't both be true . . . but somehow they're both true? That's a paradox."

re:form DVD

3. Walking in Someone Else's Shoes . . . AW p. 100

Give a chance for everyone to share his or her favorite kinds of shoes. How do those shoes change with the seasons? How do they change whether you're inside or outside? Are there any shoes that kids must wear on special occasions? Talk about why shoes are so important. What would happen if you had to wear an uncomfortable, unfamiliar pair of shoes every day? How would that feel?

Questions for conversation while you work:

- What would it feel like to walk in the shoes of someone who lives in a poor or dangerous part of the world?
- What would it have been like to walk in Jesus' shoes?
- What do you think it was like for God to walk in Jesus' shoes? What do you think God learned through Jesus about being human?

Where's this going?
Kids walk in each other's shoes and think about wh it meant for God to take human form.

4. MÖBIUS! AW p. 101

Invite a local science teacher to come in and perform a simple science experiment for your group. If a teacher is unavailable, do an Internet search for an experiment with a surprising twist, such as the egg in a bottle demonstration. Practice it a couple of times, then perform it for your group. Ask kids what was surprising about the experiment. What doesn't make sense to them? Have your guest explain how the experiment really worked. Ask kids how it feels to know that there are things going on that we can't see. Be sure to thank your guest!

Questions for conversation while you work:

- What did you think would happen when you cut the strip?
- What really does happen?
- What do you think is really happening that makes the strip do what it does?
- When you were cutting the strip and trying to understand what was happening, how did you feel?
- When you think about Jesus being fully God and fully human, how do you feel?
- Turn to your neighbor and, in your own words, explain the idea of Jesus being God and human.

Get this stuff . . .
Paper in varying lengths. Tape. Scissors.

Where's this going?
Kids experiment with the mathematical mystery of t Möbius strip and reflect or the wondrous idea of Jesu being human and God.

15-20 minutes

Gather to share the different points of view kids have discovered and developed during the session.

Regroup

On chart paper, write this sentence: "Because Jesus was human and God, he was able to ______________________________." As a group, fill in the blank as many times as you can.

Share

Invite kids to share their work and describe how and why they did it. Affirm those things you appreciate or find interesting and ask others to offer helpful observations.

Questions for conversation:

- Why would God want Jesus to be fully human and fully God?
- Using the fewest words you can, explain to your neighbor who Jesus is.
- How does Jesus bring you close to God? How does God bring you close to Jesus?
- A common saying today is "WWJD?" ("What Would Jesus Do?") How does the fact that Jesus is both God and human change how you apply this question to your life?

Send

If you haven't already, place a clear vase in the center of a table, and make sure you have enough small clear containers for each kid to have one. For each lesson in the Jesus unit, you will continue to add new sand to the vase.

Fill a third of your small containers with red sand to represent the human Jesus. Fill another third of your small containers with blue sand to represent the divine Jesus. Fill the final third of your small containers with purple sand to represent the fully human and fully divine Jesus. Go around the table and give each kid a chance to name an event in Jesus' life that represents the color of sand he or she is holding. Give thanks together for each event as each kid pours sand into the vase.

Get this stuff . . .

Chart paper. Marker. Clear vase with straight sides. Small clear containers. Red, blue, and purple sand.

Capture it . . .

Use a digital camera, camcorder, scanner, web cam, or audio recorder to capture group conversations and individual pieces of work. Upload them to your online galleries, or ask kids to do so.

Jesus Unit
Did Jesus know he was God?

Prepare

What's behind all this?

We often assume Jesus of Nazareth knew he was God, but, in fact, there is little in the Gospels to suggest he did. As an infant, angels and wise men told his parents that he was going to save Israel. As a 12-year-old, he told his parents they should have expected to find him in his Father's house.

While these were indications he was something special—maybe even the long-awaited Messiah—they alone did not imply divinity. Just before Jesus began his public ministry at age 30, the Gospels talk of his three temptations by the devil, implying that Jesus' own divinity was hidden from him, because, of course, God would not have been tempted.

As Jesus' ministry continued, he had an increasing awareness that his relationship to God was unique—unlike what anyone had experienced before. By the time he was on the cross, he knew he had the power to grant someone—the thief on the cross next to him—eternal life. But it was really the early church—especially in the writings of the Apostles as they looked back on the story, miracles, and resurrection of Jesus—that fully recognized his divinity.

Where are kids at?

- Kids this age are rapidly developing and changing in ways they don't always understand. They may feel a connection with Jesus as they study how he becomes aware of who he was and is!

Matthew 4:1
Colossians 2:9
1 Corinthians 8:6

Where's this going?
Kids play with the idea that Jesus worked at understanding his divine nature throughout his life, and consider what this means for their own self-identity.

Consider this . . .
"I mean simply that we have no way of knowing whether Jesus thought of himself as the Messiah or as the Son of God in some special sense. According to the earliest layers of the developing gospel tradition, he said nothing about having such thoughts."
Marcus J. Borg, *Meeting Jesus for the First Time: The Historical Jesus & The Heart of Contemporary Faith* (New York:Harper Collins Publishers, 1995), 29

encounter

15 minutes

Video

1. Set up

Ask kids if they have ever had their parents share a story about them that they themselves did not remember or know about. Give each kid a chance to share their story. Ask kids: How does it feel to know that there are lots of things you don't remember or don't yet realize about yourselves? Then pose today's question: Did Jesus know he was God?

2. Watch

"Did Jesus know he was God?" DVD 2, Chapter 2

3. Unpack

- What ideas from the video are new to you?
- If you were Jesus, would you have wanted to know right away that you were God? Why or why not?
- What's something new that you are learning about yourself? What has the process of discovery felt like?

What about the Bible?

Think of a time when someone asked you to do something but you weren't sure that you could. Did you say yes anyway? How did it feel as you started doing it? How did you eventually figure out that you could do it? How did that feel? Share your experience with the group. Read Mark 1:40-45 together.

Questions for conversation while you work:

- According to the passage, what motivated Jesus to heal the leper?
- What would you be thinking if you touched someone and they were healed?
- When have you been able to do something you originally thought you couldn't do? How did it feel?
- Do you see any evidence in this story that Jesus knew he was God?

Make sure you've got the obvi stuff for this session—re:form video (DVD or download), Anti-Workbooks, Bibles, pens pencils, paper, tape, etc.

mes•si•ah
[muhs-**sigh**-uh]
someone who will save or free a country or people

lep•er
[lehp-ur]
A person with the skin-and-nerv disease of leprosy. Leprosy can be cured with medicine.

Back it up . . .
"Christians often assume that Jes knew that he was God. But, in t the Bible isn't really clear on tha point."
re:form DVD

engage

25-30 minutes

Choose 1+ Anti-Workbook (AW) activities to explore the session question. The first 2 are for individual use, while the last 2 involve the whole group.

1. Anti-Glasses AW p. 102

Think of a time when you were unsure or unsettled about what was coming next in your life. Were you nervous, or even frightened? How did you cope with how you were feeling? What eventually happened? How did God's presence in your life support you through this time? Share your experience with being limited in what we can see of our lives.

Questions for conversation while you work:

- How do your Anti-Glasses change how you see the world?
- For those who wear regular glasses, what did it feel like when you first got glasses?
- What is it like to have limited vision as you try to do normal activities?
- How well do you feel like you know who you are?
- What do you think Jesus thought about the unusual events that were occurring in his life?

Get this stuff . . .

Collage-making materials such as torn paper, feathers, torn tissue paper, seeds, beads, etc. Glue sticks. Simple jigsaw puzzle.

Where's this going?

Kids create crazy glasses to experience limited vision and consider what it would be like to have limited knowledge of self.

2. Be Somebody! AW p. 103

Pick a famous person or character to be as you introduce this activity. Be sure to dress the part! Explain the activity to your group while maintaining your character. Allow kids to ask you a few questions. Gauge kids' reactions as you keep on with the charade. Use your own experience with pretending to be famous to guide your discussion with kids throughout the activity.

Questions for conversation while you work:

- What famous person did you choose to be and why?
- How did people react to you when you tried to convince them that you were a famous person?
- Were you able to keep a straight face? Why or why not?
- Why is it hard to convince others that you're famous?
- Why would it have been hard for Jesus to convince people he was God?
- Which do you think would have been harder—convincing someone you're famous or convincing someone you're divine? Why?
- If Jesus had been given a choice, do you think he would have chosen to be one with God? Why or why not?

Get this stuff . . .

Note cards.

Where's this going?

Kids pretend to be famous people and experience what it might have been like if Jesus had made any claim about being God.

Back It Up . . .

"Some would argue that Jesus never openly claimed to be God because in the Jewish faith—and Jesus was Jewish—it was unthinkable for a Jewish man or woman to think, let alone say, that they and God were one and the same. It was considered blasphemy."

re:form DVD

3. Imagine a Future! AW p. 104

Set up three baskets labeled "20 Years Ago," "Today," and "20 Years From Now." Get kids started thinking by having them write down things they know about what the world was like 20 years ago, what it's like today, and what they think it might be like 20 years from now. Get them thinking about fashion, transportation, buildings, homes, technology, and more! Have them put their scraps of paper in the respective baskets. If they need inspiration during the activity, encourage them to tap into the brainstorm baskets!

Questions for conversation while you work:

- What is your wildest prediction?
- What is your greatest hope for your life 20 years from now?
- Why can't we know what our future will bring?
- How do you feel when you think about your future? Why?
- Consider kids who live in poor countries. What do you think their futures hold?
- What do you think Jesus would have thought about his future?

Get this stuff . . .
Assorted pieces of scrap paper. Three baskets.

Where's this going?
By making predictions ab[out] their futures, kids will thi[nk] about what their futures [may] hold and about what Jesu[s] knew or didn't know abou[t] his future.

4. Who Am I? AW p. 105

Pull a card from the deck of cards you brought and, without looking at it, place it against your forehead for kids to see. Ask "yes or no" questions to figure out what card you're holding up. Once you figure it out, create an explanation of how the identity of that card is really important to you, how it fits your personality, and how it really represents who you are.

Questions for conversation while you work:

- What types of questions best helped you guess who you were?
- What questions would you ask other people to figure out who YOU really are?
- Why is it sometimes hard to know who we really are and who we are supposed to be?
- What questions might Jesus have asked God as he was learning who he really was?
- When you are confused about your life, whom do you talk to?

Get this stuff . . .
Deck of playing cards.

Where's this going?
Kids play a 20-questions-type game to discover wh[o] they are, leading to insigh[t] about what makes us who we are and what made Je[sus] who he was.

Back it up . . .
"So even if Jesus did know [he] was God, he'd probably w[ant] to keep that to himself."
re:form DVD

15-20 minutes

ather to share the different points of view kids have discovered and eveloped during the session.

Regroup

ass a note card to each kid. On the front side, ask kids to write one thing ney know about themselves. On the back side, have them write something ney want to know about themselves. Have kids share both sides of their cards vith the group. Then ask them how their cards might change in 20 years.

Get this stuff . . .

Note cards. Clear vase with straight sides. Small clear containers. Green and orange sand.

Share

nvite kids to share their work and describe how and why they did it. Affirm nose things you appreciate or find interesting and ask others to offer helpful bservations.

Capture it . . .

Use a digital camera, camcorder, scanner, web cam, or audio recorder to capture group conversations and individual pieces of work. Upload them to your online galleries, or ask kids to do so.

uestions for conversation:

- What are some new things you've learned about yourself recently?
- How does it feel when someone tells you something about yourself that you didn't realize before?
- What kinds of things do you think Jesus learned about himself as he grew up?
- Do you think Jesus knew he was God right away? Why or why not?

Send

you haven't already, place a clear vase in the center of a table, and make ure you have enough small clear containers for each kid to have one. For ach lesson in the Jesus unit, you will continue to add new sand to the vase.

ill half of your small containers with green sand to represent what we know bout ourselves. Fill the other half of your small containers with orange sand o represent what we don't yet know about ourselves. Go around the table and ive each kid a chance to name something that corresponds with the color of and he or she is holding. As kids pour their sand into the vase together, say prayer for a peaceful, healthy, and happy future for friends, family, and the hurch.

Jesus Unit

If Jesus was God, why did he have to die?

Prepare

What's behind all this?

t is clear at the beginning of the Bible, in the very first chapters of Genesis, hat the primary curse upon the human race for turning away from God is hat we will not be immortal. Only God is immortal. So the main thing that ifferentiates humans from God is the fact that we die. God does not.

But it's also clear from the beginning of the Bible that, despite our human ailings, God desires to have an intimate relationship with us. In fact, God esires that so much that the Second Person of the Trinity (the Son, or *ogos*) became incarnate in Jesus of Nazareth. God embraced the full human xperience.

he full human experience includes death. God experienced death when Jesus vas crucified. While God surely could have forgiven human sin in many ways, God chose to enter into the deepest and most tragic aspect of human life, thus euniting us to God in a way we had not been since the Garden of Eden.

Where are kids at?

Be alert to any kids who may have recently experienced the death of a family member, friend, or member of their faith or school communities. A lesson that deals with death and resurrection may trigger feelings that need reassurance and a listening ear.

Philippians 2:5-11
Romans 8:10-11

Where's this going?

Kids explore why God chose to experience human life and death and consider the purpose of the resurrection.

Consider this . . .

"In the passion of the Son, the Father himself suffers the pains of abandonment. In the death of the Son, death comes upon God himself, and the Father suffers the death of his Son in his love for forsaken man."

Jürgen Moltmann, *The Crucified God*, 192

encounter

15 minutes

Video

1. Set up

Provide each student with a piece of smooth beach glass, bark, driftwood, a smooth stone, or a shell collected from your local area. Have each kid write an initial answer to the question, "If Jesus was God, why did he have to die?" on his or her item using a fine-tipped permanent marker. Place the items pieces on the center of a table.

2. Watch

"If Jesus was God, why did he have to die?" DVD 2, Chapter 3

3. Unpack

- What ideas from the video are missing from our pile of ideas?
- If you were going to give a friend a mini movie review about the video, what would you tell him or her?
- What are some human characteristics that Jesus had to have in order to face the life events he had to experience?

What about the Bible?

Divide your group into two teams. Give one group the passage Philippians 2:5-11. Give the other group Romans 8:10-11. Give the groups 3 minutes to read their passage and write down the evidence their passage gives to answer the question, If Jesus was God, why did he have to die? After the 3 minutes, re-read the passages together and have groups share what they found.

Questions for conversation while you work:

- What evidence did you find?
- Why are these messages important for Christians?
- How does it feel to have Paul say in Philippians 2:5, "Let the same mind be in you that was in Christ Jesus"? Why is this so challenging?
- Read Philippians 2:9-11 again together. What is this passage saying about Jesus' experience?
- What questions do you still have about why Jesus had to die?

Make sure you've got the obvi stuff for this session—re:form video (DVD or download), Anti-Workbooks, Bibles, pens pencils, paper, tape, etc.

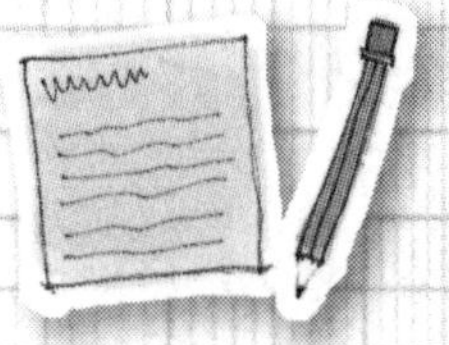

Get this stuff . . .

Beach glass, bark, driftwood, smooth stones, or shells. Fine-ti permanent markers. Paper.

sac·ri·fice
[sak-ruh-fice]
giving up one thing for another thing

Mes·si·ah
[muhs-sigh-uh]
For Jewish people, the one who come to save the people of Israe For Christians, Jesus is the Messiah.

Back it up . . .

"Death is a problem. We can't escape it. Nobody can. Not phy death. Not spiritual death. God knew something had to change here. So God sent Jesus to Ear somehow being both all God an all man . . . and died for our sin
re:form DVD

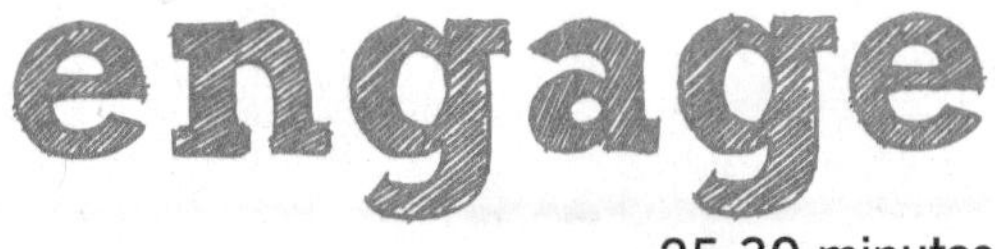

engage

25-30 minutes

Choose 1+ Anti-Workbook (AW) activities to explore the session question. The first 2 are for individual use, while the last 2 involve the whole group.

1. Human vs. God AW p. 106

Take a look through Hebrews 2 together. What particularly Godly characteristics of Jesus are highlighted here? What truly human characteristics does this letter focus on? Then take a moment to reread Hebrews 2:14-18. After kids have completed this Anti-Workbook activity, pass out blank business cards. With Hebrews 2:14-18 in mind, have kids create a business card for Jesus. Ask kids: What special things does Jesus do for you? How does this help you understand why Jesus had to die? (Hint: It's all about the resurrection.)

Questions for conversation while you work:

- What are your favorite human characteristics?
- If God can do all of these things, why do you think God chose to experience death?
- If Jesus died so he could be resurrected, what do you think that means for you after death?

Get this stuff . . .

Punch-out cards from page P11 of the Anti-Workbook. Blank business cards. Markers.

Where's this going?

Kids compare human and divine powers and explore the importance of Jesus living a fully human life.

2. What If? AW p. 107

Have kids think of a person living today whom they would consider a hero. They should limit their choice to a person from the following categories: politics, religion, the arts, humanitarians, and everyday people. Describe why that person is a hero and what they are doing for the world. What gift have they brought to the world that is unique?

Questions for conversation while you work:

- Jesus was a world changer. What was the most important part of his message to us?
- What if Jesus had lived longer? What would he have done next?
- Physical death is one of the hardest things we face as humans. Why didn't God just skip that part of being human?
- Read 1 Corinthians 15:12-19 together. What's Paul's perspective on the question, "What if God figured out some other way to change the world?"?
- If there had been no Jesus, what other way could God have sent his message of love to us?

Where's this going?

Kids imagine a world without Jesus as a way of exploring what Jesus' presence in our world has done for us.

Back It Up . . .

"God could have forgiven human sin in many ways, but God chose to experience death. And through the cross Jesus defeated death and brought us back into life, reuniting us with God."
re:form DVD

3. Anti-Workbook of the Divine Power of Second Guessing AW p. 108

Role play an argument with God for kids. Pull out your cell phone and pretend you're arguing with God about something you think God should do differently. Pick something goofy like making mud less sticky or giving us our own personal control over the weather on important days. Make it clear that you're losing the argument, and then hang up in a huff. Then let kids get started on their activity.

Questions for conversation while you work:

- Why do you think God doesn't just choose the best and easiest outcome for everything?
- What if you had control in this situation? Would you send your child to earth? Would you insist that he suffer and die? Would you raise him again from the dead? Why?
- How does God help us make decisions and survive tough things in our lives?

Get this stuff . . .
Cell phone. Tape.

Where's this going?
Kids apply the divine pow of their Anti-Workbooks to re-do some situation, whether it's Biblical or in their lives, and consider w God made things the way they are.

4. Station ANTI-TV AW p. 109

Give kids 15 seconds to name as many TV shows as they can. Discuss the shows kids brought up. Talk about the characters in each show. What do they do? Why do they do it? What can we learn about real life from TV? What isn't so helpful about TV when it comes to real life?

Questions for conversation while you work:

- How does your TV show showcase what Jesus' life might have been like today?
- How is your show useful to viewers? What can they learn about Jesus from it?
- How is the way you are telling Jesus' story today different from how Jesus' story was told 1,000 years ago?
- What would happen in your TV show when Jesus died?
- How would Jesus' resurrection be portrayed in your show? Cliff hanger? Happy ending? Why?

Get this stuff . . .
Cameras that will film vide

Where's this going?
Kids create a TV show that showcases Jesus as fully human and fully God durin any part of his life.

15-20 minutes

Gather to share the different points of view kids have discovered and developed during the session.

Regroup

Draw a large, rough jigsaw puzzle on a piece of paper. Ask each kid to write on the puzzle one thing Jesus did that showcased who he was, and whether that thing showed Jesus as God, human, or both. Cut the puzzle apart and have kids put it back together while everyone shares what they wrote down.

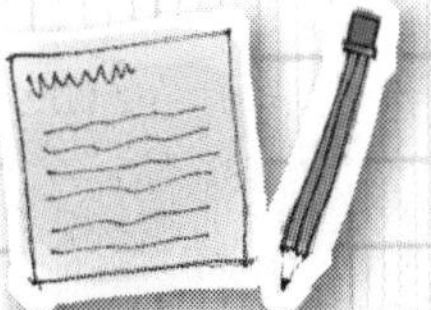

Get this stuff . . .
Mural paper. Markers. Clear vase with straight sides. Small clear containers. White sand.

Share

Invite kids to share their work and describe how and why they did it. Affirm those things you appreciate or find interesting and ask others to offer helpful observations.

Capture it . . .
Use a digital camera, camcorder, scanner, web cam, or audio recorder to capture group conversations and individual pieces of work. Upload them to your online galleries, or ask kids to do so.

Questions for conversation:

- How was Jesus' life like a puzzle? What do we know about the "final" assembly of the puzzle of his life?
- What parts of the "puzzle" of Jesus' life are most attractive to you?
- What parts are confusing?
- Why do you think it was important for Jesus to experience the most human part of being human—death?

Send

If you haven't already, place a clear vase in the center of a table, and make sure you have enough small clear containers for each kid to have one. For each lesson in the Jesus unit, you will continue to add new sand to the vase.

Fill all of your containers with white sand to represent Jesus' death. Go around the table and give each kid a chance to name a reason he or she feels it was important for Jesus to have experienced death. Give thanks to Jesus for his sacrifice as kids pour their white sand into the large vase.

Jesus Unit

Do I have to believe Jesus performed miracles in order to be a Christian?

'repare

What's behind all this?

he miracles are a big part of the Jesus story in the Gospels—although it's otable that Paul doesn't mention them much in his letters. Starting with his hanging of water into wine at a wedding, Jesus performs miracles showing is power over nature (like calming a storm) and over human ailments (like prosy and paralysis).

esus also makes it clear, when he heals a man who was paralyzed and vhose friends had lowered him through the roof of the home where Jesus vas teaching, that his ability to forgive sins and his ability to heal are both onnected. And they are both a work of the Holy Spirit, which descended on esus at his baptism.

lesus' miracles inspired awe in those who observed them. Even more mportant, they were signposts pointing to what the kingdom of God is ike—where there is no more leprosy, paralysis, or demon possession. In his niracles, Jesus was giving people a vision of the world the way that God ntends it to be.

Where are kids at?

- Kids this age are beginning to question things that might not be true in today's "real world." Miracles definitely fall into this category. Focus on how miracles make us feel. Encourage discussion about the excitement, wonder, and amazement we feel when hear stories of Jesus performing miracles. Use those emotions to help kids break into thinking of miracles as something that can strengthen our faith whether we truly believe they happened or not.

John 14:11
Revelation 21:3-4

Where's this going?

Kids plumb the meanings of miracle stories in the Bible and what they ultimately say about God.

Consider this . . .

"The truth is, nothing about the early ministry of Jesus is plainer than that it was chiefly as a wonder-worker, a benefactor and doer of good to people in physical or mental distress that he was first known."

Edgar J. Goodspeed, *A Life of Jesus*, (New York: Harper and Brothers, publishers), 1950, 53

encounter

15 minutes

Video

1. Set up

Using a long strip of mural paper, give kids 2 minutes to work together to make the longest list they can of current events that they would consider modern-day miracles. On the back of the same paper roll, give kids 2 minutes to work together to make the longest list they can of miracles that they remember happening in the Bible.

2. Watch

"Do I have to believe Jesus performed miracles in order to be a Christian?" DVD 2, Chapter 4

3. Unpack

- How do you feel about the video we just watched?
- What words can you think of that describe the word *miracle*?
- What events in the video remind you of something that has happened in your life?
- According to the video, what were some reasons Jesus performed miracles?

What about the Bible?

Split kids into two teams. Give teams 10 minutes to do a Gospel scavenger hunt for stories about miracles. Which team can create a longer list?

Questions for conversation while you work:

- To you, what is a miracle? How does this compare to what miracles were like in the Bible?
- When was a time you experienced a miracle, or what is a miracle you have heard about?
- Why do you think some people have their prayers answered by miracles?
- Why do you think some people don't have their prayers answered by miracles?

Make sure you've got the obvi stuff for this session—re:form video (DVD or download), Anti-Workbooks, Bibles, pens pencils, paper, tape, etc.

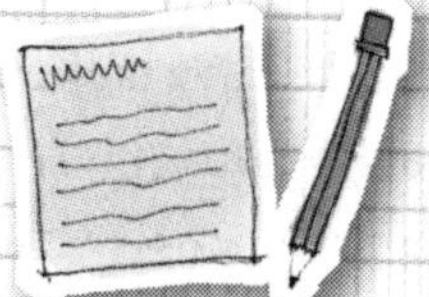

Get this stuff . . .

Long strip of mural paper. Mark

Back it up . . .

"If we look at the story about a paralyzed man who was lowered through the roof of a home Jesus was teaching in, it says that Jes then told the man that his sins were forgiven. Which some peop thought was very un-cool. But Je knowing their hearts, then prove to them that he had the authorit forgive sins by healing the man a well."

re:form DVD

engage

25-30 minutes

Choose 1+ Anti-Workbook (AW) activities to explore the session question. The first 2 are for individual use, while the last 2 involve the whole group.

1. Miracle, Any Miracle! AW p. 110

Before this activity, consider some of your favorite miracle stories from the Bible and how you have seen them come into play in your life. Tell kids about your favorite miracle story. Why is it your favorite? What does it tell you about God? How have you seen these kinds of miracles, in a similar or smaller way, come to life in your own experiences?

Questions for conversation while you work:

- What kinds of miracles do you see proclaimed in our sample tabloids?
- Why do you think some people believe in miracles today?
- How do you feel about miracles today?
- How are the miracles in our sample tabloids different from the Biblical miracles you're reading about? What is God telling us by creating these miracles?
- If Jesus had never performed any miracles, would you still be able to say he was God's Son? Why or why not?

Get this stuff . . .
Sample tabloids for kids to browse.

Where's this going?
Kids look at a variety of miracles in the Bible and rewrite them, tabloid-style.

Back it up . . .
"Walk? I can dance!"
re:form DVD

2. Humpty Dumpty AW p. 111

Select a few volunteers to act out the parts in the "Humpty Dumpty" nursery rhyme. Be sure to include a Humpty Dumpty, the king's horses, and the king's men. Read "Humpty Dumpty" aloud for your group once or twice while your volunteers act out the rhyme.

Questions for conversation while you work:

- What does Humpty Dumpty look like in your drawing?
- When you recall the nursery rhyme, is there any point where Humpty Dumpty is said to be an egg?
- Why do you think most people picture Humpty Dumpty as an egg even though he's never described as one?
- How could this assumption relate to our assumptions about miracles?
- When you read about miracles in the Bible, how do you feel?
- Do you think stories of miracles are important for your faith? Why?
- Do you think it's possible to believe in the power of miracles even if you don't know whether they really happened? Why or why not?

Get this stuff . . .
Wide variety of drawing materials, such as thin-line colored markers, colored pencils, and high-quality drawing pencils. Copy of the Humpty Dumpty nursery rhyme.

Where's this going?
Kids draw Humpty Dumpty based on the nursery rhyme—which never actually mentions an egg—and consider what this means for our assumptions about miracles.

3. Perform a Miracle! AW p. 112

Learn a simple card trick in advance of this activity. Perform the trick several times for your group. Then reveal how the trick works. Invite any kids in the group to share card tricks they know with the group.

Questions for conversation while you work:

- Why do people love watching magic tricks and shows? How do magic tricks make them feel?
- Why do people love the miracle stories in the Bible so much? How do those stories make them feel?
- What is the difference between a miracle and a magic trick?
- How do you think Jesus felt when he caused a miracle to happen?
- What do you think Jesus felt about the people to whom he could not bring miracles?
- Why do you think Jesus used miracles?

Get this stuff . . .

Spoons. Nickels. Deck of playing cards. Book of card tricks, or online card trick sources.

Where's this going?

Kids learn how to do a magic trick and explore how miracles were different from simple magic tricks.

4. My Medical Chart AW p. 113

Think of an experience you've had with illness or injury. It could be a personal experience or an experience of one of your friends or family members. What made you feel better during the experience? What things have you done for others to help them when they were ill? Share your experience with the group.

Questions for conversation while you work:

- Think of a time when you had a cold. What did it feel like when you finally realized you'd "beaten" the virus?
- Even though we know diseases are bad, why do you think some germs are good?
- Do you think there can be healing for all sick people, even those with lifelong diseases like diabetes or MS? What does healing look like for someone with a lifelong disease?
- Why do you think some people consider their medical illnesses to be gifts?
- What message does God send with a miracle?

Where's this going?

Kids reflect on their medical histories and the power of healing in order to see God's abundance and gifts to the world.

Back it up . . .

"Christians believe that in the Kingdom of God there is no more leprosy, paralysis, demon possession, parking tickets, algebra tests, or line dancing."
re:form DVD

respond

15-20 minutes

Gather to share the different points of view kids have discovered and developed during the session.

Regroup

Have kids get back into their teams from the beginning of the lesson. Pass their lists of miracles back to them and have them add any new Biblical miracles they learned about in the lesson, as well as any miracles on the back that they have heard about from the news or friends.

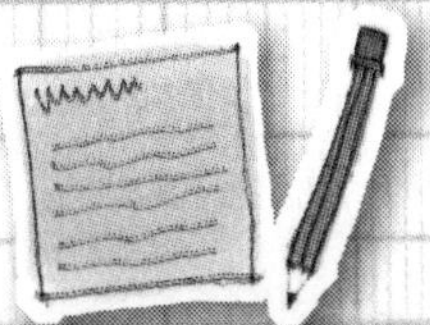

Get this stuff . . .
List of miracles from Encounter. Clear vase with straight sides. Small clear containers. Small bowls of red, blue, purple, green, and orange sand.

Share

Invite kids to share their work and describe how and why they did it. Affirm those things you appreciate or find interesting and ask others to offer helpful observations.

Questions for conversation:

- Why do you think there are so many miracles in the Bible?
- Are modern-day miracles really miracles? Why or why not?
- What's one of your favorite "everyday" miracles, like birth or sunrises?
- If Jesus had lived longer, what other miracles might he have performed?
- If Jesus were alive on Earth today, what miracles might he perform?

Capture it . . .
Use a digital camera, camcorder, scanner, web cam, or audio recorder to capture group conversations and individual pieces of work. Upload them to your online galleries, or ask kids to do so.

Send

If you haven't already, place a clear vase in the center of a table, and make sure you have enough small clear containers for each kid to have one. For each lesson in the Jesus unit, you will continue to add new sand to the vase.

Place bowls of sand out, and allow kids to fill their small clear containers with a color of sand that represents miracles to them. Go around the table and give kids a chance to name miracles they celebrate personally, either from their lives or from the Bible. As everyone pours their sand into the large vase together, pray this prayer: "Dear God, we celebrate your work in the world during Jesus' life and each and every day of our lives. Amen."

Jesus Unit
Why did Jesus get baptized?

'repare

What's behind all this?

'Baptism" literally means "washing," and it was a common ritual in Jesus' lay. In fact, some Jews would ritually wash themselves half a dozen times er day, before every meal and every prayer time, to spiritually cleanse hemselves.

Vhen Jesus' cousin John began baptizing people in the Jordan River, people vould have seen it in this context—John was baptizing people after they epented of their sins. But when Jesus showed up to be baptized, even John vas taken aback.

The dove (a symbol of God's Spirit) and the voice of God at Jesus' baptism nvoke an anointing of Jesus and inaugurate the beginning of his ministry. And Jesus' submission to baptism by John set an example that Christians have ollowed ever since.

Where are kids at?

- Kids this age will probably still think of baptism in a very concrete way. Water was poured on their heads. Words were said. Help lead them in connecting their baptism to the story of Jesus' baptism. Encourage them to think about how baptism is more than just water and words. Baptism connects us with the Holy Spirit and we are changed.

Mark 1:9-11
Acts 19:4-5
Ephesians 4:4-6

Where's this going?
Kids explore what Jesus' baptism reveals about him and how that shapes Christians' identities and lives.

Consider this . . .

"It was a sublime moment in his [Jesus'] life. For as he came up out of the water, serene in the consciousness that he was doing his utmost to carry out the will of God, a tremendous sense of vocation, selection and mission came over him. He heard a voice saying to him, 'You are my son, my beloved! You are my chosen!'"

Edgar J. Goodspeed, *A Life of Jesus*, (New York: Harper and Brothers, publishers), 1950, 42

encounter

15 minutes

Video

1. Set up

Have kids in your group share the stories of their baptism. Where were they baptized? How old were they? Who was there? What happened? Are there any special stories that make their baptism unique in their family? Allow time for kids to think about these questions and share their stories with the group. Ask if kids realized that Jesus was baptized.

2. Watch

"Why did Jesus get baptized?" DVD 2 Chapter 5

3. Unpack

- According to the video, what possible reasons was Jesus baptized?
- What about your baptism and Jesus' baptism is the same? What about them is different?
- What impact might Jesus' baptism have had on those who saw, heard, and experienced it?

What about the Bible?

Write these verses on chart paper: Matthew 3:13-17, Mark 1:9-11, Luke 3:21-22, and John 1:29-34. Have kids race to the verses listed. Whoever finds a passage first can choose another volunteer to read it. On another piece of chart paper, list similarities and differences between these four Gospel accounts of Jesus' baptism.

Questions for conversation while you work:

- What happens in each of these accounts?
- What's unique about each of these accounts?
- What does being baptized mean to you?
- What are some of your experiences with other baptisms? How do they make you feel?

Make sure you've got the obvic stuff for this session—re:form video (DVD or download), Anti-Workbooks, Bibles, pens c pencils, paper, tape, etc.

Back it up . . .

"Baptism was just what folks did the time. It helped clean them o the outside and it was symbolic getting clean on the inside."
re:form DVD

bap·tism
[bap-tizm]
a ritual that welcomes people int the Christian community and eq them to live their lives within tha community

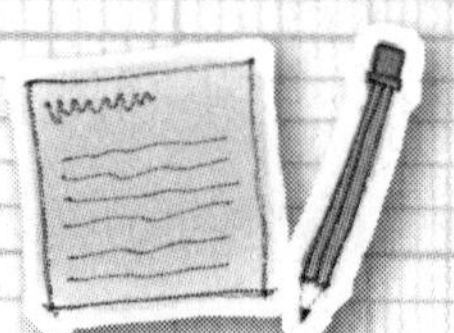

Get this stuff . . .

Chart paper. Marker.

engage

25-30 minutes

Choose 1+ Anti-Workbook (AW) activities to explore the session question. The first 2 are for individual use, while the last 2 involve the whole group.

1. Spirit Photo Shoot AW p. 114

As a group, list all the words or images for Holy Spirit and baptism that you have heard or seen. Using Legos®, create a Holy Spirit shape. What shape did you create and why? Encourage kids to use their Holy Spirit shape during their photo shoot.

Allow some time for kids to really explore your meeting space, building, and if possible, the surrounding neighborhood. Consider trekking offsite to a park, mall, or downtown city block to give kids the opportunity to stretch their imaginations in this activity. There are many things and places that can remind us of the Holy Spirit and Jesus' baptism!

Questions for conversation while you work:

- What was your first idea for a photo? Why did that come to mind first?
- Where are your photos located? In a church? Outside? In a mall?
- How do you think the people who experienced Jesus' baptism shared their story?

Get this stuff . . .

Digital cameras. Photo printer. Stapler. Legos®.

Where's this going?

Kids imagine where they might find the Spirit, and take photos of those locations in order to focus on the role of the Spirit in Jesus' baptism.

Back it up . . .

"But for Jesus, maybe it wasn't so much about the cleansing off of the old as it was the getting ready for the new. He was starting something big that would need some heavy-duty blessing."

re:form DVD

2. How Many Ways? AW p. 115

Pass out scraps of paper to kids. Have kids think of all the ways that people in Bible times used water and write one use on a piece of paper. When finished, kids should float their paper scrap in the bowl of water. Then have kids think of the modern ways of using water, write one on a piece of paper, and float those in the bowl. How has our use of water changed over the years of human life? What does this mean for our future?

Questions for conversation while you work:

- Which items did you choose and why?
- Of the alternative uses you have devised, which is your favorite? Which is most useful? Which is the wackiest?
- How might people have reacted to baptism as a brand-new, unexpected use for water?

Get this stuff . . .

Large bowl of water. Scraps of paper.

Where's this going?

Kids gather items and consider a variety of innovative ways to use each common item, and then apply this exploration to the many ways water was used in Bible times.

3. Wet Tag! AW p. 116

Have kids work together to write two sets of rules for the water tag game, making one set very strict and controlling, using the rules in the Anti-Workbook. The other set of rules should emulate the rules (or lack of rules) you might have in a neighborhood water tag game. Which game sounds more fun? As you work your way through the activity, try putting these two sets of rules to work.

Questions for conversation while you work:

- Which game was more fun—the one with lots of rules or the one with fewer rules? Why?
- What can we learn from rules? What can we learn from freestyle games? How do these ideas relate to how we look at the use of water in baptism?
- What kinds of requirements do you think come with baptism?

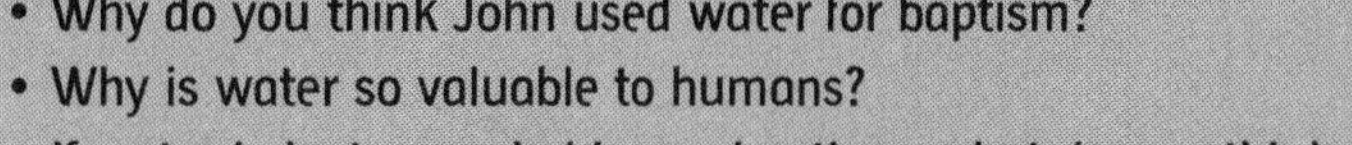

- Why do you think John used water for baptism?
- Why is water so valuable to humans?
- If water is just a symbol in our baptism, what do you think actually baptizes us?

Get this stuff . . .
Squirt bottles.

Where's this going?
By staging a game of wat
tag, kids will connect the
ancient uses of water for
purifying and cleansing
people to the new ways th
John taught in the Bible.

4. Picto-baptism-ary AW p. 117

Think about your baptism. What are the most important ways you live out your baptismal call? If you are a parent of a baptized child, what do you feel you need to do for your child now that he or she is baptized? Create a "promise note" to recite to your group, using informal jargon. For example:

"Because I was baptized, I'll always be sure to hug my children every day, help those who need it, etc."

Questions for conversation while you work:

- If you think of baptism as a command (Ready. Set. Go!), what happens after "go"? What needs to be done now that someone is baptized?
- What are a few things Jesus did after being baptized? What are some things that you have done after being baptized that are similar?
- What do you think it means that baptism is a new beginning?
- If you could choose whether to be baptized or not today, which would you choose and why?
- How is living out our baptismal call different than the checklist I recited before this activity?

Where's this going?
By playing a picture-guess
game of Jesus' work in th
world, kids explore ways t
they can emulate Jesus by
living out their baptismal c

Ho·ly Spir·it
[ho-lee speer-it]
One member of the Trinity
who works through us in
many ways, the giver of gi
and the culivator of fruits
the Spirit)

15-20 minutes

ather to share the different points of view kids have discovered and
›veloped during the session.

Regroup

ave kids think way, way, way into the future and imagine they are parents
·inging their children to be baptized. Have each kid draw a picture or write a
ory about that day. Allow time for kids to share with the group.

Get this stuff . . .
Blank paper. Clear vase with straight sides. Small clear containers. Red, orange, and blue sand.

Share

vite kids to share their work and describe how and why they did it. Affirm
ose things you appreciate or find interesting and ask others to offer helpful
oservations.

Capture it . . .
Use a digital camera, camcorder, scanner, web cam, or audio recorder to capture group conversations and individual pieces of work. Upload them to your online galleries, or ask kids to do so.

uestions for conversation:

If you think back to the video, what reasons were given by the video for baptizing someone?
What reasons would you give for baptizing your own child?
If being baptized created a physical feeling within us, what do you think it would feel like?
Why do you think Jesus chose to be baptized?
How can we live out our baptismal call in a way that emulates Jesus?

Send

you haven't already, place a clear vase in the center of a table, and make
ıre you have enough small clear containers for each kid to have one. For
ach lesson in the Jesus unit, you will continue to add new sand to the vase.

ill a third of your small containers with red sand to represent the Holy Spirit
re. Fill another third of your small containers with orange sand to represent
ıe Holy Spirit fire. Fill the final third of your containers with blue sand to
›present the water of baptism. Go around the table and give each kid a
hance to finish this prayer sentence as they pour their sand into the large
ase: "Dear God, Because I have been baptized, I . . ." Finish the prayer with
group "Amen."

Jesus Unit
Is believing in Jesus really the only way to get to heaven?

Prepare

What's behind all this?

The incarnation (God taking human form) of the Son in Jesus of Nazareth was the culmination of a long-standing, and often tortured, relationship between God and humankind. After covenants with Adam's family, Noah's family, Abraham's family, and Moses' people, Jesus Christ became the instigator of a new covenant between God and all human beings.

Jesus came to tell people about the availability of a new kind of relationship to God—a relationship filled with healing and love for the downcast and ostracized. Jesus' message was that no matter your race or tribe, God wants that covenantal relationship with you.

When Jesus was explaining this new reality to his disciples, he said he was the only way to be in relationship with God, and that statement still stands as one of the most controversial in the Bible.

Where are kids at?

- Kids this age are beginning to form their own identities and beliefs. Encountering tough faith ideas in a group setting allows them to test out their beliefs and knowledge in a safe place. Allow kids to "pass" on a question if they don't have an answer or aren't ready to answer.
- Kids of this age are also beginning to understand the importance of making and keeping their own promises. They've counted on others to keep promises, like parents and teachers, but "covenantal" relationships between peers are often being made, challenged, and even broken. It's reassuring for kids to see God as someone who keeps covenant with us.

John 3:5-6
John 14:6
Romans 10:9

Where's this going?
Kids explore the intersection between faith and salvation and construct their own response to Christianity's claims of exclusivity.

Consider this . . .
"He [Jesus] had already proved to be, in Christian experience, the way to God, and veritable truth and life, as he was to prove for subsequent centuries, and still proves to be today."
Edgar J. Goodspeed, *A Life of Jesus*, New York: Harper and Brothers, 1950, 228

encounter

15 minutes

Video

1. Set up

Have kids write an acrostic poem using the word S-A-L-V-A-T-I-O-N. Encourage them to use the words in their poems to reflect what they think salvation is, how they feel about it, how they think it happens, and what it means for us as Christians. Give everyone an opportunity to share with the group.

2. Watch

"Is believing in Jesus really the only way to get to heaven?" DVD 2 Chapter 6

3. Unpack

- Who do you know who doesn't believe in Jesus? What do they believe?
- What are some things you've heard about how to get to heaven?
- What are some kinds of covenants you encounter each day?
- According to the video, why is the covenant of salvation important?
- Why do you think there are so many beliefs in the world today?

What about the Bible?

As a group, make a list on chart paper of Jesus' actions and characteristics. Get kids thinking with some questions: Who did Jesus minister to? According to the video, what message did Jesus come to share? How did Jesus feel about kids? What kinds of miracles did Jesus do? Use your list as reference for talking about how Jesus is "the way."

Questions for conversation while you work:

- Read John 3:5-6. What might being "born of the Spirit" be like?
- Read John 14:1-6. How might our list of Jesus' actions help us understand what he meant by saying "I am the way"?
- Read John 12:44-47. What does this passage seem to say about Jesus' role in our salvation?
- What will heaven be like for you?

Make sure you've got the obvi stuff for this session—re:form video (DVD or download), Anti-Workbooks, Bibles, pens pencils, paper, tape, etc.

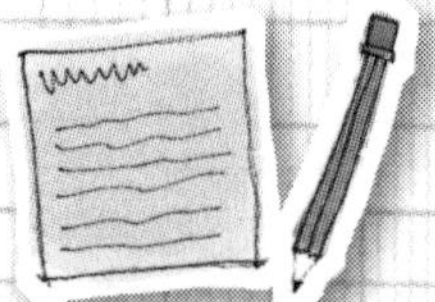

Get this stuff . . .
Blank paper. Markers. Chart pa

sal·va·tion
[sal-**vay**-shun]
deliverance from sin

Back it up . . .

"When you look at the world's m religions like Hinduism, Islam, Buddhism, Judaism, and Christi there's one thing that they pretty much agree on: humanity needs salvation."
re:form DVD

"This new Covenant is open to everyone, not just Christians. Christians aren't God's new chos people. All people are God's chos people."
re:form DVD

engage

25-30 minutes

Choose 1+ Anti-Workbook (AW) activities to explore the session question. The first 2 are for individual use, while the last 2 involve the whole group.

1. A-mazing Times AW p. 118

Think of a time when you received lots of different advice from lots of different people. What were they advising you on? What was it like to hear so many different opinions? How did you ultimately decide what to do? Was it a good decision? How did you know? Share your experience with the group.

Questions for conversation while you work:

- What are some ways you made it through the maze?
- How did it feel to try to find different paths each time you attempted the maze?
- When is a time you've had many options and had to choose one? How did it feel?
- What do you like about being a Christian? What would you like to learn about other religions?

Get this stuff . . .
Markers.

Where's this going?
Kids find lots of different ways to complete one maze and consider whether there may be many roads to heaven.

2. Digital Heaven AW p. 119

Consider the most heavenly experience you've had on Earth. What did it involve? Go through each of your senses and think about how that sense was filled with heavenly feeling. Share your experience with the group as a way for them to start thinking about their "digital heaven." Challenge kids to go beyond the sense of sight and to collect tastes, smells, sounds, and touches to attach to their pages, as well.

Questions for conversation while you work:

- What kinds of pictures are you collecting? How do those represent heaven for you?
- How does it feel to try to select one image to represent heaven? If you had no limitations, how many images would you have and what would they include?
- How do your images of heaven compare to others' images of heaven? Why is there so much variety?
- How is God's love represented in your pictures of heaven?

Get this stuff . . .
Digital cameras. Photo printer. Stapler.

Where's this going?
Kids take photos illustrating their visions of what heaven looks like and explore the mystery of eternal life.

3. GPS Not Included AW p. 120

As you begin this activity, take a roundabout route to get to your seat or position in front of the group. Weave in and out of things, crawl under something, and go in a couple of circles. When you finally arrive with your group, explain that you were taking a very personal journey to be with them. Let kids use this example as a way to get started on their activity.

Questions for conversation while you work:

- What does your map look like? Did you choose a direct route or a roundabout route?
- What happens when you draw your route on other maps? How do the routes compare?
- Is there a "best" route to get from one place to another in our church?
- Even if we doubt the promise of our own salvation, how does the idea of God's covenant in Christ help us to be confident about where we're headed?

Get this stuff . . .
Markers.

Where's this going?
Kids create various routes through the building to explore the personal natu[re] of our paths to eternal life with God.

4. Can You Tell Me How 2 Get . . . to Heaven? AW p. 121

Consider assigning this activity a week or two ahead of time to give kids enough time to complete the project before today's meeting. If you assign the video today, be sure to allow time during the next meeting to share documentaries and discuss what kids found.

Have kids practice their interview techniques with partners in preparation for the Anti-Workbook activity. Practice using easy questions and follow-up questions and listening well. Take notes on the answers and share with the group!

Questions for conversation while you work:

- What kinds of questions can you ask in addition to the first one?
- What kinds of answers did you hear? Why do you think there's so much variety?
- If you had to title your documentary, what title would you give it?
- How did hearing what everyone else has to say about this question affect how you feel about it?

Get this stuff . . .
Video recorders.

Where's this going?
Kids create an interview documentary to explore w[hat] people think about how to get to heaven.

Back it up . . .
"How God chooses to see c[...] define this quality is totall[y] up to God, whether somec[one] wears the label of Christia[n] or not. Because it isn't on[ly] about who's in or who's ou[t] or if it happens in this life or the next. It's about God['s] love for us."
re:form DVD

respond

15-20 minutes

Gather to share the different points of view kids have discovered and developed during the session.

Regroup

Pass out blank paper and have kids create an acrostic poem for the word H-E-A-V-E-N. Allow time for kids to share their poem with the group.

Share

Invite kids to share their work and describe how and why they did it. Affirm those things you appreciate or find interesting and ask others to offer helpful observations.

Questions for conversation:

- Why do you think there are so many different beliefs about how to get to heaven?
- What do you think is more important when it comes to getting to heaven—how well we believe or how well God's keeps his covenant?
- Do you think everyone gets to heaven eventually? Why or why not?
- Do you think people who never believe in Jesus will make it to heaven? Why or why not?

Send

If you haven't already, place a clear vase in the center of a table, and make sure you have enough small clear containers for each kid to have one. For each lesson in the Jesus unit, you will continue to add new sand to the vase. Fill a third of your small containers with brown sand to represent dirt. Fill another third with blue sand to represent water. Fill the final third with green sand to represent the greenness of the world. Set out the bowl of gold sand to represent heaven. As kids pour their Earth colors into the large vase, let kids name something important to them about how we live our lives on Earth. Then have each kid grab a handful of gold sand to add to the vase. As kids add their gold sand, let them whisper questions they still have about heaven. End with "Amen" together.

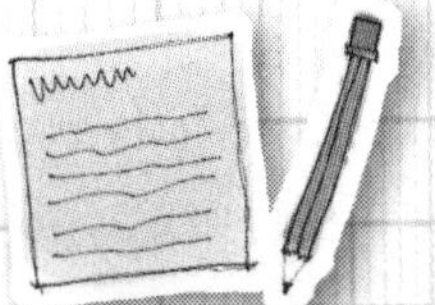

Get this stuff . . .

Blank paper. Clear vase with straight sides. Small clear containers. Brown, blue, and green sand. Small bowl of gold sand.

Capture it . . .

Use a digital camera, camcorder, scanner, web cam, or audio recorder to capture group conversations and individual pieces of work. Upload them to your online galleries, or ask kids to do so.

UNIT No. 5
OTHER BELIEFS

Other Beliefs Unit

If there is only one God, why are there so many different religions?

'repare

What's behind all this?

. "religion" is a system by which a particular group of people understands nd organizes its followers' experience of God. Because the major religions Christianity, Judaism, Islam, Hinduism, and Buddhism) have been around long time, they also come with lots of history, tradition, and ritual. And, to e honest, some of that history isn't so pretty. But that history can also be eautiful and life-giving.

'here are two common responses to the fact that there are so many religions n the world. One is to ignore the other religions and to live around other eople who share the same belief system that you do. The other is to reduce he potency of your own beliefs and claim that all religions are different and qually valid paths to the same God.

3ut the most difficult path is to maintain the distinctive beliefs, traditions, nd history of your religion, while at the same time being respectful to other eligions and open to the truth that lies in them. A primary message of God in he Hebrew Scriptures is hospitality. A primary message of Jesus was to reach ut to those who are not like you. While we believe Christianity to be true, we bserve God's hospitality when we respect the religions of all people.

Where are kids at?

- Kids today are tech-savvy. If some have access to concordances on their phones, why not encourage them to use them?
- Kids this age can be very idealistic, wanting everyone to get along together. Exploring the nature of other religious expressions may help them discover and claim that which is unique about Christianity.

Leviticus 19:9-10
Romans 12:13

Where's this going?
Kids consider Christianity in relationship to other religious traditions.

Consider this . . .

"The problem to be faced is: how to combine loyalty to one's own tradition with reverence for different traditions."
Abraham Joshua Heschel, *Moral Grandeur and Spiritual Audacity: Essays*, 242

encounter

15 minutes

Video

1. Set up

Gather in a circle. Distribute 20 to 30 blank note cards. Make a deck of cards with a different religion on each card. Talk about the difference between religions and denominations (see sidebar). Spread the cards on the floor. Challenge kids to name anything that all these religions have in common. If even one religion doesn't share something, it can't be considered a commonality. Write each commonality on another note card. Affirm commonalities and ask why are there so many religions.

2. Watch

"If there is only one God, why are there so many different religions?" DVD 2, Chapter 7

3. Unpack

- What surprised you in this video?
- What is still confusing?
- What personal experience can you describe with another religion, such as conversations or attending a different tradition's service or ritual? Did anything feel familiar? Uncomfortable? Pleasing?
- What do you wonder about other religions?

What about the Bible?

Look at Leviticus 19:9-10 and Romans 12:13. Ask one kid to read each passage. Make a list of words with similar meanings. Form pairs to find these words in concordances and to look up the verses they reference. When kids find a verse with a message connected to the Leviticus and Romans texts, they should shout, "FREEZE!" and read the verse out loud dramatically.

Questions for conversation:

- What do the Leviticus and Romans passages have in common?
- What does hospitality look like in the Bible? In our lives? In the church?
- How should we approach people who follow other religions?

Make sure you've got the obvi stuff for this session—re:form video (DVD or download), Anti-Workbooks, Bibles, pens pencils, paper, tape, etc.

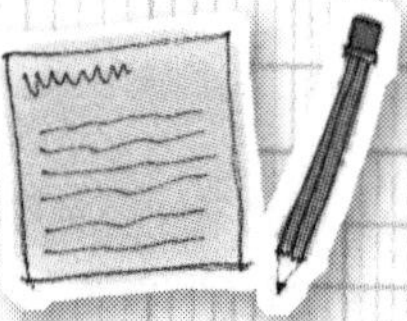

Get this stuff . . .

Note cards. Markers. Concordan Whiteboard. Dry erase markers.

re·li·gion
[rih-lih-juhn]
a way people understand and organize their experiences of what is holy

de·nom·i·na·tion
[dih-nom-ih-**nay**-shuhn]
A branch of a particular religion. example, Presbyterian or Luther to Christianity as Sunni or Shia i Islam.

hos·pi·tal·i·ty
[hahs-pih-**tal**-ih-tee]
the generous and kind reception treatment of strangers

Back it up . . .

"Bahai, Buddhism, Confucianism, Christianity, Hinduism, Islam, Jainism, Judaism, Native Americ Sikhism, Taoism, Unitarianism, Zoroastrianism all teach the golden rule in some form."
re:form DVD

engage

25-30 minutes

Choose 1+ Anti-Workbook (AW) activities to explore the session question. The first 2 are for individual use, while the last 2 involve the whole group.

1. Sand Art AW p. 126

As you invite kids to combine sand of various colors, consider your own experiences with people of different religious traditions. Do you have a positive view of other religions, or do some make you uncomfortable? Can you name why? If possible, share an experience of a personal relationship with someone from a different faith tradition. What was hard about it? Wonderful? Did you learn anything about Christianity through your experience?

Questions for conversation while you work:

- What color of sand would you pick to represent Christianity? Why?
- What happens when you combine different colors of sand? Compare your answer to what happens when people of different faiths are in the same room.
- Why do you think people of different faiths have trouble getting along?
- What could be challenging about being friends with someone who has different beliefs than you? What could be enriching?

Get this stuff . . .
Small clear jars with lids. Colored sand. Clear tape. Magnifying glasses.

Where's this going?
Kids observe the potential for retaining individual identity while mixing with others.

Back it up . . .
"Stand firm in your beliefs while respecting and staying open to understanding the beliefs of others. Because different doesn't mean bad."
re:form DVD

2. Your Drawer AW p. 127

How would you define Christianity to a friend of a different faith tradition? How would you define it to your group? What symbols signify Christianity to you? What stories do you associate with Christianity? What is central to Christianity? Is this unique to Christianity? Or could it be found in other religions as well? Do you feel uneasy about any of your responses?

Questions for conversation while you work:

- How are you deciding which images or words you include in or leave out of your Christianity folder? Has anyone or anything in your past influenced your decisions?
- Are your words and images unique to Christianity, or do they have something in common with other religions?
- Does everyone's Christianity folder look the same? Why or why not?

Get this stuff . . .
File folders. Markers. Paper. Tape. Magazines or newspapers. Scissors.

Where's this going?
Kids consider the uniqueness of Christianity as well as its commonalities with other religions.

Back it up . . .
"There are a lot of similarities among many of the major religions. Almost all major religions believe in a singular higher power and call on people to live morally."
re:form DVD

3. Build-A-Religion AW p. 128

As a leader, does it make you nervous to think about combining positive elements of multiple religions into one "super religion"? Excited? Indifferent? Trying to make sense of religion is a lifelong struggle—for teens and adults. When you are honest about the fears or concerns you bring to this activity, you are giving kids permission to be thoughtful and honest about their own questions now and in the future.

Questions for conversation while you work:

- What symbol did you choose for Christianity? Why? What other symbols could you have chosen? What about for the other religions?
- What happens when you combine them? What do you gain? What do you lose?
- What do you think would happen if you did this in real life? How might people respond? Why?

Get this stuff . . .
Clay or play dough.

Where's this going?
Kids create harmony amo
many religions by sculptin
positive attributes of each

Back it up . . .
"One [Christian response] is to ignore other religions . . . Another is to water down your own beliefs an basically claim that all religions are different but equally valid paths to the same God."
re:form DVD

4. Sugar Stack AW p. 129

Ask kids about food allergies. As a leader, where have you seen God's presence revealed through diversity? Have you ever found yourself in a situation in which diversity (of religions, races, genders, nationalities, etc.) added something unique to the group, or might have if it had been present? Have you ever seen glimpses of God in people who were strikingly different from you? What did you see? Talk with kids about these ideas as they build their sugar-cube towers, and then read Genesis 11:1-9.

Questions for conversation while you work:

- Look around as you build. What do you see that is similar? Different?
- If each cube represents one religion, what might you call your structure?
- What connections do you find among the Tower of Babel story, the existence of multiple religions, and your sugar-cube tower?
- What did people in the Tower of Babel story see when God spread them across the earth that they might have missed if the tower had actually reached heaven? Why might God have wanted this?

Get this stuff . . .
Sugar cubes (lots of them) Frosting. Food coloring. Plastic knives.

Where's this going?
Kids reflect on the Tower c
Babel and God's desire for diversity.

Back it up . . .
"There are so many differer
religions in the world no or
is completely sure how mc
there are. Experts' best gu
is several thousand."
re:form DVD

respond

15-20 minutes

Gather to share the different points of view kids have discovered and developed during the session.

Regroup

Spread out the cards with names of religions and commonalities on the floor where all can see them. Give each kid a blank note card. Ask kids to write one more thing they would like to know about another religion. Then invite them to flip their cards over and write one way they personally could show hospitality to people of different religions.

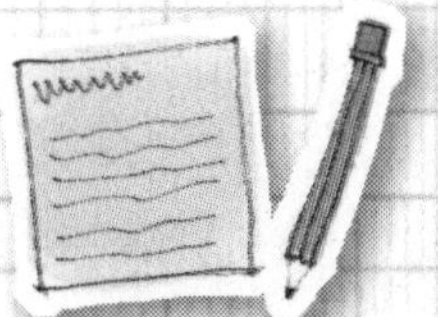

Get this stuff . . .

Note cards from Encounter. Blank note cards.

Share

Invite kids to share their work and describe how and why they did it. Affirm those things you appreciate or find interesting and ask others to offer helpful observations.

Capture it . . .

Use a digital camera, camcorder, scanner, web cam, or audio recorder to capture group conversations and individual pieces of work. Upload them to your online galleries, or ask kids to do so.

Questions for conversation:

- What was new for you today?
- What might you want to think more about?
- How do you think beliefs impact or influence actions?
- How might you respond if someone asked you why there are so many different religions?

Send

Ask kids to hold on to the cards with their continuing questions and ideas for hospitality. Gather in a circle around the cards identifying many religions and their commonalities. Offer a prayer of thanksgiving for the diversity in God's earth by inviting kids to place their cards on top of the others. Close with a blessing for the group that they might be ambassadors of God's love throughout the world.

Other Beliefs Unit

Why do Christians believe Christianity is the best religion?

repare

What's behind all this?

ther religions have many beliefs about God. They have their own practices of rayer and worship. They have their own sacred texts.

ut no other major religion claims that God came to Earth, became human, xperienced the joys and trials of human life, and ultimately entered into the reatest suffering of humanity: death. Christianity's claim to uniqueness is esus Christ: his life, his death, and his resurrection.

Where are kids at?

- Kids this age are working hard to define themselves, over and against their parents, in relationship to their peers, and in their own eyes. Allowing them to express what makes them unique helps them in this process.
- Kids this age may be getting to the point where they are embarrassed about what they don't know or reluctant to ask what feel like silly questions. Today's activities may offer an opportunity to ask those questions.

1 Corinthians 15:13-14
Philippians 2:5-11

Where's this going?

Kids dig for what makes Christianity unique among the world's religions.

encounter

15 minutes

Video

1. Set up

Christianity is the majority religion in our society, so many of us are not accustomed to naming its uniqueness. What, at its core, is Christianity? Are we aware of and do we practice Christianity daily? Ask kids to draw the first thing they think of when they hear "Christianity" on one note card. Write an adjective describing Jesus on the other card. Share responses. Save the cards to use later.

2. Watch

"Why do Christians believe Christianity is the best religion?" DVD 2, Chapter 8

3. Unpack

- What surprised you in this video?
- What don't you believe?
- How does it feel when someone doesn't believe you?
- Do you think Jesus intended to start a religion?
- Christianity proclaims that God, as Jesus, died. Is that scary? Comforting? Confusing?

What about the Bible?

Read 1 Corinthians 15:13-14. Have kids write things Christians wouldn't have if Jesus were not risen (hope, forgiveness, etc.) on paper. Have one kid stand inside the bag. Kids wad their papers and throw them in the bag. Did these things die with Jesus? (Kid in the bag plays dead.) Or did the reality come alive with Jesus? (Kid rips out and throws back wads of promises.)

Questions for conversation:

- Does Christianity exist if there is no resurrection? Why or why not?
- Is it the end of the story when you get a fresh start? How do you feel?
- How is the empty tomb the beginning—not the end—of the story?

Make sure you've got the obv stuff for this session—re:form video (DVD or download), Anti-Workbooks, Bibles, pens pencils, paper, tape, etc.

Get this stuff . . .

Blank note cards. Markers. Slip paper. Big leaf bag.

re•volt
[ri-volt]

a movement or expression of strong dissent

Back it up . . .

"But at the end of the day, the t that distinguishes Jesus' follow that they pin all their hopes to uniquely far-fetched idea that t God died...in order to conquer c and by rising again, took away death's power once and for all."

re:form DVD

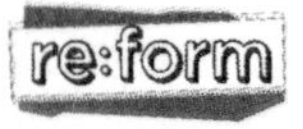

engage

25-30 minutes

Choose 1+ Anti-Workbook (AW) activities to explore the session question. The first 2 are for individual use, while the last 2 involve the whole group.

1. You-nique AW p. 130

Before asking kids to do this activity, try it for yourself. What makes you unique? Think beyond your physical traits. What gifts, skills, or personality traits have you been given by God? Perhaps it is a combination of elements that makes you unique. Is it challenging or easy to think of yourself as a child of God, created to be unique, and for a unique purpose? Why is it easy or hard?

Questions for conversation while you work:

- Is it easy or hard to name your own traits?
- Do you wish you were more like or more different than others? Why?
- What do you really like about yourself? What do you wish you could change? Why?
- Are some traits more "Christian" than others? Why?

Get this stuff . . .
Markers.

Where's this going?
Kids explore what makes them unique as they consider the unique nature of Christianity.

u•nique
[yoo-neek]
one of a kind, different, individual, singular, uncommon, novel, rare, particular

2. We Are . . . AW p. 131

If you had just five written words to let someone know what you—as a person—are all about, what would you say? Think about marquees outside a theater, billboards, political signs, or print or digital ads. What about Christianity? What could you put on a marquee outside your church to tell people what Christianity is all about? Would you highlight what you believe? What you do? What else would you highlight? Get started on page 131.

Questions for conversation while you work:

- Can you tell if someone is Christian just by what you see? By talking with them?
- What do Christians do that is uniquely Christian?
- If someone from another planet (who happened to speak your language) approached you, what is the one thing you would want them to know about Christianity?
- Is there anything you wouldn't want someone to know about Christianity? Why?
- What do you think is the best thing about Christianity? Why?

Where's this going?
Kids articulate the core foundations of Christianity.

Back it up . . .
"The third day after he died he, well, he stopped being dead. He rose. He was resurrected from death to life. And *that's* the thing that makes the Jesus-based movement known as Christianity different, unique."
re:form DVD

3. Quite a Show AW p. 132

Jesus did some bizarre things that would have been quite shocking in his time and would still be today. We may be so familiar with some stories that they lose their shock value (healing sick people, bring dead people to life, appearing out of nowhere after death, food miracles, etc.). Invite each kid to find a partner, choose a story requiring the suspension of reality, and write a short script for two hand puppets recreating an improbable Jesus story.

Questions for conversation while you work:

- How do you respond when someone says something that couldn't happen? Embarrassed? Annoyed? Curious? Hopeful? Do you think Jesus' friends felt that way?
- What message was Jesus trying to give in the story you recreated?
- Jesus talked about eating his body and drinking his blood. How might you explain that to someone who is not a Christian?
- Which story is the hardest to believe really happened?
- Do these strange stories make it easier to believe that Jesus is God in human flesh? Why? Why not?

Get this stuff . . .
Bibles with pictures. Mitte or gloves.

Where's this going?
Kids create scenes highlighting some of the unexpected things Jesus s and did.

Back it up . . .
"Jesus didn't just say crazy things. He did crazy things . . . wild things. Impossibl things . . ."
re:form DVD

4. Chalk It Up AW p. 133

Okay, leader—it's time for honesty. Do you worry that kids will ask questions about Christianity and you won't know what to say? Many adult Christians worry that there are things they *should* know but don't, so they're embarrassed to talk about these things. If you could ask your pastor or your fellow church members any anonymous question, what would you want to know? What question do you really want your kids to ask and have answered? Why that question? Work together with kids to ask some of the big questions as they determine survey questions.

Questions for conversation while you work:

- Why might some people be afraid or embarrassed to ask some questions about Christianity?
- Are you willing to take a risk and ask one of those questions right now?
- What's one question you wish people would ask you about your faith?
- Are there right or wrong answers to all questions? Who decides?
- What's the one question or issue that makes you a little unsure about joining the church?

Get this stuff . . .
Chalkboard or bulletin boa Chalk.

Where's this going?
Kids create a survey where people can anonymously enter their responses abou Christianity.

Back it up . . .
"It may be fairly said that many people who call themselves 'Christian' aren familiar enough with the tenets of other faiths to kn what makes Christianity different from them."
re:form DVD

15-20 minutes

Gather to share the different points of view kids have discovered and developed during the session.

Regroup

Invite kids to look at the cards they completed earlier. On the back of the card with the picture, have them write one adjective describing Christianity. On the back of the other card, ask kids to write something they think Jesus might say if he were living on Earth today.

Share

Invite kids to share their work and describe how and why they did it. Affirm those things you appreciate or find interesting and ask others to offer helpful observations.

Questions for conversation:

- What was new for you today?
- What might you want to think more about?
- How do you think beliefs impact or influence actions?
- What does it mean when someone says their religion is the best?

Send

Ask kids to gather in a circle holding their cards describing Jesus and Christianity. Offer a prayer of thanksgiving by asking each kid to name something on his or her card after you say, "God, we thank you for ..." Finish the prayer by thanking God for the uniqueness given to you and all people. Charge kids to live out that blessing as beloved children of God.

Get this stuff . . .
Note cards from Encounter. Markers.

Capture it . . .
Use a digital camera, camcorder, scanner, web cam, or audio recorder to capture group conversations and individual pieces of work. Upload them to your online galleries, or ask kids to do so.

Other Beliefs Unit
Why are there so many different Christian churches?

Prepare

What's behind all this?

In the book of Acts, Luke writes that everyone got along great right after the Pentecost. The church lived in harmony and peace. But that didn't last very long. Pretty soon Ananias and Sapphira were caught lying to their fellow Christians, and they were struck dead. Then Paul and Peter started to quarrel about the nature of the new faith. So, almost from the very beginning, there were challenges to church unity.

But the church held together pretty well for the first 1,000 years. Then, based on increasing theological and cultural differences, the first major split happened in 1054. Five centuries after that, the fractures multiplied exponentially, leading us to the tens of thousands of Christian denominations that we have today. And most of those splits can be blamed on the human sin of wanting to be more right than the next guy (and yes, it was almost always guys).

Jesus prayed for the unity of the church. We should pray for unity too. Maybe our generation will be the one that reverses the trend of fracture and starts bringing all Christians together. . .

Acts 2:43-47
John 17:20-23

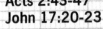

Where's this going?
Kids construct views on unity and diversity within Christian communities.

Where are kids at?

- Kids this age are struggling with their own identities, which means that activities that ask them to decide or to form opinions are particularly meaningful—and at times difficult.
- Kids this age are more likely to express their feelings through actions than through words, so encourage kids to think about what they can do to make people of other traditions feel welcomed and loved.

encounter

15 minutes

Video

1. Set up

Some differences are worth serious disagreement. Others are just preferences. Lead a forced-choice activity. Read pairs of items, asking which they prefer, and point to the spot where they should stand to indicate their preference. (Peanut butter or jelly, summer or winter, hiking or swimming, day or night, pairs of your choosing.) Were any kids always in the same spot or with the same people?

2. Watch

"Why are there so many different Christian churches?" DVD 2, Chapter 9

3. Unpack

- What surprised you in this video?
- What is still confusing?
- What do you know about other Christian denominations?

What about the Bible?

How did the Christian church become so many different groups? What was expected of people who were a part of the group of Christians in Acts 2:43-47? Talk about Jesus' vision of unity in God's love in John 17:20-23. Assign kids the first two verses of: Corinthians, Galatians, Ephesians, Philippians, and Colossians. Find the cities on a map in the Bible.

Questions for conversation while you work:

- How did 1st century communication and transportation move people toward or away from the unity Jesus described? How about today?
- Does everyone in your congregation believe the exact same things? If not, how does your congregation work toward unity in Christ?
- Look again at Acts 2:44. What do the people who gather in your church have in common?

Make sure you've got the obvi stuff for this session—re:form video (DVD or download), Anti-Workbooks, Bibles, pens pencils, paper, tape, etc.

cath·o·lic
[kath-uh-lik]
concerning the church universal; whole

Cath·o·lic
[kath-uh-lik]
referencing the Roman Catholic Church

de·nom·i·na·tion
[dih-nom-uh-nay-shuhn]
a branch of a particular religion. For example, Presbyterian or Lutheran is to Christianity as Sunni or Shia is to Islam.

non·de·nom·i·na·tion·al ch
[nahn-dih-nom-uh-nay-shuhn-uhl church]
A Christian church that isn't an official part of a larger body of churches

doc·trine
[dok-trin]
something that is taught

Back it up . . .

"Some would say that the Church can never be totally unified becau churches are made up of people c people have a tendency to disagr
re:form DVD

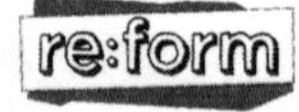

25-30 minutes

Choose 1+ Anti-Workbook (AW) activities to explore the session question. The first 2 are for individual use, while the last 2 involve the whole group.

1. Our Town AW p. 134

As a leader, what's your experience with this church or others? If you've switched from one church to another, what was your experience like? As kids note the religious or denominational options available in your community, talk about experiences you or they have with the churches on their list.

Questions for conversation while you work:

- What churches on your list have kids attended? What were they like? What was the same as your church? What was different?
- If a friend who goes to another church asked why you are a part of your church and not theirs, what would you say? Do you think your friend might have a similar answer? What does that mean? Is one of you right and the other one wrong?
- How could you learn more about other churches in your community?
- Are there people in your family who are part of another Christian group?

Get this stuff . . .
Phone books.

Where's this going?
Kids research the Christian denominations that are a part of their community.

2. The Interview AW p. 135

What emotions kick into gear when you approach someone holding different views than yours? Are you nervous? Challenged? Energized? What if you think you might have a strong disagreement with that person? People's comfort level with people they don't know well depends on their personality, the subject of the conversation, and past experiences. Working in pairs may lower kids' anxiety levels. Use your time together to write interview questions. Tell kids that you'll talk about their experiences the next time you meet.

Questions for conversation while you work:

- What's exciting about discovering other people's beliefs? What's scary?
- How can knowing someone else's beliefs help you know your beliefs?
- Before you ask someone else the questions you write, think about the answers you would give.
- Be sure everyone doesn't call the same church! How will the responses differ if you interview someone who works at the church or someone (an adult or a kid) who goes to the church? Why?

Where's this going?
Kids write questions to discover the similarities and differences among Christian churches.

Back it up . . .
"So really, when it comes down to it, all these churches may not agree on everything. But they are unified on the most important thing—the reason the Christian church was started in the first place: Jesus."
re:form DVD

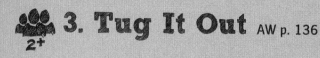

3. Tug It Out AW p. 136

When we err on the side of minimizing our differences to avoid conflict or just to get along, we can be in danger of minimizing something that is very important for us or for others. It is more honest to admit our differences and work together to see how we can still cooperate. As a leader, what do you think would be worth fighting for? Worth splitting apart for? Churches within one denomination may have differences, and can sometimes get into a verbal tug of war rather than finding a way to settle their differences. As kids determine an unimportant difference via a tug of war, talk about options for standing up for their personal beliefs.

Questions for conversation while you work:

- Is fighting always bad or always good? Why? Is it important? Is it inevitable?
- Can you remember a time when you disagreed with a really good friend about something? What was that like? How important does that seem now? Are you still friends?
- What Christian beliefs or practices are the most important for you?

Get this stuff . . .
Rope.

Where's this going?
Kids consider which differences are worth standing up for and explore options for settling disagreements.

Back it up . . .
"During the reformation mc groups started analyzing and challenging the way t church did things. This led to all kinds of schisms tha happened over all kinds of disagreements in the chur
re:form DVD

4. You're Invited AW p. 137

As a leader, can you remember a time when being together helped resolve an argument or differences between yourself and a friend or among a group? Sometimes just being together can help us focus on the things we agree upon rather than on our disagreements. Help kids consider all the things they have in common with people from other Christian churches, both as people of faith and as human beings.

Questions for conversation while you work:

- Why might having fun with someone be important even if we don't agree about everything?
- What you would put on a list of things you have in common with all the invited guests?
- Are there needs in your community that could be met more effectively by all the churches working together? How could you help get this started?

Where's this going?
Kids look for ways Christia churches can celebrate together while agreeing to disagree.

Back it up . . .
"Today, at last count, there are over *40,000* different Christian denominations. That's a lot."
re:form DVD

respond

15-20 minutes

Gather to share the different points of view kids have discovered and developed during the session.

Regroup

Ask each kid to take four note cards and to write his or her name on each card. Then have kids write a name for God on one card; a noun on the second; a verb on the third; and an adjective on the fourth. Make four piles of cards. Mix up each pile. Ask kids to get one card from each pile, but not their own. Give kids time to create a prayer for another church by gluing the four cards on another piece of paper, along with additional words or art.

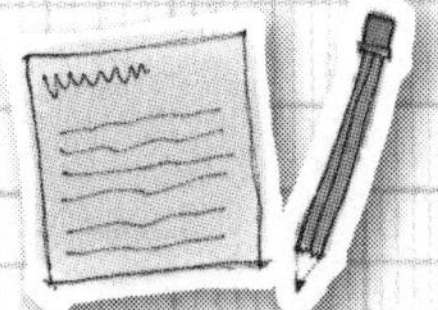

Get this stuff . . .
Note cards. Paper. Glue sticks. Markers.

Capture it . . .
Use a digital camera, camcorder, scanner, web cam, or audio recorder to capture group conversations and individual pieces of work. Upload them to your online galleries, or ask kids to do so.

Share

Invite kids to share their work and describe how and why they did it. Affirm those things you appreciate or find interesting and ask others to offer helpful observations.

Questions for conversation:

- What was new for you today?
- What might you want to think more about?
- How do you think beliefs impact or influence actions?
- What can you do to work toward unity in the Christian church? By yourself? With others?

Send

Have the group stand in a circle with the prayers they created. Offer a prayer of thanksgiving for people of all faiths and denominations. Invite each person to read his or her prayer or to say a word that models or conveys openness (e.g., respect or love). Close by blessing your group to be a blessing for the world.

UNIT No. 6
Tough Questions

Tough Questions Unit
Is it a sin to think about sex?

repare

What's behind all this?

o be blunt, if it weren't for sex, none of us would be here. In some ways, ex is the most natural thing in the world, so it's no surprise to read about throughout the Bible. But sex can also be confusing, as Adam and Eve iscovered when they suddenly became aware of their nakedness.

n the Hebrew Scriptures, sex is both celebrated (e.g., Song of Solomon) and hown to be a stumbling block (e.g., David and Bathsheba). Jesus doesn't talk nuch about sex, but Paul does, mainly telling the people in the early church o demonstrate self-control and not engage in the same sexually promiscuous ehaviors as those around them.

he biblical bottom line is that sex is wonderful and beautiful and creative vhen engaged in appropriately—but it can also lead to a great deal of hurt nd sin when engaged in inappropriately.

Where are kids at?

- Some kids this age may be sexually active while others have never even held hands. Be aware of all experiences!
- Most kids will be uncomfortable talking about sex with an adult. Create a safe and non-judgmental environment by focusing on concepts rather than specifics or personal information. Don't feel like you have to answer personal questions, either.
- If you hear anything that clues you in to abusive situations, consult the appropriate authorities.

Song of Solomon 1:2

Where's this going?
Kids think about sex as a God-given part of real life and consider what this means for healthy physical, spiritual, and emotional relationships.

encounter

15 minutes

Video

1. Set up

Images and words about sex are everywhere. Ask kids to use sticky notes to write categories of people or things in their lives that have been sources of information about sex. (School, home, church, magazine, movie, TV, Internet, friend, etc.) Stick the notes on chart paper, grouping similar responses. Who controls how sex is portrayed in each group? At what age do people first see or hear some of these words or images? Did anyone name church as a source?

2. Watch

"Is it a sin to think about sex?" DVD 2, Chapter 10

3. Unpack

- Why do some words make people feel uncomfortable?
- How do you feel right now talking about sex? (Awkward, funny, excited, confused, etc.)
- Is it possible to avoid hearing sexual words or seeing images of sex?
- How can we think about sex in a healthy and life-giving way?

What about the Bible?

Ask kids to skim the Song of Solomon in 90 seconds by assigning 1 chapter to each pair of kids. Tell them to tally the number of similes they find that compliment the writer's beloved. Share the results. Expect giggling and laughter.

Questions for conversation:

- What comparisons are the most ridiculous? Which ones made you laugh?
- What does this love letter tell us about how the Bible views sex?
- How would you feel if someone gave you lots of compliments? Would that make their love feel true? Why or why not?
- How do you show people you care for them?
- When is sex an appropriate way for people to show their feelings for each other?

Make sure you've got the obvi stuff for this session—re:form video (DVD or download), Anti-Workbooks, Bibles, pens pencils, paper, tape, etc.

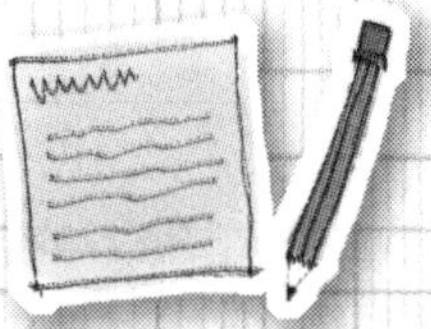

Get this stuff . . .
Sticky notes. Chart paper. Mark

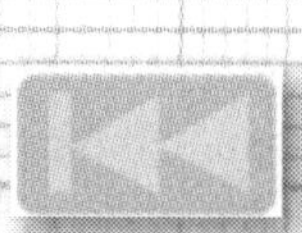

Back it up . . .

"God chose sex as the means for many creatures to propagate th species . . . including us human It's part of creation, and it's a p of who we are as children of Go So obviously it's OK to think ab it . . ."
re:form DVD

"Historically speaking, Christians have always believed that sex is sacred. It's special. It's a gift fro God. And . . . let's face it, it's . awesome."
re:form DVD

sim·i·le
[sim-ih-lee]
a comparison that uses "like" or

25-30 minutes

Choose 1+ Anti-Workbook (AW) activities to explore the session question. The first 2 are for individual use, while the last 2 involve the whole group.

1. Pieces of Pie AW p. 142

Tell kids about a time someone wooed you. Did they use compliments? Cards? Flowers? Flirting? How did you know? Hearing about an adult's healthy relationship can help kids figure out how to treat one another. Brainstorm a list of things important in a relationship. Write the ideas on chart paper. Then let kids work individually to complete their own relationship pie charts. After everyone is finished, tally everyone's biggest pieces of pie on the chart paper. Encourage kids to ask important adults in their lives to fill out pie charts, too.

Questions for conversation while you work:

- How do you decide if you have a crush on someone?
- How do you know if someone likes you back? What does that feel like?
- What's the hardest part about asking someone out?
- Is dating worth all the hassle it can cause? Why or why not?

Get this stuff . . .
Chart paper. Marker.

Where's this going?
Kids use a pie chart to show the relative importance of all the pieces in a relationship.

Back it up . . .
"So *everything* God creates is good! Everything. Including you. And everything has its role to play. Even . . . you know."
re:form DVD

2. Culture Shock AW p. 143

You can begin this activity at the end of a prior session and talk about kids' findings today, or assign it now and talk about it the next time you meet. Always be sure you follow up on things you ask kids to do between meeting times.

Ask kids where they've seen images of sex in the past day. Then encourage them to pay attention throughout the week, maybe working together with their friends. Whenever one friend sees an image of sex, he or she can say a code word such as "Pineapple!" and everyone can record the image in their Anti-Workbooks.

Questions for conversation while you work:

- Where do you see images of sex most often?
- Why do you think the media uses sex to advertise things?
- Are you more or less likely to buy something using sex to sell the product?
- Would you buy something stating it would make you sexier? Why or why not?
- Why do you think we strive to be more beautiful?

Where's this going?
Kids pay attention to how often they are exposed to images of sex in their everyday lives.

Back it up . . .
"If sex is supposed to be this holy, sacred gift from God, but we're constantly bombarded with a different idea of it in popular culture . . . what's the deal?"
re:form DVD

3. Dating Game AW p. 144

Excitedly introduce your "date," telling kids everything that's great about this new love interest. How did you meet? Why are you sure this one is *the* one? Be sure your date is in the Dating Game audience. Recruit the volunteers listed on p. 146. The bachelors and bachelorettes select a character card and use the information to get into their roles. Everyone else gets the set ready. The host introduces the show and helps the contestant keep the questions rolling.

Questions for conversation while you work:

- What are your criteria for a person whom you would . . . Smile at? Wink at? Shake hands with? Hug? Hold hands with? Kiss?
- What are your criteria for a person whom you would . . . Ask for directions? Talk to about the weather? Ask for help on homework? Sit next to at lunch? Ask for advice? Share all of your secrets with?
- How do your criteria differ for each level of interaction and why?
- Why are these expectations important in dating and friendship?

Get this stuff . . .

A prop as your date (stuffed animal, movie st poster, etc.). Divider wall Microphone prop. Chairs. Character cards (AW p. P

Where's this going?

Kids play a dating game to consider characteristic important in a romantic partner.

Back it up . . .

"But, we *can* be intention *about how* we think abou sex. A healthy and life-giv approach might look a litt different."

re:form DVD

4. Stomp Session AW p. 145

Play several rounds of this game, using different rules in each round. Designate one color of balloon the "offense" and the other color the "defense." If you have an offense balloon tied to your leg, try as hard as you can to pop everyone else's balloons. If you have a defense balloon, try as hard as you can to protect your balloon. Try different mixes of offense and defense. Ask kids to keep track of their emotions while stomping or protecting.

Questions for conversation while you work:

- What did it feel like to be on offense? On defense?
- What is it like if everyone is on offense or defense?
- Do healthy relationships involve more offense or defense? Why?
- What emotions did you feel or observe while playing?

Get this stuff . . .

Lots of balloons (2 colors, String. Scissors. Tape.

Where's this going?

Kids consider the nature healthy relationships.

Back it up . . .

"Those thoughts are fuelec a powerful biological ener that God gave to human beings as part of creation and if it is feared, shamec or misdirected, that enerc can become problematic, even destructive. And no wants that."

re:form DVD

respond

15-20 minutes

Gather to share the different points of view kids have discovered and developed during the session.

Regroup

Have kids write their favorite compliments from the Song of Solomon on note cards. Share what they wrote and why. Encourage everyone to slip this card into his or her Bible as a reminder of how we can keep spirituality at the center of our lives and still have healthy sexual relationships.

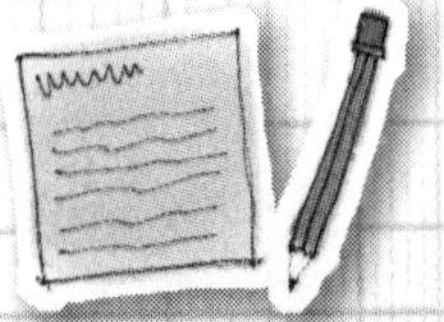

Get this stuff . . .

Note cards. Mural paper or cardboard (labeled and designed as a "Tough Questions Toolbox" and displayed where many people can see it). Tape.

Share

Invite kids to share their work and describe how and why they did it. Affirm those things you appreciate or find interesting and ask others to offer helpful observations.

Capture it . . .

Use a digital camera, camcorder, scanner, web cam, or audio recorder to capture group conversations and individual pieces of work. Upload them to your online galleries, or ask kids to do so.

Questions for conversation:

- How does God view sex? How does the Bible support this view?
- What does a healthy spiritual and emotional relationship look like?
- How can we show one another that we value our relationships?
- When can sex become a bad thing? How do we avoid that?
- Even though we know sex is natural, God-given, and a part of our lives, how do we figure out the right timing?
- Finish the sentence "According to the Bible, sex is . . ."

Back it up . . .

"God creates life and re-creates life for good."

re:form DVD

Send

Give kids note cards and some time to record one tool they acquired today that will help them when thinking and talking about sex. Tape the tools to the toolbox; then gather around and pray for guidance as we tackle the world of tough questions. Encourage people in your congregation to check out the toolbox to see what kids are encountering in re:form. Take a picture of your toolbox each week. Post it to the re:form online gallery.

Tough Questions Unit

How do I stop doing things I know I shouldn't do?

Prepare

What's behind all this?

The first thing Jesus did after his baptism was to spend 40 days in the wilderness, during which time he was tempted by the devil. And though we might think otherwise, *Jesus really was tempted.* In fact, the wonder of the incarnation is that in Jesus, God truly experienced all of human life, including temptations. That should give us comfort.

We should also take comfort that virtually every person we read about in the Bible, from the Hebrew patriarchs, kings, and prophets to the New Testament apostles, struggled with doing the very things they knew they should not do. And yet, whether it was after worshipping a golden calf or denying Jesus, God consistently offered forgiveness and love to those who did what they should not.

How do we stop doing things we know we shouldn't do? First, recognize that failures are endemic to the human experience. Christians call this "confession." Christians confess together that we fall short of God's glory. And second, exhibit self-control over those things that tempt you, turning to God for extra strength. Christians call this "prayer and self-examination." We do not do the things that tempt us because we are called to love our neighbors as we love ourselves. It's neighbor love that guides our actions.

Luke 4:1-2a
Romans 7:15-20

Where's this going?

Kids explore the consequences, for themselves and for others, of God's gift of free will.

Where are kids at?

- Kids this age take risks. They may know something isn't a good idea, but they may try it anyway to see what happens. If stories come up today, your role is to listen and ask questions rather than to punish or give advice.
- Kids need to be reminded of forgiveness. This will help kids learn to look at their own choices critically and learn from the decisions they make.

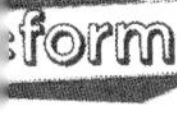

encounter

15 minutes

Video

1. Set up

Begin by playing a short "forced-choice" game (purchased or comprised of questions you made up—being sure to include a bit of the gross factor). Ask kids why they made their decisions. Did anyone consider factors outside their own well-being? Pose the question: How do we make decisions with positive consequences?

2. Watch

"How do I stop doing things I know I shouldn't do?" DVD 2, Chapter 11

3. Unpack

- What was the last choice you made that you knew you shouldn't have?
- What factors do you think about when making a decision?
- Why do people make poor choices?
- What does it feel like when you do something you shouldn't and don't get caught? When you do get caught?
- Would knowing God is paying attention change the choices you make?
- How can we use God's presence to help us make more good choices? Fewer bad choices?

What about the Bible?

Help kids think about the consequences of choices by disclosing a time when you did something you knew you shouldn't do. This isn't the time for a big story that could sound like you're bragging. Choose something as simple as grabbing a doughnut instead of a healthier breakfast. Did you consider the consequences? Did you feel guilty afterward? Why did you make this choice?

Questions for conversation:

- Read Luke 4:1-2a. Do you ever feel tempted? Can you tell if you are tempted *by the devil?* What do some of your personal devils look like?
- How often do you feel guilty about something? What makes you feel guilty?
- Read Romans 7:15-20. Have you ever experienced this same thing? What is Paul saying about why we make bad choices?

Make sure you've got the obvic stuff for this session—re:form video (DVD or download), Anti-Workbooks, Bibles, pens pencils, paper, tape, etc.

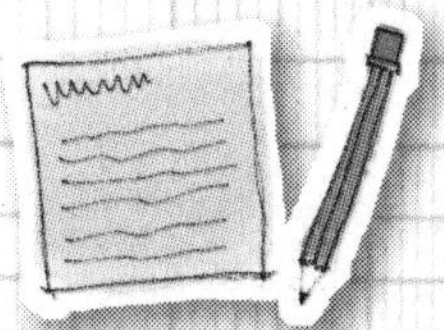

Get this stuff . . .

Zobmondo!! "Would You Rather . . . ?"™ (or other forced-choice game).

Back it up . . .

"Self-righteousness is when you'r doing the right things, but you're really doing them for yourself an not for God or other people."
re:form DVD

"When we act selfishly, we are not only turning our backs on ou relationship with God; we often h others around us as well."
re:form DVD

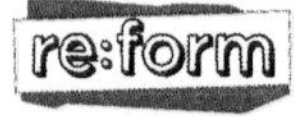

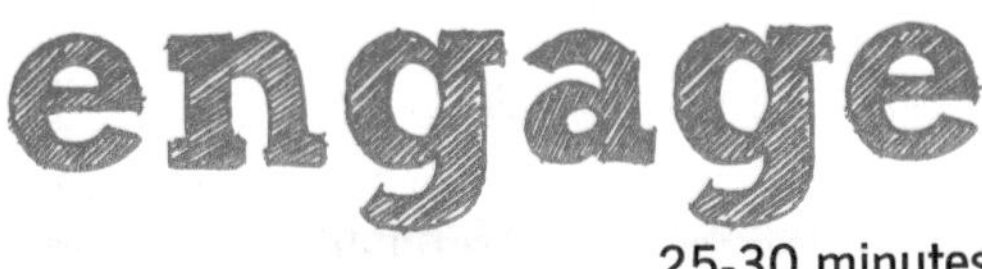

25-30 minutes

Choose 1+ Anti-Workbook (AW) activities to explore the session question. The first 2 are for individual use, while the last 2 involve the whole group.

1. Hit or Miss AW p. 146

Set out blindfolds, chairs, and stuff kids can use for target practice. Practice saying the Biblical Hebrew and Greek words for sin/missing the mark. (See sidebar.) After kids do the activity a few times on their own, invite them to work together to create a contraption that makes hitting the mark an even bigger challenge.

Questions for conversation while you work:

- What's your SDAP (Stuff Drop Accuracy Percentage)? How does this relate to your estimated PCMP (Poor Choice Making Percentage)?
- How does it feel when you miss the target because it's too hard? Can you do anything to improve this?
- Why can't your PCMP ever reach 0%?
- How can you decrease your miss the mark (sin) percentage?

Get this stuff . . .
Stuff to drop or throw. Blindfolds. Stuff to build a contraption (clips, tape, rubber bands, cardboard, string, etc.). Chairs. Dropcloth.

Where's this going?
Kids consider the often-unintentional nature of missing the mark.

het (Biblical Hebrew)
[heht]
sin, missing the mark

ha•mar•ti•a (Biblical Greek)
[hah-mahr-**tee**-ah]
sin, missing the mark

2. Carry the Cross AW p. 147

Before your group meets, practice folding the origami cross using directions on page P15 of the Anti-Workbook. Think about ways you already carry the cross with you every day. Do you wear a cross necklace? Have a key chain? Tattoo? Or do you just carry the cross within you? Show kids the cross you folded and invite them to begin.

Questions for conversation while you work:

- Does carrying a cross create feelings of guilt (sinning in light of Christ's sacrifice) or of being freed (confidence in Christ's forgiveness)? Which is more prominent for you?
- How can carrying the cross help us make better decisions?
- Do you think Jesus forgives us even when we knew we were doing something bad? Why?
- What might you think of every time you touch your cross this week?

Get this stuff . . .
Origami cross punch-out (AW, p. P15).

Where's this going?
Kids make visual reminders of confession and forgiveness.

Back it up . . .
"Free will means that much of the time we can choose our own actions."
re:form DVD

3. Rewind AW p. 148

Help kids pick an angel, a devil, and a decision-maker for each situation in the Anti-Workbook. Lead one trio of kids through the role-play of one possibility, attending to the persuasions used by the angel and the devil. Then invite another trio to role-play another way this could turn out. Do you see any patterns? Consider expanding some of the situations into moral dilemmas, such as stealing bread because your family can't afford groceries, or running a stop sign on the way to the emergency room.

Questions for conversation while you work:

- What does it feel like to be an angel? A devil? The decision-maker? Which role do you prefer and why?
- What if Jesus were the decision-maker? How would his decisions compare to yours?
- How would your decision be affected if you knew no one would find out what you did?
- Who are you thinking about when you make your decision? You? God? Your mom? Someone else?
- What happens if you factor in God? How does that affect your decision?

Get this stuff . . .
Angel and devil props (optional).

Where's this going?
Kids role-play tempting situations to practice resisting temptation in rea life.

Back it up . . .
"But there are times when our ability to choose wisel is overtaken by our deepe more primal desires. That' when things start to becor all about you."
re:form DVD

4. Almighty Dice! AW p. 149

This activity is all about the things kids have control of in their lives, so give them control of the activity itself. If needed, help start the brainstorming session by offering ideas. Then let kids lead themselves through the rest of the activity. Don't forget to join in the game!

Questions for conversation while you work:

- What's the worst answer you got from the Almighty Dice?
- What would it be like not to have control over any of your decisions?
- What could you get away with if you didn't have to take responsibility for any of your decisions?
- How does it feel not to agree with a decision the Almighty Dice made for you?
- What's better about being able to make decisions for ourselves? What's worse?

Where's this going?
Kids list daily decisions an consider what would happe if their actions were left to chance.

Back it up . . .
"Finding the courage and presence of mind in the he of the moment to choose wisely and do the right thir is very hard, because it requires you to step away from what you want and focus on what God wants."
re:form DVD

respond

15-20 minutes

Gather to share the different points of view kids have discovered and developed during the session.

Regroup

Regroup with another round of "Would You Rather . . . ?"™ or other forced-choice game. This time be intentional about making decisions that have positive consequences for others. Remember there is never a perfect answer. Sometimes decisions may seem "wrong" at first and prove to be "right" later.

Share

Invite kids to share their work and describe how and why they did it. Affirm those things you appreciate or find interesting and ask others to offer helpful observations.

Questions for conversation:

- Why is decision-making so hard?
- How can you make the most positive decisions possible?
- Will you ever reach the perfect decision-making percentage? Why not?
- How can you put your free will to the best use?
- When you do mess up, what should you do?

Send

Give kids note cards and some time to record one tool they acquired today that will help them when making decisions in their lives. Tape the tools to the toolbox; then gather around and pray for guidance as we tackle the world of tough questions. Encourage people in your congregation to check out the toolbox to see what kids are encountering in re:form. Take a picture of your toolbox each week and post it to the re:form online gallery.

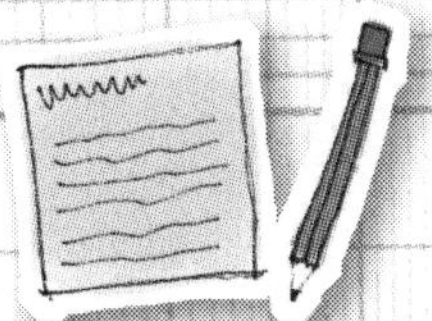

Get this stuff . . .

Zobmondo!! "Would You Rather . . . ?"™ (or other forced-choice game). Note cards. Mural paper or cardboard (labeled and designed as a "Tough Questions Toolbox" and displayed where many people can see it). Tape.

Capture it . . .

Use a digital camera, camcorder, scanner, web cam, or audio recorder to capture group conversations and individual pieces of work. Upload them to your online galleries, or ask kids to do so.

Back it up . . .

"And when we let God's love flow through us, then doing the right thing isn't just something you feel like you should do—it is something you want to do."

re:form DVD

Tough Questions Unit
Is divorce a sin?

'repare

What's behind all this?

'ne of the tragic facts about human life is that relationships that were meant ɔ last sometimes end. People enter into a covenant with each other with the ıll expectation that it will endure until death, but then it doesn't. There are ıl sorts of reasons that divorce happens, but, regardless of the reason, it's a ɑinful and sad experience.

esus spoke directly about divorce, saying there is only one reason it's ıppropriate. But we know that God offers forgiveness, grace, and healing even ɔ those who fall short of Jesus' teachings.

Where are kids at?

- Kids this age have a varying range of personal experiences with divorce, but it's likely that most kids know someone whose parents have divorced. This is almost always an emotionally traumatic experience, so don't be surprised if those emotional memories show up while you are together.
- Support kids' stories by sharing how God supports us through tough times and how we can support one another, too.

Mark 10:10-12
1 Corinthians 7:10-11

Where's this going?
Kids consider the power of God's love and forgiveness within the brokenness of divorce.

Consider this . . .
"That June, Kurt wrote on his bedroom wall, 'I hate mom. I hate dad. Dad hates mom. Mom hates dad. It simply makes you want to be so sad.'"
Heavier than Heaven: A Biography of Kurt Cobain, Charles R. Cross

encounter

15 minutes

Video

1. Set up

Show kids the supplies you gathered. Give everyone time to pick one or two items and create a way to represent how divorce sometimes happens. Give each kid a chance to present his or her sticky item becoming unstuck. Pose the question: We all know that divorce happens, but is it a sin?

2. Watch

"Is divorce a sin?" DVD 2, Chapter 12

3. Unpack

- Do you think we can do anything about being sinful?
- What's more important than our sinfulness?
- What are your experiences with divorce?
- How do you cope when something bad is happening and you can't do anything about it?

What about the Bible?

Prepare several "If" statements for kids to complete with "then" statements. Read them out loud for the group, such as:

"If you text message during class, then . . ."
"If you cheat on a test, then . . ."
"If you drive recklessly, then . . ."
"If you experiment with drugs, then . . ."

Questions for conversation:

- Read Mark 10:10-12 and Matthew 19:3-9. Does Jesus say divorce is a sin? What if-then statements fit these passages?
- Read 1 Corinthians 7:10-11 and Ephesians 1:5-7a. What if-then statements fit these passages?
- Why do you think Jesus' and Paul's warnings against divorce are so harsh?
- Why does Jesus repeatedly reassure us that we can ask for forgiveness?

Make sure you've got the obv
stuff for this session—re:form
video (DVD or download),
Anti-Workbooks, Bibles, pens
pencils, paper, tape, etc.

Get this stuff . . .

A variety of things that stick bu
come undone (Velcro®, magnet
sandwich cookies, Chinese fing
trap, food storage container wit
paper, stapler, tape, peanut but
sandwich, zipper).

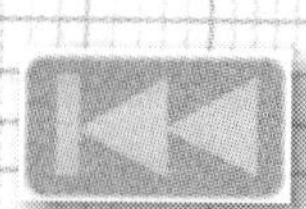

Back it up . . .

"The word 'sin' refers to a single
bad act, a nefarious deed that
violates an accepted moral law
or rule . . . Christians believe th
underlying problem in everyone
is a state of being called 'sin.' W
have it. And it completely separ
us from God and each other."
re:form DVD

"But most Christians believe sim
that sin is part of divorce, regar
of whether it arises from our fal
condition as human beings, or
is the direct result of particular
sinful acts."
re:form DVD

for·give·ness
[for-gihv-ness]
the act of excusing a mistake or
offense

engage

25-30 minutes

Choose 1+ Anti-Workbook (AW) activities to explore the session question. The first 2 are for individual use, while the last 2 involve the whole group.

1. Perfection? Busted. AW p. 150

Think of your entire neighborhood as an exploration laboratory today. Weather permitting, go out and explore. If your regular meeting space isn't located in an area conducive to outside-the-building exploration, consider an alternate site this week or bring a variety of things kids can use. Before beginning, spend some time pondering some of the most beautiful things in the world. Do they have any broken parts or imperfections? Why do you think our world is filled with imperfections? Use your thoughts to guide today's discussion.

Questions for conversation while you work:

- What imperfections are you finding in your collected items?
- Why do you think everything contains imperfections?
- What beauty have you found in the broken items you are photographing?
- How does God create beauty in brokenness?
- How can goodness be found in the brokenness created in divorce?

Get this stuff . . .
Digital cameras. Photo printers. Sticky notes. Tape. Magnifying glasses.

Where's this going?
Kids ponder how God can work toward good in the midst of brokenness.

2. Pin the Apple AW p. 151

Find a way to challenge yourself while giving kids directions for this activity. Can you find a way to help them while blindfolded and/or without words? How will you communicate what to do? With your hands? Through other body language? How does it feel to be limited in what you can do?

Questions for conversation while you work:

- How was your ability to place the stickers accurately affected when you had limited ability to see or were faced with other challenges?
- How is this like being limited by our sinfulness?
- What are some of the challenges faced in marriage?
- What are the consequences of missing the mark with apple stickers?
- What challenges are faced when people divorce? Who is affected?

Where's this going?
Kids challenge themselves to attain accuracy in spite of limitations.

Back it up . . .
"The hard truth is that human relationships break—sometimes beyond repair—and when they break, the people in the relationship get hurt. Often, people outside the relationship get hurt, too."
re:form DVD

3. Fruit Bowling AW p. 152

Think of a time when something didn't go the way you had planned. Did you feel bruised and battered? Maybe you felt out of control. How did you cope? Talk about this experience with the kids. Share both the bruised and battered part and how you were able to move forward and try again.

Questions for conversation while you work:

- How hard is it getting the fruit to go where you want it to go?
- How does it feel when the fruit doesn't go where you planned?
- What did you try to get it to work the next time?
- What's happening to the fruit the longer we bowl? Is some of it still edible?
- How is this like relationships with people we love?
- When have you felt like this fruit looks?

Get this stuff . . .

Assortment of small fruit. Plastic bowling pins or em liter bottles. Painter's tape Plastic tarp (optional).

Where's this going?

Kids experience how thing can get bruised or broken when they get out of contr

Back it up . . .

"The God you read about in the Bible seems much mo interested in forgiveness and in repairing brokennes in healing relationships— between people and God, and between people."
re:form DVD

4. Tower Time AW p. 153

Carry a deck of cards into the room with you. "Trip" and drop the deck. Start picking up the cards, slowly trying to put them in the order they were before dropping them. Ask kids if they think there's any chance you can get them back in the same order. Why? Keep rearranging the cards as kids split into teams and start building (and destroying) towers. Be sure kids finish all three steps before checking page P9 for the final instruction.

Questions for conversation while you work:

- What's unique about your Lego® tower?
- How does it feel to have someone else destroy your tower?
- What was different about trying to rebuild the exact same tower? Were they identical?
- When have you had to put yourself back together after something bad happened? How were you different after that experience?
- What "building blocks" require repair after divorce?
- How can we depend on God when we feel broken? How can we depend on one another?

Get this stuff . . .

Legos®. Digital camera. Photo printer. Deck of carc Final Tower Time instructi (AW p. P9).

Where's this going?

Kids use blocks to recogniz that people and relationshi may not look the same wh we reconstruct them.

Back it up . . .

"But in the end, when it comes to broken relationships, God doesn't seem all that interested in assigning blame . . . or punishing people."
re:form DVD

15-20 minutes

Gather to share the different points of view kids have discovered and developed during the session.

Regroup

Check for food allergies! Give each kid a jumbo marshmallow. Have kids use their index fingers and thumbs to repeatedly pull apart and squish back together the marshmallows. Continue this process until the marshmallows take on a new (taffy-like) form. If appropriate, let kids eat their newly formed marshmallow taffy. "Broken" marshmallows are still marshmallows. People broken by sin are still beloved children of God.

Share

Invite kids to share their work and describe how and why they did it. Affirm those things you appreciate or find interesting and ask others to offer helpful observations.

Questions for conversation:

- How were the marshmallows different after being pulled apart? How were they the same?
- How are you different because of tough situations you've survived? How are you the same?
- How does Jesus' forgiveness help when divorce happens?

Send

Give kids note cards and some time to record one tool they acquired today that will help them deal with their experiences with divorce. Tape the tools to the toolbox; then gather around and pray for guidance as we tackle the world of tough questions. Encourage people in your congregation to check out the toolbox to see what kids are encountering in re:form. Take a picture of your toolbox each week and post it to the re:form online gallery.

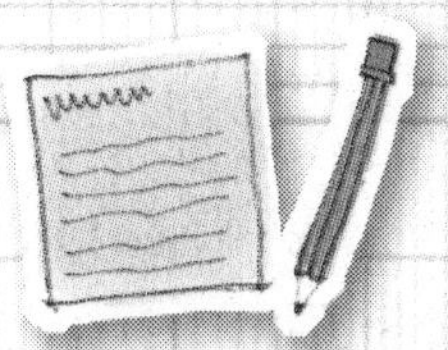

Get this stuff . . .

Jumbo marshmallows. A way to wash hands. Note cards. Mural paper or cardboard (labeled and designed as a "Tough Questions Toolbox" and displayed where many people can see it). Tape.

Capture it . . .

Use a digital camera, camcorder, scanner, web cam, or audio recorder to capture group conversations and individual pieces of work. Upload them to your online galleries, or ask kids to do so.

Back it up . . .

"Sometimes healing means near-complete restoration, where things can maybe be even better than before. And sometimes healing means the long, difficult process of moving on. But either way, Christians believe God is constantly working to make all things new."
re:form DVD

Tough Questions Unit

What does it mean to be "born again"?

repare

What's behind all this?

icodemus visited Jesus in the middle of the night so that his peers wouldn't e him. He complimented Jesus' godliness, and Jesus responded by saying at for one to experience the kingdom of God, one must be "born from bove." Nicodemus had never heard this phrase before, so he asked what it eant. Jesus replied that it's not like being born from your mother's womb, ut is a different, second birth—birth in the Spirit.

or centuries theologians have debated the exact meaning of this phrase—hich shows up only in this passage—wondering whether it implies a ramatic "born again" experience or is instead symbolic of a process. The ebate will continue. But the bottom line is this: God offers new life to those ho open themselves to God's Spirit.

Where are kids at?

Kids this age live their lives by fulfilling (or actively choosing to not fulfill) requirements. Paper due dates, school assignments, chores, and work (for some) dominate how they look at the world. Don't be surprised if they look at their faith in a similar way. They may believe there is a list of things they have to do in order to be born again.

Kids are curious about reproduction, birth, and life. Look for opportunities to make connections between learning at school and at church.

John 3:1-10
Revelation 21:5a

Where's this going?

Kids consider God's transforming power as we are born of the Holy Spirit, our lives changed forever.

encounter

15 minutes

Video

1. Set up

Brainstorm some things that go through experiences of being born again (caterpillars, deciduous trees, perennial flowers, bears during hibernation, etc.). How are they different after being born again? Do they make a conscious choice to go through transition?

2. Watch

"What does it mean to be born again?" DVD 2, Chapter 13

3. Unpack

- What do you think it means to be reborn in the Spirit?
- What are some ways Christians think about being born again?
- Do you feel qualified to decide if you've been born again? Why or why not?
- If being born again like a caterpillar becoming a butterfly, where are you in the process? Still an egg? A caterpillar? Cocoon? Full-fledged butterfly?

What about the Bible?

Pick three readers—one to read Nicodemus's words, another Jesus' words, and another everything else in John 3:1-10. While the readers prepare, set the stage. It's nighttime. Jesus is chilling out at home, probably surfing the web or watching sitcom reruns. Nicodemus is *sneaking* over to Jesus' house because Jesus is an outcast (crrraaazzyyyy person) and Nicodemus doesn't want anyone to know he's headed over there.

Questions for conversation:

- If you could ask Jesus any question, what would you ask?
- Did you hear the words "born again" in the translation you read? If not, what word did follow "born"?
- What does Jesus use as an analogy to explain being born from above?
- What would you describe as your most spiritual moment?
- How does Jesus' promise of new life in the Spirit relate to Jesus' promise of eternal life in John 3:16?

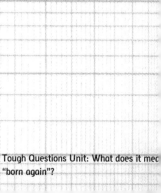

Make sure you've got the obvi stuff for this session—re:form video (DVD or download), Anti-Workbooks, Bibles, pens pencils, paper, tape, etc.

Back it up . . .

"Other Christians believe accept Jesus Christ as your Lord and S is only the first step in a spiritu process toward being born agai process that calls for you to see God's plan for you to let the Ho Spirit lead you so that you may in the love, grace, and knowled Jesus Christ."

re:form DVD

25-30 minutes

Choose 1+ Anti-Workbook (AW) activities to explore the session question. The first 2 are for individual use, while the last 2 involve the whole group.

1. Today I . . . AW p. 154

Begin by giving kids confusing directions. (Open Anti-Workbooks to page 42, close them, change seating positions, stand up, turn around, go back to their original seats, switch Anti-Workbooks with someone, draw a doodle somewhere, and switch back.) Finally, tell them the correct page (154). Ask kids to note—small and in pencil—every decision they made today. Ask them to carry the book for a day, recording every decision that affects them.

Questions for conversation while you work:

- What everyday decisions do you have a say in? No say?
- Why are some choices confusing?
- Do you ever feel like God has more control over your life than you'd like?
- What are some good things about not having complete control?
- What choices can you make about your faith? About God?

Where's this going?

Kids reflect on how much control they have over decisions in their lives.

Back it up . . .

"Some Christians believe that being born again happens instantly the moment you first decide to accept Jesus Christ as your Lord and Savior."
re:form DVD

"Others [Christians] believe it's a combination of accepting Jesus into your heart and then being baptized, upon which you are instantly transformed by the Holy Spirit."
re:form DVD

2. My Big Day AW p. 155

Before meeting with kids read John 3:8 and consider your understanding of the relationship between physical birth and finding new life in the Spirit. What's especially important and exciting about a baby's birth? About recognizing new life in the Holy Spirit? How does this analogy about the power of wind help you connect with what the Spirit does to spark spiritual life? Make two columns on the chart paper labeled "Physical Birth" and "Born of the Spirit." Use one marker color to write things that fit in both columns and the other to write things specific to one column.

Questions for conversation while you work:

- Why are people excited when a baby is born?
- How have you learned about your birth?
- What do babies need to live into being all they can be?
- What do people need to live into having new life in the Spirit?
- What new relationships are established when a baby is born?
- What new relationships are established when someone is born again?

Get this stuff . . .

Chart paper. Markers (two colors).

Where's this going?

Kids consider what they know about the day of their physical birth and about the impact of their birth in the Spirit.

Back it up . . .

"Nicodemus hadn't heard this phrase before either, and when he asked what it meant Jesus explained that it's not like being born from your mother's womb but a different, second birth—a birth in the Spirit."
re:form DVD

3. The Biggest Decision AW p. 156

Come up with a real or fake decision you need to make. Make a couple of big lists of pros and cons on chart paper and ask kids to give you input. After awhile, become exasperated and pull out your decision-making tool to make your decision for you. Then ask it whether your kids should begin work on their activity. Do whatever it says! (If it says no, you can always try again.)

Questions for conversation while you work:

- What's the biggest decision you've ever made? How did you make it?
- Were there parts of the decision you didn't really have control over?
- In what situations might a Magic 8 ball be a good source of guidance? Not such a good source?
- Think of times when you wished someone else would just make a decision for you. Why didn't you want to be in charge of that decision?
- What is part of a decision to be born again? What can you control? What is up to God?

Get this stuff . . .

Magic 8® ball or other decision-making tool. Cha paper. Markers.

Where's this going?

Kids discern the elements over which they have cont in the complexity of the decision-making process.

Back it up . . .

"And then there are other Christians who speak of being born again as something that happens to people. That your brain ha nothing to do with being b again."

re:form DVD

4. I See . . . AW p. 157

Think about an event in your life that forever changed the way you viewed something. What was the experience like? How did it change you for the better? Share your experience with your group.

Questions for conversation while you work:

- What do you see in the inkblot? What images did other kids help you see?
- Is it possible to un-see an image that you saw? Why? What other kinds of things can't you undo?
- How is seeing something new in the inkblot like having an experience that changes how you see the world?
- Does everyone interpret Bible stories the same way?

Where's this going?

Kids share what they see ir inkblots to help transform what others may see.

Back it up . . .

"Christians can agree that what Jesus was saying to Nicodemus is that God graciously gives new life to us through God's Spirit."

re:form DVD

15-20 minutes

Gather to share the different points of view kids have discovered and developed during the session.

Regroup

Draw a picture or write a description of what you think spiritual rebirth might look like. Explain your drawing or read your description to the group.

Share

Invite kids to share their work and describe how and why they did it. Affirm those things you appreciate or find interesting and ask others to offer helpful observations.

Questions for conversation:

- What questions do you still have about being born again?
- How do you see your relationship with God right now? How might it change in the future?
- What do you find difficult about understanding being born again?
- How has your faith changed from when you were little to right now?
- How do you think it will continue to change?

Send

Give kids note cards and some time to record one tool they acquired today that will help them when thinking and talking about being born again. Tape the tools to the toolbox; then gather around and pray for guidance as we tackle the world of tough questions. Encourage people in your congregation to check out the toolbox to see what kids are encountering in re:form. Take a picture of your toolbox each week and post it to the re:form online gallery.

Get this stuff . . .

Blank paper. Note cards. Mural paper or cardboard (labeled and designed as a "Tough Questions Toolbox" and displayed where many people can see it). Tape.

Capture it . . .

Use a digital camera, camcorder, scanner, web cam, or audio recorder to capture group conversations and individual pieces of work. Upload them to your online galleries, or ask kids to do so.

Back it up . . .

"A person's salvation shouldn't really depend on something as flimsy and fickle as the human will. Like the Apostle Paul wrote in Ephesians, 'For by grace you have been saved through faith, and this is not your own doing; it is the gift of God.'"
re:form DVD

Tough Questions Unit
What if my friends aren't Christian?

Prepare

What's behind all this?

While Christianity is the largest religion in the world, its members/followers/faithful still only make up about one-third of the world population. That means there are a lot of people who aren't Christian, including people you know. This situation is not unlike that in the early church. The first Christians, too, had to figure out how to treat their friends and neighbors who didn't follow Jesus. How they did it, according to the book of Acts, was by telling people about Jesus and by attempting to live lives that exemplified Jesus' love for the world.

It's important to remember that the work of saving someone is not ours. It's God's. People are saved by God's Spirit alone. Sometimes God uses us in that work, and sometimes not. Our job is to be available to God and to be the best friends (and sons, daughters, brothers, sisters, etc.) we can be to everyone we know.

Where are kids at?

- When it comes to friendships among kids this age, conformity is key. They value being just like their friends—enjoying the same movies, making fun of the same people, hanging out at the same places, getting the same grades, etc. Kids don't want to stick out. Help kids wrestle with the tough task of standing up for their beliefs while maintaining friendships.
- Some kids are lonely, truly having no friends, or feeling no one is their friend. Be careful about assumptions you make while talking about kids and friendship.

Galatians 3:28

Where's this going?
Kids consider Jesus' love, compassion, and acceptance of all people as a role model for friendship.

encounter

15 minutes

Video

1. Set up

Have kids draw images showing what friendship looks like. Talk about all the things kids see in the drawings—people, activities, movies, songs, or places to hang out. Make a quick list of non-negotiable elements of friendship. Throughout your time together today, be alert for kids with few friends.

2. Watch

"What if my friends aren't Christian?" DVD 2, Chapter 14

3. Unpack

- What religions are practiced by kids in your school?
- When do you sometimes disagree with friends?
- What are your criteria for a good friend? Did you hear any of your ideas in the video?
- When is it hard to stand up to your friends and say what you know is right?

What about the Bible?

Think of a time when you had a disagreement with a friend. Was it hard to stand up for what you believed in? Did your friend listen to you? How did you know you were right? What feelings did you experience? Did you ever doubt yourself? How did you convince yourself to stick it out? Share your story with the group.

Questions for conversation:

- What could cause you to end a friendship with someone?
- Read Galatians 3:28. How can you maintain your Christian identity while respecting the beliefs of others? Do you think that would be hard to do? Why or why not?
- How can you spread the love of Jesus to people who aren't Christian?
- What would it be like if you brought your friends to confirmation?
- What can you learn from people of other religions?

Make sure you've got the obv stuff for this session—re:form video (DVD or download), Anti-Workbooks, Bibles, pens pencils, paper, tape, etc.

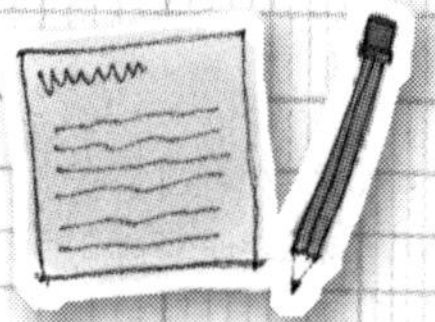

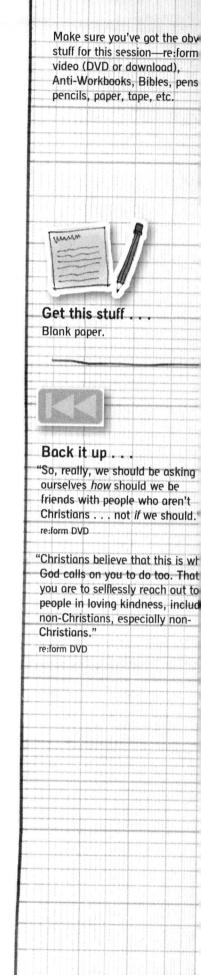

Get this stuff . . .
Blank paper.

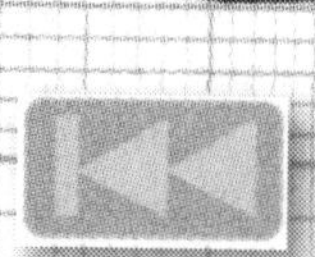

Back it up . . .
"So, really, we should be asking ourselves *how* should we be friends with people who aren't Christians . . . not *if* we should."
re:form DVD

"Christians believe that this is wh God calls on you to do too. That you are to selflessly reach out to people in loving kindness, includ non-Christians, especially non-Christians."
re:form DVD

engage

25-30 minutes

Choose 1+ Anti-Workbook (AW) activities to explore the session question. The first 2 are for individual use, while the last 2 involve the whole group.

1. Yearbook AW p. 158

Pull out your old yearbook and flip through the pages, showing kids some of the friends you had in high school or middle school. Share some stories of you and your friends in high school. How were times different then? Enjoy the laughter that comes from kids seeing you as an awkward youngster! Do this activity while together or ask kids to complete it at home or school and bring it back to share the next time you meet.

Questions for conversation while you work:

- What do you and your friends do together?
- Is it necessary for friends to spend time together?
- How have you been a good friend? Is this always easy? Why or why not?
- How have people been good friends to you?
- How was Jesus a good friend to the people he met?
- What role does faith play in your friendships?

Get this stuff . . .

Old yearbook or photo album. Digital camera. Photo printer. Glue or tape.

Where's this going?

Kids consider, illustrate, and label their roles as friends.

Back it up . . .

"So . . . maybe ask yourself what is motivating you to be friends with anyone, really."
re:form DVD

2. Me: A Composite AW p. 159

Gather your collection of paraphernalia from your junk drawer, a dollar store, or a basket of stuff you've been meaning to sort through. Give one item to each kid, creating a corny (or thoughtful) explanation of why you think that item represents that kid (e.g., bouncy ball / you bounce when excited; Pez dispenser / you dispense many smiles, etc.). Then ask kids to share positive aspects they see in other kids by drawing or attaching collage items in their Anti-Workbooks. Allow time for kids to share with the entire group.

Questions for conversation while you work:

- How do you represent who a person is through art?
- What kinds of things are appearing in your collage?
- What kinds of things are you adding to others' collages?
- How accurate do you think your collage is?
- Is there anything on this collage that wouldn't be on a collage for someone who is not a Christian?
- If you created a collage for yourself, what would it look like?

Get this stuff . . .

Paraphernalia collection (knick-knacks, Pez® dispensers, snow globes, bumper stickers, bouncy balls, etc.). Collage supplies (paper, sequins, feathers, pom-poms, string, magazines, newspapers, etc.). Glue. Markers.

Where's this going?

Kids get a glimpse of how others see them.

3. Speed Meeting AW p. 160

Give speedy instructions for today's speed-meeting activity. Dramatically hold your stopwatch and speak as quickly as possible to explain what kids should do to set up and participate in the activity. You might need to repeat the directions. Click the stopwatch and let kids get started! Time 48 seconds for each speed-meet. Keep going until all kids speed-meet all other kids.

Questions for conversation while you work:

- What kinds of questions are you asking?
- What new things are you finding out about your confirmation friends?
- If you were given another 48 seconds with each person, what else would you ask?
- What do you have in common with the kids in your confirmation group?
- How do you see some people differently than you did before this activity?

Get this stuff . . .
Stopwatch. Chairs.

Where's this going?
Kids attempt to uncover n information—commonaliti and differences—within th group.

Back it up . . .
"It's really good to know th are people out there who s the world basically the wa you do. That there are oth people who try their best t follow Jesus. It's good to g refreshed, recharged, and realigned. Motivated. That a huge part of what the church is all about."
re:form DVD

4. Autographs AW p. 161

Sign your autograph on one napkin (or other item of limited value) for each kid in your group. Pass these napkins out, explaining that you are positive these will be valuable when you are given the best-confirmation-leader-ever award. Maybe kids will want to tape your signed napkins in their Anti-Workbooks for safekeeping. Then invite kids to begin collecting autographs.

Questions for conversation while you work:

- Whose autographs are you getting for each category?
- Are there any categories you're having a hard time filling?
- What categories might you want to add for people in our group?
- What kinds of qualities do you look for in a friend?
- How can you be a good friend to those people who don't necessarily fit your criteria?
- Where do you think Jesus would sign? Why?

Get this stuff . . .
Napkins. Tape.

Where's this going?
Kids ponder the characteristics they look fo in friends as they collect autographs.

Back it up . . .
"According to the Bible, Jes wasn't ever trying to fit in, to get people to accept him He was demonstrating God unlimited love for all people by reaching out to them, caring for them, letting the know that he accepted ther and loved them no matter what."
re:form DVD

15-20 minutes

ather to share the different points of view kids have discovered and eveloped during the session.

Regroup

lave your kids draw pictures or write descriptions of "The Perfect Friend." Not friend they have, because we all know those friends mess up sometimes, ut The Perfect Friend. The Friend that fits each kid's ideal picture of what a riend should be. What is he or she like? What does he or she like to do? How s he or she The Perfect Friend? Is this friend a Christian? Why or why not?)oes it matter? Let kids share their drawings or descriptions.

Share

nvite kids to share their work and describe how and why they did it. Affirm hose things you appreciate or find interesting and ask others to offer helpful bservations.

Questions for conversation:

- What are the most important qualities you look for in a friend?
- Is religion among those qualities? Why or why not?
- How can you show Christian love to all people? Why is this important?
- Do you feel called to talk about Christianity with non-Christian friends? Why or why not?
- How does this go along with being a good friend?

Send

Give kids note cards and some time to record one tool they acquired today that will help them deal with being the best friend they can be to everyone. Tape the tools to the toolbox; then gather around and pray for guidance as we tackle the world of tough questions. Encourage people in your congregation to check out the toolbox to see what kids are encountering in re:form. Take a picture of your toolbox each week and post it to the re:form online gallery.

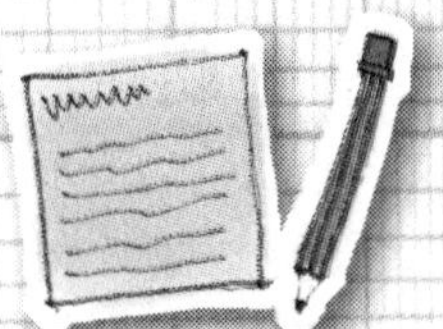

Get this stuff . . .

Blank paper. Note cards. Mural paper or cardboard (labeled and designed as a "Tough Questions Toolbox" and displayed where many people can see it). Tape.

Back it up . . .

"Ask yourself what is motivating you to be friends. Is it concern for them? Genuine concern? Even if they don't want you to be concerned? Or is it fear and selfishness?"
re:form DVD

"Be a friend to people who aren't like you. A good friend. A real friend. And get together with fellow believers to encourage each other and remind each other why we're doing this."
re:form DVD

Capture it . . .

Use a digital camera, camcorder, scanner, web cam, or audio recorder to capture group conversations and individual pieces of work. Upload them to your online galleries, or ask kids to do so.

Tough Questions Unit
Is it okay to be angry at God?

Prepare

What's behind all this?

Throughout the Bible, God is portrayed as a passionate God. And God created humankind to be in passionate relationships—with one another and with God. It's why God did not create a race of obedient robots, but instead created human beings with free will. So, since God created us as passionate, relational beings, we can assume God can handle our passionate emotions.

The Christian practice of prayer is the practice of emoting before God. It is in moments of righteous anger that we come before God with questions of purpose and meaning for our lives. God also hears the cry of the guilty. This is called confession. The lament Psalms are filled with confessions of the guilty and the innocent.

Where are kids at?

- Kids this age have strong emotions and don't always know how to deal with them. Anger, especially, can often be channeled in a bad direction, such as violence. Help kids gain the tools to deal with their anger. Yelling into a pillow, writing angry poems, banging drums, and running around are all great ways!
- Kids will likely have experienced anger when they were unjustly accused or punished (whole-class consequences), as well as having experienced anger at times when they were indeed guilty.

Job 15:12-13
Mark 15:33

Where's this going?
Kids get angry at God! And discover that God can handle their anger.

Consider this . . .

"Those who believe that they believe in God, but without any passion in their heart, without anguish of mind, without uncertainty, without doubt, without an element of despair even in their consolation, believe only in the God-Idea, not in God Himself."
Miguel de Unamuno, *Tragic Sense of Life*, 213

"That is my son that is. I tell ya ever since he was an itty bitty boy, sometimes he talks to the Lord and sometimes he yells at the Lord, tonight he just happens to be yellin' at him."
Momma (June Carter Cash) in *The Apostle* (1997)

encounter

15 minutes

Video

1. Set up

Show kids the old leather-bound Bibles, notebooks and pencils, and old, musty books. Tell kids God informed you kids are having too much fun in confirmation. Put all re:form items (Anti-Workbooks, DVD, etc.) in the box. Tell kids that from now on, you will do all the talking. They will only listen, take notes, and join you in reciting memorized prayers. Assuming kids protest, keep reminding them that God made this decision, not you.

2. Watch

"Is it okay to be angry at God?" DVD 2, Chapter 15

3. Unpack

- What makes you angry?
- When have you been angry at God?
- What does the word *fair* mean?
- According to the video, why is it okay to be angry at God?
- What did Job learn from his experience of losing everything?

What about the Bible?

Before asking kids about experiences that have been hard in their lives, consider a difficult experience in your life. What happened? Why were you angry? How did you cope? Did you wonder what would happen next? Share this experience with your group.

Questions for conversation:

- What's one of the hardest experiences you've ever had to live through?
- What did you learn about yourself during that time? About God?
- Read Job 42:2-5. What does Job say about his experience?
- How hard is it to stop being angry at God? What can we learn from Job about this?

Make sure you've got the obvi
stuff for this session—re:form video (DVD or download), Anti-Workbooks, Bibles, pens
pencils, paper, tape, etc.

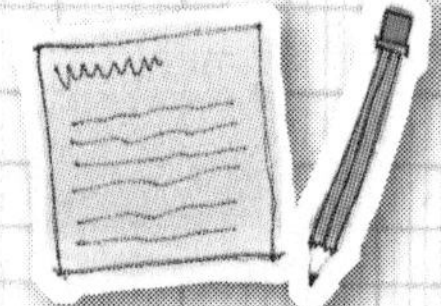

Get this stuff . . .
Old leather-bound Bibles. Noteb
Pencils. Old books. Marker. Box labeled "To Be Destroyed."

Back it up . . .
"Now there are lots of times in everyone's life when things happen that aren't very fair."
re:form DVD

"Job lets his emotions fly for days and days, 20 chapters in all, whi
is just under half of the entire bo
of Job. That's a lot of venting. Ar
God listened patiently to all of Jo
anger, anguish, and frustration."
re:form DVD

25-30 minutes

Choose 1+ Anti-Workbook (AW) activities to explore the session question. The first 2 are for individual use, while the last 2 involve the whole group.

1. Angry Prayers AW p. 162

Anger has many faces. Some people show anger with loud voices and banging. Other people become withdrawn and quiet. Find verses in one of the Psalms listed on page 162 of the Anti-Workbook where the writer is filled with hopelessness. Read the verses to the kids in a quiet but passionate voice.

Invite kids to write their own Psalm expressing something they are or have been angry about. When kids finish writing ask them to form groups of two or three to quietly share their lament.

Questions for conversation while you work:

- What kinds of things do you pray for or about?
- Does God cause the things you are angry about?
- Do you feel like God listens to you? Why or why not?
- Do you become louder or quieter when you are angry? What else do you do?
- What do you do to release your angry feelings?

Where's this going?
Kids, like lots of people in the Bible, sometimes become angry at God.

la•ment
[luh-**ment**]
A sad or angry poem that expresses frustration about something. You can find a lot of these in Psalms and Lamentations.

Back it up . . .
"When we're mad at God we're really angry because we don't understand why God is doing or not doing certain things in our life or the lives of others."
re:form DVD

2. Shout It Out AW p. 163

Yell the instructions for this activity with the pillow over your face like you're really angry. Then let kids brainstorm things that make them feel anger. Allow kids to practice Shouting It Out through the various supplies you have brought, including the punch-out megaphone from page P17 of their Anti-Workbooks.

Questions for conversation while you work:

- Which tool is the most rewarding to shout into?
- How is shouting a good practice when you're angry? When is it appropriate? Not so much?
- Is it possible to shout angrily but keep the rest of your body calm?
- Would you consider yelling at God a prayer? Why or why not?
- How does God respond to your anger?

Get this stuff . . .
Pillow. Oversized cups. Blanket. Lamp. Fan. Paper bags. Window. Paper-towel tubes. Megaphone punch-out (AW p. P17).

Where's this going?
Kids consider things that anger them and practice shouting them through various apparatuses.

3. God's Complaint Box AW p. 164

Ask kids to help you make a list of the places where they have seen a complaint box. Do they know what happens to the complaints people put in the box? Who reads them? Does anything change? Has anyone taken the time to submit a complaint?

Get started on the first part of the activity. Then make a plan for making and using a "Complaints to God Box." How could this box be a positive way to express sadness and anger to God?

Questions for conversation while you work:

- What's the purpose of complaining about something?
- What's the difference between complaining *to* God and complaining *about* God?
- What are the top three complaints you would make to God? Do they affect other people? Did anyone else share these complaints?
- How does God give you the power to solve some of these problems?
- How does praying over these complaints help?

Get this stuff . . .
Chart paper. Shoeboxes. Scissors. Glue. Markers. Paint. Magazines and newspapers.

Where's this going?
Kids consider the value of complaining to God.

Back it up . . .
"It was important for Job tc let God know how he was feeling, because keeping o anger inside of us, stifling emotions, separates us fro our relationship with God."
re:form DVD

4. You're Covered AW p. 165

Pull out your phone and pretend to be text messaging. Tell kids you're sending a text to God. Then read this exchange to your kids. (They can help you if you're having trouble!)

To God: god ur so big!
From God: i no thx.
To God: no srsly, yru so big?
From God: wut?
To God: ur big! wutd u eat?!
From God: im angry at u!
To God: god i wuz jking!
From God: whatevs.
To God: sry!
From God: s'ok. i 4giv u.

Questions for conversation while you work:

- When has someone been really angry at you? Was it justified? How did that feel?
- How is forgiveness like covering something up? How is it different?
- When is it hard to offer forgiveness to someone?
- How does it feel to know we can always ask for and receive forgiveness from God?

Get this stuff . . .
Stopwatch. Cell phone. You're Covered Sticker (AV p. S8).

grace
[grays]
the free and unmerited fav of God

15-20 minutes

ather to share the different points of view kids have discovered and eveloped during the session.

Regroup

ave all the kids in your group write a text message conversation with God. o they include anything they are angry about? How will they know if God plies? Is there anything they need forgiveness for? Have everyone share their onversations with the group and then attach their conversations to their Anti-orkbooks.

Share

nvite kids to share their work and describe how and why they did it. Affirm ose things you appreciate or find interesting and ask others to offer helpful bservations.

uestions for conversation:

- Why is it important to find good ways to deal with your anger? How can you do this?
- How do you let God know you're angry? How can you deal with this anger?
- What can we learn from Job about being angry at God?
- How do you feel knowing that through all our emotions—including anger—God loves us?

Send

ive kids note cards and some time to record one tool they acquired today hat will help them when they are angry at God. Tape the tools to the toolbox; hen gather around and pray for guidance as we tackle the world of tough uestions. Encourage people in your congregation to check out the toolbox to ee what kids are encountering in re:form. Take a picture of your toolbox each eek and post it to the re:form online gallery.

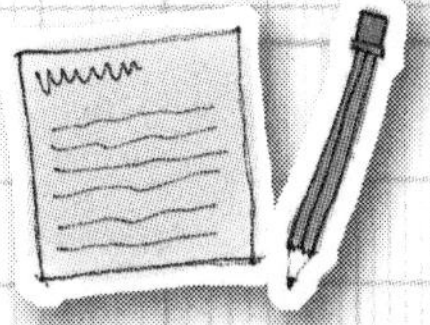

Get this stuff . . .

Blank paper. Tape. Note cards. Mural paper or cardboard (labeled and designed as a "Tough Questions Toolbox" and displayed where many people can see it).

Capture it . . .

Use a digital camera, camcorder, scanner, web cam, or audio recorder to capture group conversations and individual pieces of work. Upload them to your online galleries, or ask kids to do so.

Back it up . . .

"So in the end, Job's heart was re-opened to his relationship with God."
re:form DVD

Tough Questions Unit
Did God create the devil?

Prepare

What's behind all this?

God created all things and declared it good. But while passages like Psalm 5:4 remind us that God is not the author of evil, God does allow for its existence. Giving humanity free will was a risk that opened creation up to the possibility of both good and evil, joy and sorrow. Today it seems like the easiest way to know and work for good is to understand it in contrast to the evil that's been allowed to infiltrate God's good creation.

Our theological ancestors told their stories with personifications of evil, sometimes called Satan and sometimes the devil. In Genesis, the personification of evil and temptation is a sly serpent that lures creation away from intimacy with God.

People are still divided on whether Satan is an actual being or a symbolic personification, but we can all agree that evil does exist. The good news is that Jesus defeated evil on the cross. Christians are called to live into a new reality in which the powers of sin, death, and the devil have been bound by God's grace in Christ. In Jesus we see that, when it comes to temptation, resistance is anything but futile!

Where are kids at?

- Kids this age are wired to take risks as they attempt to test the limits of themselves and the world around them. Some may partake in such risks without even realizing where the desire to go against the rules is coming from. Help kids discover that, like Jesus, they can learn to recognize and resist temptation.

Luke 10:17-20

Where's this going?

Kids explore good and evil, light and darkness, honesty and deception, as they consider the devil's influence.

Consider this . . .

"The greatest trick the Devil ever pulled was convincing the world he didn't exist."

The Generous Gambler, Charles Baudelaire
Used in the movie *The Usual Suspects*, 1995

encounter

15 minutes

Video

1. Set up

Remove all seating. Ask kids to sit on the floor away from any walls. Tell them you sold the chairs after responding to an infomercial for MegaBands that will increase concentration and metabolism and strengthen your inner core. Pass out basic rubber bands. Tell kids to hold their knees against their chests, loop the MegaBand around both of their index fingers, raise their arms over their heads, and repeatedly stretch the bands.

2. Watch

"Did God create the devil?" DVD 2, Chapter 16

3. Unpack

- Some people believe the devil was a good angel who went bad. When have you seen see people or things going bad in your life?
- How are we easily fooled by false promises? Does that mean we think infomercials are the work of the devil?
- Should Christians fear the devil?

What about the Bible?

Split kids into groups of three or four. Give each group a few minutes to create a silhouette cartoon strip retelling how evil comes into existence and how they understand the devil's role in this. Have kids mount each scene on white paper. Allow time for kids to narrate their stories for the whole group.

Questions for conversation:

- Read Luke 10:17-20. Who's "he" in this passage? How does this passage suggest that Satan once had some say with God (see also Isaiah 14:12-20 and Job 1:12.)
- What do you think was happening in Matthew 4:1-11?
- What are some times when you've given into temptation?
- What tools do passages like Luke 10:17-20 and 1 Peter 5:6-11 give us when it comes to dealing with the devil in our lives today?

Make sure you've got the obvi stuff for this session—re:form video (DVD or download), Anti-Workbooks, Bibles, pens pencils, paper, tape, etc.

Get this stuff . . .
Rubber bands. Black constructic paper. White paper. Scissors. Gl

dev•il
[dehv-ihl]
from the Greek for accuser, tattletale; Lucifer (from Old Engl for morning star); Satan (from Hebrew for adversary, enemy) the supreme spirit of evil

Back it up . . .
"While there is disagreement as t whether the devil is an actual be and the source of all evil or just symbolic personification of evil, b sides can agree that there is inde evil in the world."
re:form DVD

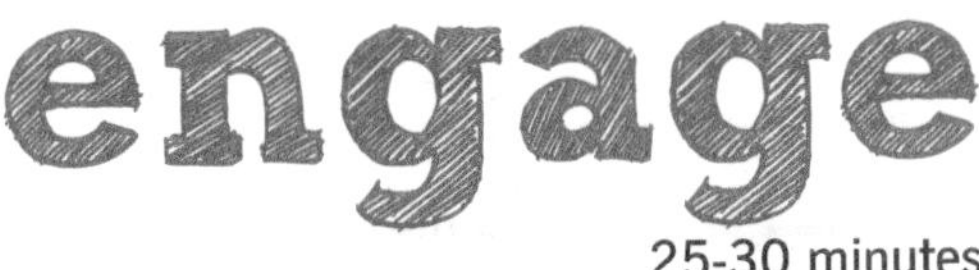

25-30 minutes

Choose 1+ Anti-Workbook (AW) activities to explore the session question. The first 2 are for individual use, while the last 2 involve the whole group.

1. Chain of Lies AW p. 166

Flash back to childhood by playing a quick game of "Who Stole the Cookie from the Cookie Jar?" Make sure everyone gets a chance to be accused. If you don't remember the words, kids can help you.

Questions for conversation while you work:

- Why do we often deny something even though we know we are guilty?
- What is the first lie in your chain? Why did you choose that lie? How big is your chain?
- How can a "small" lie in your life turn into a chain of lies?
- How can we avoid chains of lies?
- If you think God created the devil, does that mean God created lies?

Get this stuff . . .

Paper. Stapler and lots of staples. Scissors or paper trimmer.

Where's this going?

Kids explore how the devil leads us down wrong paths through trickery and lies.

Back it up . . .

"Sin can be really tricky, subtle. It can make it seem like not that big of deal, like it wouldn't hurt to be a *little* dishonest, cruel, or selfish."

re:form DVD

2. Light vs. Dark AW p. 167

Turn off all the lights in your classroom. Use a flashlight and the handheld mirrors to reflect light into different places in the room.

Invite kids to create ways to add light to the darkness on page 167. If kids choose to use a flashlight and mirror to reflect light onto their Anti-Workbook pages, catch it with the digital camera and be sure to post it to the re:form online gallery.

Questions for conversation while you work:

- How can mirrors help us bring light to dark places?
- How can God help us bring good to evil places?
- How are you bringing light to the darkness on your page? Does this have to be a physical light source?
- Is it easier to bring light or to cause darkness?
- How would you connect this activity about light and dark with your understanding of good and evil?

Get this stuff . . .

Flashlight. Handheld mirrors. Digital camera. Stuff to add light to a dark page (glow-in-the-dark paint, markers, gel pens, light-colored paper, white-out, reflecting tape, colored pencils, spray bottle with bleach and water mix, cotton balls, stapler, paperclips, etc.).

Where's this going?

Kids consider the existence of good and evil as they play with the properties of light and dark.

3. That's EVIL AW p. 168

Before kids arrive reflect on your definition of evil by browsing news articles, the Internet, and your memory. Where do you find the evil in these things? In the act? In the motivation? Let kids see or explore the stuff you gathered to represent evil. Ask them whether each item is evil and why. List their responses on chart paper, posted where they can refer to it while writing their definition of evil. Remind them to consider the Anti-Workbook questions as they work.

Questions for conversation while you work:

- What was the most evil item or article you saw while we were talking? Why?
- Who do you think would have a better idea of what evil is—the devil or God? Why?
- How do your definitions compare to the ones your friends wrote?
- How can we really know what evil is if there are so many different definitions and ideas?

Get this stuff . . .
Chart paper. Markers. Miscellaneous "evil" stuff (news articles, pictures of guns, pictures of mosquit or other troublesome bugs etc.).

Where's this going?
Kids develop a personal definition of evil.

Back it up . . .
"Evil can arise within our hearts and our minds—th times when we turn away from God, when we give i to temptation and act out selfishness instead of God love."
re:form DVD

4. Sales Pitch AW p. 169

Think of a time when you've been duped by an ad, salesperson, contractor, or someone else. Who was it? What were you buying? How did they convince you of something that wasn't true? Who do you blame? Why? How could you have avoided the situation? Share your story.

Browse through the print and other media ads. Ask these questions about each ad: Are you tempted to buy this? Why? Begin writing the used-car ad.

Questions for conversation while you work:

- What might be some good reasons that people would want to buy your car?
- How are you bending the truth to make the car sound better than it is?
- What are the differences between advertisement and deception?
- How do you know when you cross the thin line between good (advertising that is honest) and evil (boasting that is deceptive)?
- In what ways could a deceptive ad become a dangerous ad?
- Read John 8:44. How does the devil, as the master of deception, tempt you in your life? When does this become a matter of life and death?

Get this stuff . . .
Advertisements from print sources or the Internet.

Where's this going?
Kids tap into temptation a write an ad to sell a rundo beat-up car.

15-20 minutes

ather to share the different points of view kids have discovered and eveloped during the session.

Regroup

ass out MegaBands again. Have kids come up with some new uses for the MegaBand. As a finger exerciser? As a special, powerful bracelet? As an anklet hat encourages circulation? Have them share their sales pitches with the roup. Post new MegaBand uses to the online re:form gallery.

Get this stuff . . .

MegaBands (from Encounter). Note cards. Mural paper or cardboard (labeled and designed as a "Tough Questions Toolbox" and displayed where many people can see it). Tape.

Share

nvite kids to share their work and describe how and why they did it. Affirm hose things you appreciate or find interesting and ask others to offer helpful bservations.

Capture it . . .

Use a digital camera, camcorder, scanner, web cam, or audio recorder to capture group conversations and individual pieces of work. Upload them to your online galleries, or ask kids to do so.

Questions for conversation:

- Where do you see the devil popping up in your life?
- In what ways are you being tempted toward evil?
- What are some tools you can use to avoid temptation?
- How will you be on the lookout for the devil in your life from now on?
- Did God create the devil? If not, how do you explain evil in the world?

Send

Give kids note cards and some time to record one tool they acquired today that will help them overcome the devil and temptation. Tape the tools to the toolbox; then gather around and pray for guidance as we tackle the world of tough questions. Encourage people in your congregation to check out the toolbox to see what kids are encountering in re:form. Take a picture of your toolbox each week and post it to the re:form online gallery.

Tough Questions Unit
Can you accept the theory of evolution and still be a Christian?

Prepare

What's behind all this?

For some Christians, the veracity—and therefore the value—of the Bible hinges on the historical and/or scientific factuality of every verse. In other words, if the cosmos was not created in seven 24-hour days, as Genesis seems to say, then we can't believe anything else the Bible says, such as the resurrection of Jesus.

However, much of the Bible uses poetic and symbolic language in order to communicate truths about God. The Psalms is an entire book of poetry. The prophets often use symbolic and hyperbolic language to try to get through to the Israelites. And the book of Revelation is written in a special genre called apocalyptic. Therefore, we can believe the message of Genesis—that God alone is the Creator of the cosmos—and also accept the scientific consensus that our cosmos has been expanding and evolving for billions of years. The evolution of humankind is part of that process.

Where are kids at?

- Kids this age are in the process of developing their ability to wrestle with complex issues. Today's issue is one that scholars have been wrestling with for many years. Approach today on a pretty basic level: creation of humans, evolution of humans, or both? Allow kids to articulate their personal beliefs, bounce ideas off one another, and share things they may have heard. As with all tough questions, your role is to help kids think critically about their faith.

Psalm 19:1-4

Where's this going?
Kids consider the relationship between the "objective" nature of science and the "subjective" nature of faith.

Consider this . . .

"Authors of the highest eminence seem to be fully satisfied with the view that each species has been independently created. To my mind it accords better with what we know of the laws impressed on matter by the Creator, that the production and extinction of the past and present inhabitants of the world should have been due to secondary causes, like those determining the birth and death of the individual. When I view all beings not as special creations, but as the lineal descendants of some few beings which lived long before the first bed of the Silurian system was deposited, they seem to me to become ennobled."

The Origin of Species (1859), Charles Darwin

encounter

15 minutes

Video

1. Set up

Start with a cool (and safe!) science experiment. Mix equal parts of baking soda and lemon juice. What evidence leads your group to your conclusions about the experiment?

2. Watch

"Can you accept the theory of evolution and still be a Christian?" DVD 2, Chapter 17

3. Unpack

- How do science experiments influence what you believe is true?
- What have you learned about how we all got here from science? From the Bible? How do those things support or conflict with one another?
- What is the role of humans in creation?
- How can we care for what God has given us?

What about the Bible?

The Bible often utilizes personification, symbolism, and hyperbole. (See sidebar.) Split kids into teams, giving each kid this list of Bible citations (without answers). Teams have 3 minutes to decide which literary technique is used.

Isaiah 24:23 (personification)
John 4:13-14 (symbolism)
Matthew 23:24 (hyperbole)
Genesis 2:17 (symbolism)
Matthew 5:29 (hyperbole)
Deuteronomy 1:28 (hyperbole)
Revelation 20:4-9 (symbolism)
Proverbs 1:20-21 (personification)
Mark 9:23b (hyperbole)
Amos 8:2 (symbolism)
Psalm 77:16 (personification)

Questions for conversation:

- Why can't we take these examples literally? How do you know when the Bible is using literary devices or when it's speaking directly and literally?
- Can we understand whole stories in the Bible as symbolic? Why or why not?
- What does Psalm 19:1-4 tell us about creation?

Make sure you've got the obvi[ous] stuff for this session—re:form video (DVD or download), Anti-Workbooks, Bibles, pens [or] pencils, paper, tape, etc.

Get this stuff . . .
Lemon juice. Baking soda. Bowl. Spoon. Copies of Bible citations.

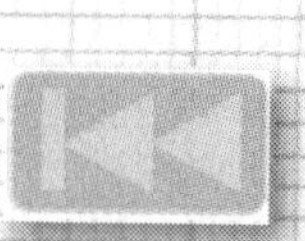

Back it up . . .
"What's truly important is knowin[g] that all life comes from God, and that we owe our very existence t[o] God. God gave us this great gift a[nd] entrusted it to our care."
re:form DVD

hy•per•bo•le
[hy-**purr**-buh-lee]
A non-literal statement showing obvious exaggeration. For exampl[e] "I'm so hungry I could eat a horse"

sym•bol•ism
[**sim**-buhl-izuhm]
The use of figures, marks, or word[s] to represent something else. For example, "And she was fair as is t[he] rose in May." (Chaucer)

per•son•i•fi•ca•tion
[purr-**sahn**-uh-fih-kay-shuhn]
Giving human characteristics to non-human things. For example, "Fear knocked on the door. Faith answered. There was no one there." (proverb)

engage

25-30 minutes

Choose 1+ Anti-Workbook (AW) activities to explore the session question. The first 2 are for individual use, while the last 2 involve the whole group.

1. Cosmos AW p. 170

Make labels out of paper for Sun, Mercury, Venus, Earth, Moon, Mars, Jupiter, Saturn, Uranus, Neptune, One of Jupiter's Moons, Milky Way, Really Far-Away Star, Black Hole, Dead Star, Really Far-Away Planet with Life. Give a label to each kid, adding or omitting labels as necessary. Give kids time to arrange themselves into a model they believe represents the universe; then ask them to draw their individual ideas. Catch the activity on camera!

Questions for conversation while you work:

- The names of the planets aren't in the Bible. Who created them?
- How does your view of the universe compare to the other cosmologies listed on the page?
- How has the world's view of the universe changed over time?
- Is it harder for us to change what we believe about where we came from (human evolution) or to change what we believe about the order of the universe (cosmology)? Why?

Get this stuff . . .

Digital camera or video recorder. Paper. Marker.

Where's this going?

Kids consider how historical scientific understandings influence how we see the world.

cos•mol•o•gy
[kahz-mahl-uh-jee]
a theory or model for the origin and evolution of the universe (and the place of humans within the universe)

2. Myth or Fact AW p. 171

Okay, leader: can you think of a time you found yourself in a discussion or a debate with someone over a science/faith topic? What was your emotional reaction? Were you able to have a civil conversation? Tell kids that this is their chance to think about and record their current thinking.

Questions for conversation while you work:

- What do you know about the theories of evolution?
- Why might you believe we evolved from apes?
- Why might you believe we were created as we are by God?
- How does it feel to be defending something you might not be sure about yet?

Where's this going?

Kids consider ways Christians reconcile evolution and creation.

Back it up . . .

"Did God create everything instantly, as many folks believe the book of Genesis says?
Or did God create things through a much more gradual process over billions of years, one that's still underway, as the scientific evidence suggests?"
re:form DVD

3. I Believe . . . AW p. 172

Think about your own experience with Christmas. What was it like when you were a kid? How about right after you stopped believing in Santa? How about now? How has your view of Christmas changed? How has it remained the same?

Questions for conversation while you work:

- What sights, sounds, smells, and emotions arise when you think of Christmas? Are they different than when you were 6?
- What is the main focus of your Christmas celebration now?
- How does your Christmas celebration merge or blend old and new perspectives?
- How does that translate into ways we incorporate new information into our existing belief systems?

Where's this going?
Kids reflect on the changi nature of personal understandings and belie

4. What Do You Think? AW p. 173

Consider assigning this activity a week or two ahead of time so you can show the videos today. Or, if you assign this activity today, be sure you plan a time to view the videos. Help kids schedule a screening that your wider congregation can attend. If equipment is a problem, plan a panel dicussion.

Consider finding YouTube® videos showing different perspectives on creation and evolution to show as you begin. Pay attention to themes and the people or group who made the videos as you do your search. What are the most common opinions on the origin of life? What opinions do you find impossible to believe?

Questions for conversation while you work:

- What questions are in your interview?
- Was the relationship between science and religion a big deal for people? What were the most common views?
- What differing opinions do people hold on evolution?
- Did you mostly agree or disagree while interviewing? How did that feel?
- Did you have any really awkward conversations? How did you deal with those?
- Which statements most closely resembled your views on evolution?
- Which interviewee did you like the most? Why?

Get this stuff . . .
Video recorder. YouTube® videos (optional).

Where's this going?
Kids document communit perspectives on the relationship between religi and science.

Back it up . . .
"Absolutely, God made us; the question is, *how* did God make us? . . . Were we created in the flash of a moment, or did humankin evolve?"
re:form DVD

respond

15-20 minutes

Gather to share the different points of view kids have discovered and developed during the session.

Regroup

Have kids create a "Creation Timeline" based on your discussions today. Allow time for each person to share his or her timeline.

Share

Invite kids to share their work and describe how and why they did it. Affirm those things you appreciate or find interesting and ask others to offer helpful observations.

Questions for conversation:

- How are our Creation Timelines similar? How are they different?
- How does it feel to know you might never be able to say with 100% certainty that you believe in evolution or you believe in biblical creation?
- Why are symbolism, personification, and hyperbole important in the Bible?
- What's one question you still have after today's meeting?
- What's one NEW question you came up with today?

Send

Give kids note cards and some time to record one tool they acquired today that will help them engage in the evolution-versus-creation debate. Tape the tools to the toolbox; then gather around and pray for guidance as we tackle the world of tough questions. Encourage people in your congregation to check out the toolbox to see what kids are encountering in re:form. Take a picture of your toolbox each week and post it to the re:form online gallery.

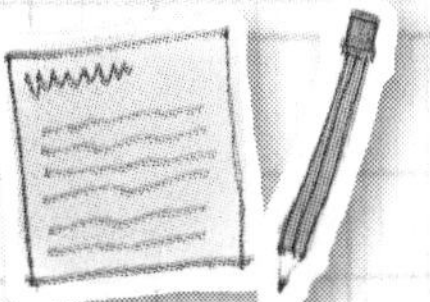

Get this stuff . . .

Blank paper. Note cards. Mural paper or cardboard (labeled and designed as a "Tough Questions Toolbox" and displayed where many people can see it). Tape.

Capture it . . .

Use a digital camera, camcorder, scanner, web cam, or audio recorder to capture group conversations and individual pieces of work. Upload them to your online galleries, or ask kids to do so.

Back it up . . .

"The truths revealed to us in the Bible don't have to be threatened by scientific facts. You can believe the message of Genesis—that God alone created everything—and also accept the scientific consensus that our universe has been expanding and evolving for billions of years, and that the evolution of humankind is part of that process."

re:form DVD

Tough Questions Unit

Why does God let bad things happen?

Prepare

What's behind all this?

If God is all-good and all-powerful, why is the world full of pain and evil? This question is considered the most perplexing of all. Theologians call this argument theodicy. For some, the response is that God is not all-powerful—meaning, God has abdicated some divine power in order to give human beings freedom, and with freedom comes the ability to make bad choices and have bad things happen.

Another way to think of it is this: In the beginning, God created order out of chaos (separating the lands and the sea, the day and the night, etc.). Then, briefly, the world was in perfect harmony. There was balance among human beings—endowed with free will—creation, and God. But when Adam and Eve exercised their free will selfishly, the balance was destroyed and they were expelled from the Garden. Then chaos re-entered creation, but on a different scale than before. And we have lived with a world that is a mix of chaos (bad) and harmony (good) ever since.

Most significantly, God experiences the chaos—the pain, the suffering, the evil—with us, even to the point of death on the cross.

Where are kids at?

- Kids will vary in the kinds of bad things they have experienced. Be sensitive to kids who have suffered tragedy in their life. Allow kids to share stories, but never require more than they are ready to tell.
- Kids are savvy to what's happening around the world. Remind them that we don't have to feel hopeless when bad things happen. God wants us to help others! Talk about ways youth can serve others in your community and around the world.

Romans 8:28

Where's this going?

Kids reflect on whether chaos and suffering are consequences of God's gift of free will.

Consider this . . .

"In order to be a person, exercising some measure of genuine freedom, the creature must be brought into existence, not in the immediate divine presence, but at a distance from God."

The Problem of Evil and Suffering, John Hick

"Behind me I heard the same man asking: 'Where is God now?' And I heard a voice within me answer him: . . . 'Here He is—He is hanging here on this gallows . . .'"

Elie Wiesel, *Night*, p. 65 (*on watching the hanging of a child by the Nazis at Auschwitz*)

encounter

15 minutes

Video

1. Set up

Set out the bucket of freezing-cold ice water and a bucket of towels soaking in warm water. Invite kids who are willing to try soaking their hands in the icy water for 5 seconds. Give each kid who tried a soaking wet warm towel. Ask them what it felt like when their hands were soaking in the water. What were the consequences of making the choice to try this? Is God responsible for letting your hands get cold?

2. Watch

"Why does God let bad things happen?" DVD 2, Chapter 18

3. Unpack

- How has someone you know experienced bad thngs? How about you?
- What emotions were a part of this experience?
- According to the video, why does God give us the ability to make choices?
- What do you think it would be like to have absolutely no control over any part of your life?

What about the Bible?

Share a time when something bad happened in your life. What did it feel like? What questions did you ask? How did you cope? Did any good come from this event? Allow kids to ask questions as you share.

Questions for conversation:

- Read 2 Corinthians 12:7b-10. What do you think Paul was trying to say?
- How hard would it be for you simply to accept when bad things happen because you know that God's grace keeps you strong?
- Read Romans 8:28. What is Paul saying here?
- What kinds of good might be possible when tragedy happens in the world?
- What makes it hard to see the potential for good or renewed happiness in the middle of sad, angry, and confused times?

Make sure you've got the obvi stuff for this session—re:form video (DVD or download), Anti-Workbooks, Bibles, pens pencils, paper, tape, etc.

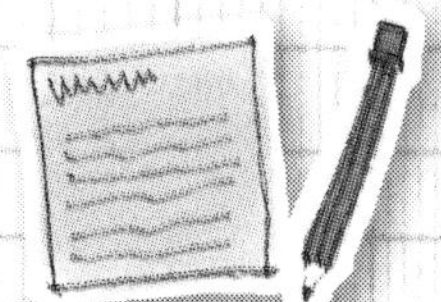

Get this stuff . . .

Bucket of ice water. Bucket of w water. Towels.

Back it up . . .

"God chooses to relinquish, or giv some divine power in order to gi human beings freedom, the free to . . . make our own choices."
re:form DVD

"What truly matters most for us i how we respond to bad things th happen. We can let God work in and let God's love flow out of us others in need, in pain—even pe who have hurt us."
re:form DVD

engage

25-30 minutes

Choose 1+ Anti-Workbook (AW) activities to explore the session question. The first 2 are for individual use, while the last 2 involve the whole group.

1. CHAOS! AW p. 174

Have kids stand in a *chaos zone* (a room within a room created by hanging bed sheets from the ceiling). Set fans to blow the sheets around, shut off the lights, play obnoxiously loud music, and invite volunteer adults to move the "walls" in and out by flapping the sheets. Then set kids to work creating chaos in their Anti-Workbooks—using the art supplies, doing a crazy dance on the page, sharing their Anti-Workbook with someone else, or spinning in the air while working. What else can your group think of?

Questions for conversation while you work:

- What did it feel like to be in the chaos zone?
- Why does chaos just happen sometimes?
- What's the most chaotic experience you've ever had?
- Why do you think God sometimes gets blamed for chaos?

Get this stuff . . .

Old bed sheets. Twine. Fans. Volunteer adults. Loud music. Collage-making stuff.

Where's this going?

Kids consider the consequences of chaos and confusion.

Back it up . . .

"Sometimes bad things just happen to people, even to really nice people, innocent people—things that no one can control."
re:form DVD

2. Confession Card AW p. 175

So, leader, what might you write on a confession card? How does this compare to what you may have confessed as a 13-year-old? Have your bad choices, thoughts, or experiences shaped who you are? Keep your thoughts in mind as you work with kids on this activity. Then set up a burning station where kids—and you—can safely burn your confession cards.

Questions for conversation while you work:

- How can your bad choices affect people around you?
- How do other people's bad decisions impact your life?
- How have your experiences with bad things changed you?
- If we can't help doing bad things because we are sinful, what can we do?
- Talk about times when it is hard to forgive someone else.
- Talk about the experience of burning your confession cards. How does it feel to know God always forgives—always?

Get this stuff . . .

Old magazines and newspapers. Scissors. Glue. Markers. Fire pit or burning bucket. Matches.

Where's this going?

Kids consider the human condition of sin as they record and burn bad thoughts, or experiences.

a·tone·ment

[uh-tohn-ment]
becoming one again with God by asking for and receiving forgiveness, repairing the damage caused by sin

3. Word Band-Aids AW p. 176

Create an "uncomforting" competition out of today's activity. Create a few "bad things" situations for kids to role-play (relationship breakup, death of a grandparent, bad car accident, etc.). Ask kids to think of the least helpful things they could say to the person who is suffering. Give small awards in these categories: Most Uncomforting, Most Awkward, Most Creative, Wordiest, and Best Zinger.

Questions for conversation while you work:

- What phrases have you heard in response to bad things? Do some of them trouble you? Why?
- What emotions do you feel when you try to think of something comforting to say?
- What emotions have you experienced when someone tries to comfort you with his or her words?
- What are some things we can do (not say) for other people when bad things happen?
- Does saying or doing feel more supportive to you?

Get this stuff . . .
Small awards (stickers, candies, etc.).

Where's this going?
Kids contemplate words actions that support peo when bad things happen

Back it up . . .
"When we stay open to a relationship with God, w we allow God to work in us and let God's love flo through us, some really things can happen."
re:form DVD

4. Half Sorrow AW p. 177

Consider the worst thing that's ever happened to you. What emotional memories do you experience? How does your body feel when you think about this bad thing? Did you feel the support from a faith community? Keep your feelings in mind as you set up guidelines for a safe environment today. If some kids don't want to share or are worried that others will eventually see their Anti-Workbook writings or drawings, give them blank paper. As kids work, brainstorm ways they can support one another when sharing. Avoid canned phrases.

Questions for conversation while you work:

- What emotions are you feeling as you remember the worst thing that's ever happened to you? Is it hard to tell others about this? Why?
- Where do you think God was when this happened?
- How do you deal with bad things? What community do you turn to?
- Can you find any good in this bad situation? If so, what was it?

Where's this going?
Kids examine the power community when sufferir bad experiences.

Back it up . . .
"At the same time, God is constantly doing everythi possible to transform dec death, and destruction in abundant life, including dying on a cross—true, sacrificial, undeserved suffering for us."
re:form DVD

respond

15-20 minutes

ather to share the different points of view kids have discovered and eveloped during the session.

Regroup

ive kids a few minutes to draw pictures of what they think hope looks ke. Encourage them to share their drawings with the group and to post eir drawings somewhere at home where they'll see it often. Ask kids how membering hope might help when bad things happen.

Share

nvite kids to share their work and describe how and why they did it. Affirm ose things you appreciate or find interesting and ask others to offer helpful bservations.

uestions for conversation:

Have you ever blamed God for something bad happening? Would you stand by that blame today?

What are some reasons that bad things happen?

What do you think the world would be like if God took control of everything?

How can you do God's work when bad things do happen?

Send

Give kids note cards and some time to record one tool they acquired today hat will help them when thinking and talking about why bad things happen n our world. Tape the tools to the toolbox; then gather around and pray for uidance as we tackle the world of tough questions. Encourage people in your congregation to check out the toolbox to see what kids are encountering in e:form. Take a picture of your toolbox each week and post it to the re:form online gallery.

Get this stuff . . .

Blank paper. Markers. Note cards. Mural paper or cardboard (labeled and designed as a "Tough Questions Toolbox" and displayed where many people can see it). Tape.

Capture it . . .

Use a digital camera, camcorder, scanner, web cam, or audio recorder to capture group conversations and individual pieces of work. Upload them to your online galleries, or ask kids to do so.

Back it up . . .

"In the end, no one has a satisfactory answer about why God lets bad things happen, but the fact of the matter is that God does let bad things happen."

re:form DVD

Tough Questions Unit

Can I do something bad enough to make God stop loving me?

'repare

What's behind all this?

in can have various consequences. It can, for instance, hurt other people murder, gossip, etc.). And even "victimless crimes" hurt us psychologically nd emotionally (lying to ourselves, viewing pornography, etc.). Those are the eal-world consequences of sin.

'eople turn away from God, and God is anguished. Jesus bore nails in his ands and feet . . . certainly that hurt God.

'he point is that sin is rebellion. It's a turning away from our dependence pon God as the source of life. God's desire for us to turn toward God is what aptism is all about. We are claimed as Children of God. We belong to one vhose mark on us is forever. God's grace overflows from life to death, and othing can separate us from that love.

Though we continue to sin against God and others, the good news is that God vill continue to reach out to us in an embrace, even when we do things that lamage those relationships.

Where are kids at?

- Kids this age are wired to take risks—stretching the boundaries of their independence and seeing where parents or other authorities will push back. And sometimes, they're going to mess up seriously. Today's conversation is a great opportunity to highlight God's unceasing love. Neither kids nor the rest of us can ever do anything bad enough to condemn our eternal selves. But there are always consequences. Help kids think about the importance of making smart decisions.

Luke 15:20
Psalm 136:1-3

Where's this going?

Kids test the claim that nothing can separate them from God's love.

Consider this . . .

"On the whole, God's love for us is a much safer subject to think about than our love for Him. . . . But the great thing to remember is that, though our feelings come and go, His love for us does not. It is not wearied by our sins, or our indifference; and, therefore, it is quite relentless in its determination that we shall be cured of those sins, at whatever cost to us, at whatever cost to Him."

Mere Christianity, C.S. Lewis, (1952) book 3, chapter 9

encounter

15 minutes

Video

1. Set up

Hold up—and break—a single strand of thread. Twist two strands together. You should still be able to break the threads. Finally, show how three threads twisted together are not easily pulled and broken. When we are in a loving relationship with God, we are stronger than when we are alone. Pose the question: Can I do something that will break that relationship?

2. Watch

"Can I do something bad enough to make God stop loving me?" DVD 2, Chapter 19

3. Unpack

- What does the video say happens when we sin?
- How do consequences from our parents and others compare to how God reacts?
- How does it feel when you mess up?
- How do you make it right with the people you affected?
- How do you make it right with God?

What about the Bible?

Split into two groups. Assign one group to read and dramatize The Prodigal Son as told in Luke 15:11-31. Tell the other group to read the parable and present a skit representing a modern-day version of the story. Allow both groups to speed-plan and perform their skits.

Questions for conversation:

- What happens in this parable?
- Why do you think the father celebrates his son's return?
- How does the modern-day skit change the story? How does it keep it the same?
- How does the father's love for his son compare to God's love for you?
- Read Psalm 136:1-3. Which person in the parable might have said the words in Psalm 136:1-3?

Make sure you've got the obv stuff for this session—re:form video (DVD or download), Anti-Workbooks, Bibles, pens pencils, paper, tape, etc.

Get this stuff . . .

Spool of thread. Props and cost for biblical and modern parable Paper.

sin
[sihn]
1. to miss the mark (literal translation from Hebrew and Gr
2. to make decisions that distan from God

par·a·ble
[pare-uh-buhl]
a simple story illustrating a mor religious lesson

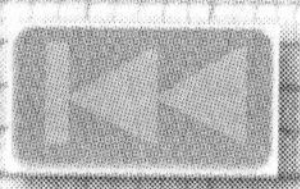

Back it up . . .

"Because God's love is unconditi and limitless, it never runs out. Because God *is* love. You can't l it no matter how hard you try."
re:form DVD

"When we act selfishly and do things that are morally wrong we hurt others around us and also ourselves. And these consequenc are real."
re:form DVD

25-30 minutes

Choose 1+ Anti-Workbook (AW) activities to explore the session question. The first 2 are for individual use, while the last 2 involve the whole group.

1. Citation AW p. 178

Write a bunch of fake—and goofy—citations and consequences to hand out as kids arrive. (Wearing sweatpants: run in place for one minute; have a nose piercing: place a paper cup over nose; etc.) Make light of your citations before setting kids loose on the activity.

Questions for conversation while you work:

- What did these biblical characters do? Were there earthly consequences?
- What kinds of citations are you writing?
- What's the worst consequence you've ever suffered?
- How do earthly consequences encourage you to change your actions?
- How does separation from God encourage you to change your actions?
- What does it feel like to know that God still loved all of these people even though they really messed up? How does that give you hope for yourself?

Get this stuff . . .
Paper.

Where's this going?
Kids discover biblical characters who committed serious offenses and were still loved and chosen by God.

Back it up . . .
"Now, of course, this doesn't get anyone off the hook for the earthly consequences of their actions. We still have to live with those."
re:form DVD

2. Stuck on You AW p. 179

If you can get your hands on a Weeble®, bring it in for kids to play with. If not, find a YouTube® video showcasing what Weebles® are all about (they wobble but don't fall down). Can you do anything to keep the Weeble® from popping back up? See if kids can tell you how Weebles® relate to today's lesson as they watch or play.

Questions for conversation while you work:

- What stuff is the stickiest?
- What stuff isn't quite sticky enough?
- What does it feel like to play with sticky stuff?
- How do you stick with your friends?
- What causes human relationships to become unstuck?
- How does it feel to know the stickiness of God's love for you is permanent?

Get this stuff . . .
Weeble® or video of Weebles®.
Sticky stuff (see AW).

Where's this going?
Kids compare sticky stuff to God's persistent love.

Back it up . . .
"The good news is that no matter how hard we push God's love away, God will keep reaching out to us with infinite love . . . All we need to do to stop pushing God away is to repent and receive God's love again."
re:form DVD

3. Pop! AW p. 180

When have you felt like you were about to pop? Too much pressure? Unreasonable expectations? Work responsibilities too great? How did you deal with the pressure? Did you "pop," or find a way to deflate safely? Share your experience with the group.

Provide supplies for additional balloon experiments: books to balance without popping, filling with water before exploding, cutting a slit before inflating. What experiments can kids think of?

Questions for conversation while you work:

- What happens when you poke the balloon with a pin? Tape it before poking?
- What might the pressure experiments show about physical or emotional limits?
- Why can't you put a popped balloon back together?
- How does God protect you from the pins and needles that try to burst your balloon?

Get this stuff . . .
Balloons. Tape. Pins. Vide
recorder. Books. Water
supply. Scissors.

Where's this going?
Kids discover that God's
unconditional love can still
have earthly consequences

Back it up . . .
"Christians believe that God
still loves us even when we
sometimes do bad stuff."
re:form DVD

4. Bad-o-Meter AW p. 181

Hold up one puppet. Tell kids she really messed up today by looking at her neighbor's paper during a math test. She claims it was just to double-check her answer. The work was all hers. We're pretty sure she cheated. Hold up the second puppet and inform everyone he took $10 from his dad's wallet to go to a movie with his friend. He claims his dad says it's okay as long as he asks first. But he didn't ask. We're pretty sure he stole.

Which puppet committed the bigger sin? Ask kids to vote by applauding loudly for the biggest sinner. Hold up one puppet and then the other. Which offense received louder applause? Ask your group why. Ask kids to rank the degree of badness in their Anti-Workbooks.

Questions for conversation while you work:

- How does your badness meter compare to other kids' meters? On what basis did you decide?
- How do you think God's badness meter would look?
- If God counts all sin as equal, why doesn't the justice system do the same?
- Do you think humans are qualified to decide consequences for other humans? Why or why not?

Get this stuff . . .
Two hand or stick puppets.

Where's this going?
Kids give human rankings
to sin while trying to grasp
God's unconditional love.

Back it up . . .
"For I am convinced that
neither death, nor life, nor
angels, nor rulers, nor thing
present, nor things to come,
nor powers, nor height, nor
depth, nor anything else in
all creation, will be able to
separate us from the love of
God in Christ Jesus our Lorc
Romans 8:38
re:form DVD

respond

15-20 minutes

Gather to share the different points of view kids have discovered and developed during the session.

Regroup

Play a few rounds of the game tug of war. One side is the God side and the other side is the sin side. Switch it up so everyone gets a chance to be on both sides. Does the God side win every round? Was God still there when the sin side won? How might this represent God's unconditional love?

Share

Invite kids to share their work and describe how and why they did it. Affirm those things you appreciate or find interesting and ask others to offer helpful observations.

Questions for conversation:

- Can you ever do something bad enough to make God stop loving you? How do you know? How does this make you feel?
- Name a few things you enjoyed today.
- How can earthly consequences encourage you to follow rules and laws?
- What's something you can add to your daily routine to remind yourself of God's love for you?
- Does God's unconditional forgiveness make you want to sin more or sin less? Why?

Send

Give kids note cards and some time to record one tool they acquired today that will help them deal with sin, consequences, and repentance. Tape the tools to the toolbox; then gather around and pray for guidance as we tackle the world of tough questions. Encourage people in your congregation to check out the toolbox to see what kids are encountering in re:form. Take a picture of your toolbox each week and post it to the re:form online gallery.

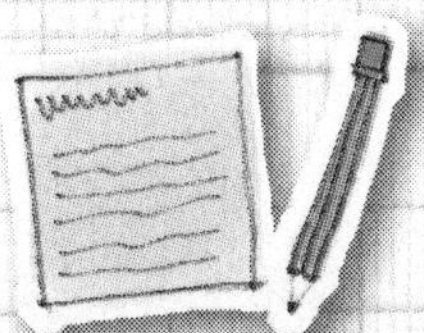

Get this stuff . . .

Tug-of-war rope. Note cards. "Tough Questions Toolbox" (made from paper or cardboard, labeled, and displayed where people in your congregation can see it. Tape.

Capture it . . .

Use a digital camera, camcorder, scanner, web cam, or audio recorder to capture group conversations and individual pieces of work. Upload them to your online galleries, or ask kids to do so.

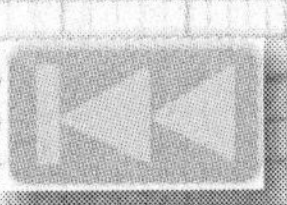

Back it up . . .

"You see, being bad doesn't hurt God the way it hurts us or other human beings. Instead of hurting God, it damages our relationship with God. It's like a wall between us and God."
re:form DVD

Tough Questions Unit
Does Revelation really describe how the world will end?

Prepare

What's behind all this?

The first thing for us to understand is that apocalyptic literature (Revelation and the Book of Daniel, in the Bible) was a common genre in the first century, much as science fiction or fantasy literature is today. And just as science fiction and fantasy authors often use those genres to make commentary on current political and cultural realities, the author of Revelation used the apocalyptic genre to make a commentary on what it was like for the first-century church to live under the thumb of the Roman Empire. In fact, writing open critique of the Empire was punishable by death, so the message John of Patmos was giving to the early church was hidden in apocalyptic language.

His message? God—and all God's people—will ultimately prevail against the forces of darkness. In Revelation God will wipe away all tears. And God will respond to those who call. The establishment of God's kingdom is about the reign of God's steadfast love and faithfulness that has been consistent throughout the Biblical witness.

The end of the world, described in Revelation, is less about the end and more about the sustaining promises of God that are with us. God's grace covers us each day.

Basically, John was writing to let his fellow first-century Christians know that, while things seemed bad and frightening—Christianity was a small, illegal, persecuted religion—Christ would eventually triumph over all of the forces that oppressed the church.

Where are kids at?

- Kids this age may know Revelation as the end-of-the-world book of the Bible. In addition, doomsday movies and apocalyptic books have given kids many graphic images of how the world will end. Help them see the historical significance of Revelation, while listening to their questions and honoring their fears and curiosities about the apocalypse.

Revelation 1:8

Where's this going?
Kids encounter apocalyptic vision in the book of Revelation as a message of encouragement, hope, and victory in Jesus Christ.

Consider this . . .
"'Apocalyptic' of this sort is a type of language-game. It regularly involves vivid metaphors which enable the writer to say, and hopefully the reader to understand . . . the significance, within God's dimension of reality, of events that happen within our dimension, within the world of space, time and matter."
NT Wright, *The Millennium Myth* (1999)

encounter

15 minutes

Video

1. Set up

Ask kids to flip to a random page in the book of Revelation and mold a sculpture of one image found on that page. Have kids share their sculptures and the verses they depict. Ask: What does Revelation describe?

2. Watch

"Does Revelation really describe how the world will end?" DVD 2, Chapter 20

3. Unpack

- According to the video, who wrote Revelation and why did he write it?
- How can we know John of Patmos's intended meaning?
- Why was symbolism so important in John's message?
- How do you think the image you molded fits John's message?
- What do you think the end of the world might look like?

What about the Bible?

Organize a Revelation imagery scavenger hunt. Split your group into two or three teams. Give each team the following list:

Rev. 1: Who is the Alpha and the Omega? What is represented by the seven lampstands? What is represented by the seven stars?
Rev. 4: Who is sitting in the 24 thrones? Describe the four living creatures.
Rev. 5: How many seals sealed the scroll? What does the lamb look like?
Rev. 8 and 9: What happened when each of the angels blew their trumpet?
Rev. 13: What did the second beast look like?
Rev. 18: What happens to Babylon?
Rev. 21: What is the New Earth like?

Questions for conversation:

- How does John's use of symbolism affect your understanding of Revelation?
- What seems to be happening in this book of the Bible?
- Why is the message that God prevails an important one?

Make sure you've got the obvio stuff for this session—re:form video (DVD or download), Anti-Workbooks, Bibles, pens c pencils, paper, tape, etc.

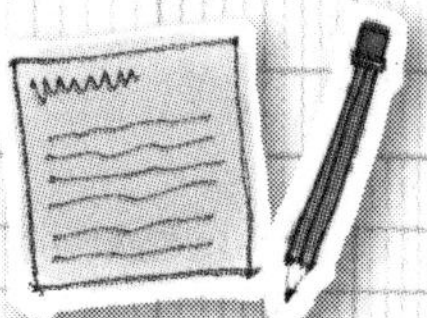

Get this stuff . . .
Play dough.

sym•bol•ism
[sim-buhl-ihz-uhm]
using figures, marks, or words to represent something else

rev•e•la•tion
[rehv-uh-lay-shun]
a dramatic disclosure of somethir not previously known or realized

Back it up . . .
"First, Revelation is sometimes called 'the book of the apocalypse' Now, *apocalypsis* in Greek literal means 'lifting the veil.' Second, apocalypsis also refers to a genre of literature that was common in ancient times."
re:form DVD

"Revelation is ultimately a message of encouragement, hope, and victory in Jesus Christ."
re:form DVD

engage

25-30 minutes

Choose 1+ Anti-Workbook (AW) activities to explore the session question. The first 2 are for individual use, while the last 2 involve the whole group.

1. Build-a-Beast AW p. 182

Use your Mr. or Mrs. Potato Head® to create a really funny-looking creature and explain to kids what your potato creature represents to you. Why did you put the arms where the arms are? Why does it only have one eye? Why are the lips coming out where the nose should go? Help kids get started thinking about what their creatures will look like, do, and represent.

Questions for conversation while you work:

- What does each part of your creature represent?
- What if your creature had to look like you? Would it still be able to represent something? Why or why not?
- What beastly images in Revelation cause you to be afraid or confused?
- What if John had stuck to human beings in the book of Revelation? How might the book have been different?

Get this stuff . . .

Mr. or Mrs. Potato Head® (or other creature-making game). Markers or colored pencils.

Where's this going?

Kids consider the value of using imagined creatures as symbols.

Back it up . . .

"Literary science fiction uses future settings and possible technology to bring analysis and criticism to its own times, to help people see things differently *right now*."

re:form DVD

2. Secret Message AW p. 183

Think about some of the ways you apply the Bible to your life. Do you use it to make decisions or judgments? Do you look to it for answers? Share with your group a few verses that are meaningful to you and why.

Some messages in the Bible sound pretty straightforward. Other parts of the Bible, like Revelation, were written at a time when the growing Christian movement faced persecution. These messages can be harder to understand. Invite kids to look for the secret message on page 183 of their Anti-Workbooks.

Questions for conversation while you work:

- How difficult is it to decode this secret message?
- What is the purpose behind codes and secret messages?
- Why might the writer of Revelation speak symbolically?
- What happens when you interpret a symbol the way you want it to be and quit trying to see what the writer intended?
- How might trying to decode the Bible take away from its meaning?
- How can we decode symbols in Revelation without the decoder key?

Where's this going?

Kids experience how meaning can be undermined when decoding messages.

se·di·tion
[suh-**dih**-shun]
the organized incitement of rebellion or civil disorder against authority or the state

Back it up . . .

"In [John's] days, writing and speaking out against the Empire were considered sedition—which was the crime Jesus was executed for, by the way."

re:form DVD

3. Secret Society AW p. 184

Research secret societies before you meet. Why do they exist? How have they been dramatized in movies and TV? What can you find about how they may have helped or hindered society throughout history? Share some of your findings with kids.

Then set kids loose covering up and coding their own secret society. Make sure your group stays focused on their secret society's main focus.

Questions for conversation while you work:

- What does your underground group do?
- How might a religious movement or church benefit from being a secret society? What unintended problems might arise?
- What ideas, beliefs, and hopes unite your secret society?
- What does it feel like to be a part of an important and totally secret society?
- What kinds of symbols does your secret society utilize?
- How do you think John's secret message in Revelation built community among the seven churches?

Get this stuff . . .

Markers. Old magazines (newspapers. Scissors. Gl

Where's this going?

Kids explore the power of secret codes to communic essential information to people within your community.

Back it up . . .

"It's pretty much the same with apocalyptic literature like the book of Revelatio The author, one John of Patmos, addressed the book of Revelation to seve Christian communities around 69 CE, like a letter but not as a message of doom and gloom, and definitely not as a literal prediction about how the world would end."

re:form DVD

4. Sci-Fi Show and Tell AW p. 185

Let kids page through the magazines and newspapers. Ask these three questions: What stands out to you? What's the most tragic event you saw? Why should we be positive even within the tragedy? Then ask kids to get to work creating a hope-filled sci-fi show from the Anti-Workbook suggestions, the magazines or newspapers, or another situation that they worry about.

Questions for conversation while you work:

- What problem or challenge did you select? Who are your characters?
- How are you portraying hope in the middle of a bad situation?
- How does it change your view of the situation to look at it from a sci-fi perspective?
- How do you think it changed John's perspective—or that of the people who heard him—to look at his situation from a different perspective?
- Imagine your great-grandchild sees this video. What might they assume about your behaviors, friends, religion, etc.?

Get this stuff . . .

Magazines or newspapers. Video recorder. Assorted paper and fabrics for costumes. Assorted props.

Where's this going?

Kids create a sci-fi show th portrays hope in somethin happening in the world to

respond

15-20 minutes

Gather to share the different points of view kids have discovered and developed during the session.

Regroup

Have kids mold creatures of their own desires. Ask each to use the creature he or she molded to tell a quick story about an event that happened during the past day. Take pictures of all the moldings and post them to the re:form online gallery!

Share

Invite kids to share their work and describe how and why they did it. Affirm those things you appreciate or find interesting and ask others to offer helpful observations.

Questions for conversation:

- How has your understanding of the book of Revelation changed?
- If the end of the world were coming, what do you think it would look like?
- How do you know that God always wins?
- How did the book of Revelation unite a large group of people?
- How can you spread the word of God to unite people you know?

Send

Give kids note cards and some time to record one tool they acquired today that will help them deal with thinking and talking about the book of Revelation, the end of the world, and how God always wins. Tape the tools to the toolbox; then gather around and pray for guidance as we tackle the world of tough questions. Encourage people in your congregation to check out the toolbox to see what kids are encountering in re:form. Take a picture of your toolbox each week and post it to the re:form online gallery.

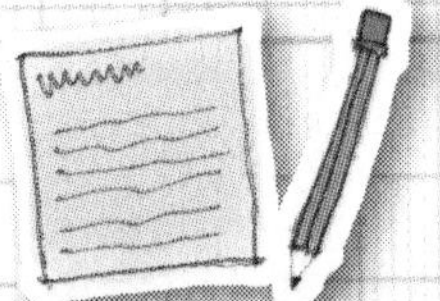

Get this stuff . . .

Play dough. Note cards. Mural paper or cardboard (labeled and designed as a "Tough Questions Toolbox" and displayed where many people can see it). Tape.

Capture it . . .

Use a digital camera, comcorder, scanner, web cam, or audio recorder to capture group conversations and individual pieces of work. Upload them to your online galleries, or ask kids to do so.

Tough Questions Unit
What does God think about war?

Prepare

What's behind all this?

The Bible appears to be conflicted about war and violence. There's a lot of both in the Hebrew Scriptures, and even Jesus' disciples carried swords on occasion. But Jesus also makes it clear that the best response to violence is to "turn the other cheek." And the Bible promises that God's perfection at the end of time is a perfectly peaceable kingdom in which "the wolf shall dwell with the lamb" and swords are made into plows because they're no longer necessary. God's steadfast love and mercy are constant throughout both Testaments.

Today, some Christians are pacifists and believe that violence should never be perpetrated on another human being, no matter the cause. Others believe in the idea of "just war," in which there are certain times when Christians must take up arms to fight injustice. But all Christians can agree that war and violence are an evil part of the world that will disappear in God's final consummation.

Where are kids at?

- Kids this age know war, but may not yet have a personal stance. Some are familiar with war through media and history class, while others may have siblings, parents, family friends, or neighbors who are or have been in the military. Give kids the freedom to explore their own beliefs and draw their own conclusions.
- Keep the conversation focused on discerning what the Bible is saying about war rather than debating the virtue of current military conflicts.

Isaiah 2:4
Revelation 21:3-4

Where's this going?
Kids examine their own ways of thinking about war and the potential for peace in light of the Christian witness.

Consider this . . .
"It is no longer a choice between violence and nonviolence in this world; it's nonviolence or nonexistence."
Martin Luther King, Jr., "I've Been to the Mountaintop" (1968)

encounter

15 minutes

Make sure you've got the obvic stuff for this session—re:form video (DVD or download), Anti-Workbooks, Bibles, pens c pencils, paper, tape, etc.

Video

1. Set up

Divvy up the cardboard tubes and encourage kids to use them for pretend sword fighting. After a short time, ask how it feels to be a toilet paper roll fighting against a wrapping paper roll, etc. When they're done, ask everyone to notice their emotions (excited, cautious, energized, puzzled, undecided, etc.).

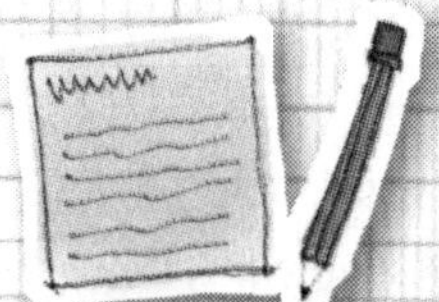

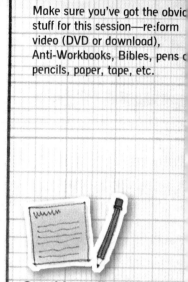

Get this stuff . . .
Empty cardboard tubes (from t.p. paper towels, or wrapping paper).

2. Watch

"What does God think about war?" DVD 2, Chapter 21

3. Unpack

- According to the video, what does the Bible say about war?
- Why do you think there are so many contradictions about war in the Bible?
- What do you hear about war from your parents? Friends? TV?
- What do you personally think about war at this time in your life?
- Have you ever been in a fight? If so, what was it about? In your opinion, was it really the best way to resolve the argument?

pac·i·fist
[pass-uh-fist]
a person who opposes war and violence as means of solving disputes

What about the Bible?

Think about a time when you were in a violent dispute, witnessed one, or were part of a dispute that could have resulted in violence. What was your experience like? How did you feel? How was the dispute resolved? What could you have done differently? How did it change your view on fighting? Share your experience with the group.

Back it up . . .
"Throughout the Old Testament, God is portrayed as being on the Israelites' side, even in brutal act of war and violence. . . . In the New Testament, Jesus' message i overwhelmingly against violence (any kind. Jesus taught forgivenes: love, and turning the other cheek.
re:form DVD

Questions for conversation:

- What are some nonviolent ways you have resolved conflicts with your family and friends?
- Read Isaiah 2:4. What did the video say about this passage? Why do some people think all violence will be gone from the world when Jesus returns?
- Read Revelation 21:3-4. What's this verse saying? How does it compare to the verse in Isaiah?
- What vision of a world without war do these verses suggest?

25-30 minutes

Choose 1+ Anti-Workbook (AW) activities to explore the session question. The first 2 are for individual use, while the last 2 involve the whole group.

1. War AW p. 186

Bring in pictures of soldiers, war, and destruction. Be sure to keep them PG-rated and to show all sides of war, from soldiers playing cards and laughing to soldiers in the middle of battle. Invite kids to look through the supplies you gathered to find items to illustrate war in their Anti-Workbooks. Encourage them to find ways to show where they think God can or cannot be found in war.

Questions for conversation while you work:

- What materials are you using in your collage and why?
- What colors dominate your collage?
- What feelings does your collage represent?
- How is God present in your collage?
- How is God with us when we are deeply broken and suffering?

Get this stuff . . .

Pictures of war. Paint. Paintbrushes. Unusual collage-making items (empty soda cans, metal cutters, old keys, paper clips, sandpaper, puzzle pieces, etc.).

Where's this going?

Kids create visual interpretations of war as they consider how God is with us in our deepest brokenness and suffering.

Back it up . . .

"And sometimes God even goes to battle, like in Joshua 10:11, where God sends giant hail stones down to kill enemy soldiers who were fleeing from the Israelite army."
re:form DVD

2. No! No! We Won't Go! AW p. 187

Is there something you would like to rally for? (More free time, kids who arrive on time, church leaders who listen to you, better lighting in the room where you meet, etc.) Make a sign and write a chant. Begin your personal rally as kids start to illustrate their views of war on their signs and write chants of their own. When the signs are complete, ask kids to defend their positions based on Biblical evidence of where God stands on war.

Questions for conversation while you work:

- Why are you pro- or anti-war?
- Who do you know who shares your views? Who disagrees with you?
- What might change your position on war?
- Do you think God would be on the pro- or anti-war side of a debate? How is this reflected in the position you defended?
- Which side of our protest is more convincing?
- What are some of the catchiest slogans in our group?
- How does it feel to be protesting against your friends across the room?

Get this stuff . . .

Sticks or dowels. Poster board.

Where's this going?

Kids design protest signs to show what they think about war.

Back it up . . .

"The Christian community may always be divided over the issue of war."
re:form DVD

3. Memories of War AW p. 188

Talk with your guest before kids arrive. Tell him or her you want to know what caused this war, what it was like to be in the middle of war, and what he or she thought peace would look like when the war was over. This will vary depending on the war. Plan an introduction comfortable for the speaker (just the facts, or a dramatic entrance like the beginning of a sports game). Have questions that are relevant to the guest's situation ready to begin the conversation—simple at first (where he or she served), and leading to emotions or analysis. Be alert for discomfort caused by any questions and be sure to thank your guest speaker before he or she leaves!

Questions for conversation while you work:

- What was the most interesting thing you heard the guest say?
- How do his or her experiences affect your view on war?
- How would your beliefs influence your willingness to volunteer to go (or not go) to war?
- How is volunteering different than being drafted? How do you feel about these two options?
- Is it possible to support people in a war but not support the war itself? Why?

Get this stuff . . .
Guest speaker with war experience.

Where's this going?
Kids interact with a war veteran to reflect on the causes and consequences war, and on hope for peac

Back it up . . .
"Many Christians througho history have been and continue to be pacifists. T believe violence should ne be committed toward ano human being, no matter what. Other Christians believe in the idea of a 'Ju War.' This theory claims t there are certain times th Christians must take up a to fight injustice."
re:form DVD

4. The Jesus Show! AW p. 189

Set the scene by taking the role of show's announcer. Tell kids that today's show guests were part of a bloody battle and are here to talk about it. Read 1 Samuel 17:38-51. Invite kids to create the set for The Jesus Show! (including places to sit, books Jesus can reference, prizes, etc.) and to develop the characters (David, Goliath, Jesus, announcer, audience, and videographer). Offer guidance when requested. Post the show to the re:form online gallery.

Questions for conversation while you work:

- How does the character Jesus reflect peaceful conflict resolution?
- What happens between David and Goliath in the Bible story?
- How could Jesus convince David and Goliath to work it out without violence?
- How do you feel about changing a Bible story?
- Violent movies and shows are very successful. What is entertaining about violence?

Get this stuff . . .
Couch. Bible. Conflict resolution books. Costume (David, Goliath, and Jesus Poster board. Paints. Vide recorder.

Where's this going?
Kids role-play peaceful wa to resolve conflicts.

respond

15-20 minutes

Gather to share the different points of view kids have discovered and developed during the session.

Regroup

Pass out the empty cardboard tubes again. This time challenge kids to argue, disagree, fight, and resolve without violence. Can they find nonviolent ways to use the cardboard tubes? Are the tubes helpful? A hindrance? Annoying?

Share

Invite kids to share their work and describe how and why they did it. Affirm those things you appreciate or find interesting and ask others to offer helpful observations.

Questions for conversation:

- Why do you think war exists?
- What do you think about war?
- Why do you think there's so much debate about whether war is right or not?
- How can you find ways to resolve conflicts without violence?
- How does Jesus lead us to nonviolent resolutions?

Send

Give kids note cards and some time to record one tool they acquired today that will help them when thinking and talking about war. Tape the tools to the toolbox; then gather around and pray for guidance as we tackle the world of tough questions. Encourage people in your congregation to check out the toolbox to see what kids are encountering in re:form. Take a picture of your toolbox each week and post it to the re:form online gallery.

Get this stuff . . .

Empty cardboard tubes from Encounter. Note cards. Mural paper or cardboard (labeled and designed as a "Tough Questions Toolbox" and displayed where many people can see it). Tape.

Capture it . . .

Use a digital camera, camcorder, scanner, web cam, or audio recorder to capture group conversations and individual pieces of work. Upload them to your online galleries, or ask kids to do so.

Back it up . . .

"However, there is one thing that Christians can all agree on: that war and violence are an evil part of the world that will disappear when Jesus returns and God makes all things new in the New Jerusalem."

re:form DVD